The **N** Word

The **N** Word

Who can say it,
who shouldn't,
and why

JABARI ASIM

HOUGHTON MIFFLIN COMPANY

BOSTON · NEW YORK 2007

For information about permission to reproduce selections from
this book, write to Permissions, Houghton Mifflin Company,
215 Park Avenue South, New York, New York 10003.

Visit our Web site: www.houghtonmifflinbooks.com.

Library of Congress Cataloging-in-Publication Data
Asim, Jabari, date.
The N word : who can say it, who shouldn't,
and why / Jabari Asim.
p. cm.
Includes bibliographical references and index.

ISBN: 978-0-547-05349-3

1. United States — Race relations — History.
2. Racism — United States — History. I. Title.
E185.A85 2007 305.896 073 — dc22 2006026872

Printed in the United States of America

Book design by Robert Overholtzer

MP 10 9 8 7 6 5 4 3 2 1

To Liana, Force of Nature

Acknowledgments

I bow down in gratitude to all the generations of ancestors in my blood family. As a continuation of my ancestors, I gratefully accept their energy as it flows through me. I ask for their continued support, protection, and strength.

Endless gratitude also:

To my parents, Irving and Joyce Smith, for generously providing me with life, sustenance, and example.

To everyone whose contributions large and small helped animate this humble offering: my siblings, Dale, Seitu, Karen, Guy and Boyce; Susie Ward, Mark and Bridgette Arnett, Lonnae and Ralph Parker, Brian and Elanna Gilmore, Jamel and Tracey Richardson, Wil Haygood, Johari Jabir, Fred and Lisa McKissack, Carla Broyles, Natalie Hopkinson, David Nicholson, my patient and supportive colleagues at Book World; Chris Lehmann, Jennifer Howard, and Mark Trainer, Joy Harris, Eamon Dolan, Lori Glazer, Sasheem Silkiss-Hero, Luise Erdmann, Janet Silver, and the rest of the team at Houghton Mifflin; Elaine Robnett-Moore, Charles and Paula Nabrit, James and Elsie Richardson, Richard and Ellen MacKenzie, the Reverend Mark Scott, Kevin Powell, Colin Channer, Rohan and Angela Preston, Bridget Warren and Todd Stewart, Sylvester and Victoria Brown, Ira Jones, Thich Nhat Hanh, and Leland Ware; Joseph, G'Ra, Nia, Jelani, and Gyasi.

To anyone whom limited space and memory have caused me to omit, please forgive me and know that I am thankful.

Contents

Introduction

I as much as any other man am in favor of having the superior position assigned to the white race.

— Abraham Lincoln, 1858

The white man was wrong, I was not a primitive, not even a half-man. I belonged to a race that had already been working in gold and silver two thousand years ago.

— Frantz Fanon, *Black Skin, White Masks,* 1952

The failure of the Negro race, as a race, to achieve equality cannot be blamed wholly on white oppression. This is the excuse, the crutch, the piteous and finally pathetic defense of Negrophiles unable or willing to face reality. In other times and other places, sturdy, creative, and self-reliant minorities have carved out their own destiny; they have compelled acceptance on their own merit; they have demonstrated those qualities of leadership and resourcefulness and disciplined ambition that in the end cannot ever be denied. But the Negro race, as a race, has done none of this.

— James J. Kilpatrick, 1962

FAILURE OF NERVE

W.E.B. Du Bois wasn't exactly prophetic when he famously observed that the problem of the twentieth century would be the problem of the "Color Line." It was 1903, after all, and the color line had been a growing problem ever since whites first confronted Native Americans centuries earlier. But Du Bois was indisputably accurate. Few were as aware of history's long reach as he, and perhaps even fewer felt the sting of the past as acutely. By the time of his writing, the Native American threat to white dominance had been emphatically eliminated, leaving only blacks between the conquerors of the New World and the bountiful destiny they envisioned.

The slaves' many talents — contributed under threat of death — had once made African Americans crucial to white ambitions in North America. Even then, the white ruling class imagined a day when their captives' services would no longer be required. George Washington expressed a typical desire in a 1778 letter to his plantation manager. "To be plain," he wrote, "I wish to get quit of Negroes."

Presidents from Jefferson to Lincoln took Washington's wish a step further, entertaining fantasies of large-scale black exportation that ultimately went nowhere. In contrast, taking steps to ensure that the blacks in their midst would not become citizens of the Republic proved much easier. Early on, the Founding Fathers removed us from the Declaration of Independence, an act Ralph Ellison called a "failure of nerve." The Founders committed "the sin of American racial pride," Ellison wrote. "They designated one section of the American people to be the sacrificial victims for the benefit of the rest . . . Indeed, they [blacks] were thrust beneath the threshold of social hierarchy and expected to stay there."

How whites from all levels of society worked to keep us there — through a combination of custom, law, myth, and racial insult — is the subject of this book.

Reflecting on this potent, destructive blend in 1903, Du Bois condemned whites' "personal disrespect and mockery, the ridicule and systematic humiliation, the distortion of fact and wanton license of fancy, the cynical ignoring of the better and the boisterous welcoming of the worse, the all-pervading desire to inculcate disdain for everything black, from Toussaint to the devil." Nearly four decades after his "Color Line" comment, Du Bois attributed the still-yawning divide between whites and blacks to that same white hostility, a virulent contempt that "depended not simply on economic exploitation but on a racial folklore grounded on centuries of instinct, habit and thought and implemented by the conditioned reflex of visible color." *The N Word* looks closely at that folklore tracing its path as it sustained the entwined ideas of white supremacy and black inferiority, supplemented the nation's ever-growing popular culture, and influenced the scope and direction of its legal system. It explores in depth various categories of literature, science, music, theater, and film, the legislative policies and judicial decisions designed to keep blacks in their place, and the language of racial insult that runs like an electric current through them all.

A WAR OF WORDS

The decision to exclude blacks from the Declaration enabled race to emerge as "a new principle or motive in the drama of American democracy," Ellison persuasively observed. Race, in his view, "was to radiate a qualifying influence upon all of the nation's principles and become the source of a war of words that has continued to this day." The battle of wills, initially between planters and their human property, has gradually and painfully evolved into an increasingly harmonious albeit fitful coexistence between white and black Americans. At no time has it been a one-sided conflict: *The N Word* also takes note of the acts of defiance that I and many others regard as a form of counternarrative challenging the majority culture's myth of conquest and superiority. That myth, in effect, attempts to erase the real history of blacks in America and replace it with a fictional tale of futility and mediocrity. Blacks who have actively campaigned against the majority narrative have been, as it were, writing themselves into existence.

Although the fusillades traded over the years have diminished considerably, language continues to convey formidable and occasionally savage force. For much of the history of our fair Republic, the N word has been at the center of our most volatile exchanges. Because no discussion of American race relations — and no consideration of white supremacy — can be complete without it, "nigger" appears early and often in these pages.

If it is true, as Henry Demarest Lloyd has noted, that "history is condensed in the catchwords of the people," then "nigger" properly belongs in the company of such all-American terms as *liberty, freedom, justice,* and *equality.* As Randall Kennedy and others have shown, the N word is certain to provoke strong reactions whenever it is encountered. Its remarkable durability, coupled with Americans' historical willingness to find uses for this epithet in nearly every facet of their everyday lives — from the geographical to the philosophical to the culinary — may also illustrate the extent to which racial unease continues to permeate our culture.

As part of my examination, I will heed Ellison's observation that black American consciousness does not reflect a will to historical forgetfulness but derives instead from our memory, "sustained and constantly reinforced by events, by our watchful waiting." If Ellison is right, how does our attitude toward past wrongs and struggles affect our conduct in the ever-changing present? I will also attempt to show that the word "nigger" serves primarily — even in its contemporary "friendlier" usage — as a linguistic extension of white supremacy, the most potent part of a language of oppression that has changed over time from overt to coded. While "jigaboo," "coon," "pickaninny," and "buck" have been largely replaced by such ostensibly innocuous terms as "inner-city," "urban," and "culturally disadvantaged," "nigger" endures, helping to perpetuate and reinforce the durable, insidious taint of presumed African-American inferiority. Within this context, *The N Word* also discusses blacks' adoption of the epithet to describe themselves, an increasingly popular habit among younger African Americans. Are they in fact removing the word's power to harm or merely succumbing to an immense, inscrutable, and bizarre failure of the imagination?

CURIOUSER AND CURIOUSER. . .

The N Word is divided into five sections. Part I, "Birth of a Notion," begins in 1619, when African captives first set foot on British North American territory. It extends to the end of 1799 with Thomas Jefferson, the new nation's foremost promoter of Negro inferiority, poised to occupy the White House. Part II, "The Progress of Prejudice," begins in Jefferson's first term and ends in 1857. That year, blacks' dehumanized status was dramatically emphasized by *Dred Scott v. Sanford*, which determined that they "had no rights which the white man was bound to respect." Part III, "Dreams Deferred," picks up immediately after *Scott* and continues until 1896, when *Plessy v. Ferguson* formalized the Jim Crow restrictions that circumscribed life for most African Americans. Part IV, "Separate and Unequal," covers the period from 1897 until 1954, the year of the landmark *Brown v. Board of Education* decision striking down racial segregation. Part V, "Progress and Paradox," spans the dramatic changes that took place between 1955 and the present.

Thus far in this nation's development, it has been the long, sick, and twisted history of tangled relations between blacks and whites that has both defined and propelled America's unique status on the planet. If the United States remains a noteworthy international symbol as a melting pot and laboratory of interracial experiment, then the persistence of white supremacist strains in the national culture is an especially useful gauge by which progress (or the lack of it) is measured. With that in mind, this book is an extended inquiry into the wages and consequences of our peculiarly American saga of racial conflict.

Because I wanted to prevent *The N Word* from being a multivolume project certain to exhaust both its author and its audience, I have in various instances limited my focus to particular examples, discarding or bypassing others in the interest of brevity. Inevitably, some of my choices will strike others as unwise or arbitrary. To them I can only humbly plead forbearance and offer encouragement to await other examinations of this topic, which will undoubtedly and deservedly follow.

PART I

Birth of a Notion
1619–1799

1

Founding Fictions

Names have always been a problem for black people in America . . . our names bespeak the tangles of American culture — miscegenation, issues of property and ownership, the peculiar violence of our past — in the same way our skins do.

— C. S. Giscombe, *Into and Out of Dislocation,* 2000

"THE WORD NIGGER to a colored person," Langston Hughes once observed, "is like a red rag to a bull."

Christopher Darden echoed this argument decades later in a Los Angeles courtroom. Working as a prosecutor in the murder trial of the disgraced athlete and celebrity pitchman O. J. Simpson — a legal skirmish the media were fond of calling "the trial of the century" — Darden described the epithet as the "filthiest, dirtiest, nastiest word in the English language." It was so filthy, he contended, that the African Americans on the jury could not hear it without losing their ability to consider the details of the case fairly.

Johnnie Cochran, the lead defense counsel for Simpson, scoffed at Darden's suggestion and called it demeaning. If centuries of oppression had failed to impair the judgment of African Americans, he argued, how could two little syllables do the job?

The Simpson case was not about the N word, of course, but the epithet did function as the pivotal metaphor for the racial themes that ultimately decided the outcome of the trial, thus demonstrating its enduring potency as an instrument of white supremacy and a symbol of lingering sentiment against blacks. Similarly, the positions staked out by the two black lawyers at the heart of the case conveniently illustrate the opposing views that frame the contemporary use of the N word. In one corner, Christopher Darden argued that the word has no proper place in public settings. In the other, Johnnie Cochran argued that "nigger," while inflammatory, could be heard and encountered without destroying civilization as we know it.

The origin of the pair's famous tussle can be traced all the way back to 1619, when the Jamestown colonist John Rolfe noted in his diary the first time African captives came to live and toil in British North America. "Twenty negars," he wrote, had arrived on a Dutch man-of-war.

Did he mean "niggers" or "Negroes"? Most lexicographers trace both words to "niger," the Latin word for "black." Some of them also contend that "nigger" was intended initially as a neutral term. Citing the presence of "nigers" in the "learned discourse" of the seventeenth-century anti-slavery activist Samuel Sewall, they suggest that the word acquired a derogatory character over time, picking up various spellings along the way. However, little other than Sewall's discourse is offered as evidence to support this argument. Other usages, while not necessarily hateful, clearly are not sympathetic either. Reginald Scot's *Discoverie of Witchcraft* (1584), for example, described an "ouglie divell" with "fanges like a dog, a skin like a Niger, and a voice roring like a lion." The merchant Nicholas Crisp, writing in 1637, described one of his ships as equipped to "take nigers and carry them to foreign parts." In 1651 two British traders placed orders with the Guinea Company, each specifically requesting a shipment of "lusty negers."

Some scholars have attributed the modern, all-too-familiar spelling to the Scottish poet Robert Burns, whose 1786 poem "The Ordination" includes among its scintillating lines:

> Come, let a proper text be read,
> An' touch it aff wi' vigour,

How graceless Ham leugh at his dad,
Which made Canaan a nigger.

Others, most notably J. E. Lighter, have suggested that Burns probably spelled it the same way Sewall did. By the time Burns got around to cranking out his verse, black people had no doubt become accustomed to hearing the N word as an insult — regardless of how it was spelled. Twenty years before "The Ordination," the Afro-British memoirist Ignatius Sancho wrote to a correspondent, "I am one of those whom the vulgar and illiberal call '*Negurs.*'"

Eleven years before Burns, the British Redcoats concocted their own illiberal doggerel to taunt the black and white patriots who had bravely assembled at such places as Brandywine Creek and Saratoga to fight and die for freedom:

The rebel clowns, oh what a sight
Too awkward was their figure
'Twas yonder stood a pious wight
And here and there a nigger.

The Redcoats' spelling can't be confirmed, but their pronunciation seems pretty clear. With the N word appearing in verse (such as it was), could song be far behind? An item in the *Virginia Gazette* from this period referred to the black militiamen who had joined the British marching to the tune of "Hungry Niger Parch'd Corn." By then it was reasonable for Ignatius Sancho and his dark-skinned fellows to hold in low regard anyone who chose to use the term in any form — nigger, niger, negur, negar — especially since "Negro" (as a term for black Africans) had been part of the English vocabulary as far back as 1555.

Not that "Negro" conferred much more respect. It was, after all, synonymous with "black," which was and continues to be an unmistakably negative term in most English-language contexts. The lamentable tendency of contemporary journalists and others to refer to unfortunate events as "Black September" or "Black Friday" stems from centuries-old connotations. Common definitions in the *Oxford English Dictionary*, dating back to the 1500s, include "foul," "dirty," "wicked," and "horrible." The sentiments of the British traveler George Best, recorded in 1578, were hardly atypical. He speculated that the Africans' black skins "proceedeth of some natural infection of the first inhabitants of that country, and so all the whole progenie of them descended, are still polluted with the same blot of infection."

The intensity of English neuroses regarding most things black practically ensured that the language they chose to describe Africans and their "progenie" would be anything but neutral. Instead, it reflected their obsessions. In the historian Winthrop Jordan's words, "Blackness had become so thoroughly entangled with the basest status in American society that at least by the beginning of the eighteenth century it was almost indecipherably coded into American language and literature."

From the outset, the British and their colonial counterparts relied on language to maximize the idea of difference between themselves and their African captives.

ALL PERSONS EXCEPT NEGROES

Black people continued to be imported as the British stake in the New World grew. By 1649, about 300 had been "taken and carried to foreign parts"; they had landed in Virginia and formed roughly two percent of the colony's 15,000 residents. They weren't yet officially slaves — and, indeed, a few were free — but they had already become exposed to separate and unequal treatment. Virginia's first census takers listed blacks separately from white men and rarely bothered to note their names. In 1639 the colony's assemblymen passed a statute to establish a militia, declaring, "All persons except Negroes to be provided with arms and ammunition or be fined at the pleasure of the Governor and Council." All of the colonies would enact similar measures by the end of the century. Such restrictions were inconsistently enforced and presaged the varying degrees of unease with which American patriots regarded armed and trained slaves throughout the Revolutionary War. The wording of the statute is almost whimsical compared to the exclusionary codes of the modern era. In the 1930s, for example, black visitors to Hawthorne, California, encountered a sign at the city limits that warned, "Nigger, Don't Let the Sun Set on YOU in Hawthorne." Still, the 1639 legislation was uncharacteristically blunt for its time. In the near future, Virginia lawmakers would turn to genteel, coded language to deny the rights of blacks and whites without property. At the 1776 state convention, for instance, George Mason and his peers preferred limiting equality to men who had "entered into a state of society."

"Official" slavery, confirmed through statute laws that distinguished blacks from indentured whites by establishing lifetime servitude for Negroes and their subsequent generations, was well under way by the late 1660s. In 1680 Virginia passed a law requiring slaves to carry passes when traveling without their masters. Ten years later, South Carolina passed an "Act for the Better Ordering of Slaves," then enacted a stricter, more comprehensive code in 1696. While maintaining the pass system, it required all whites to apprehend slaves and give them "a moderate whipping" if they had no pass. It also provided that a slave who resisted could be beaten, maimed, assaulted, or, if necessary, killed. Slave quarters were subject to biweekly inspections for the purpose of locating stolen items. In 1705 Virginia assembled a systematic code very similar to South Carolina's, and other states eventually followed suit.

Among the most influential factors that influenced the movement to codify the slave laws were (1) the need for free labor to work the tobacco, rice, and indigo fields beginning to flourish in the colonies' expanding plantation economy, (2) the swelling black population, which exacerbated fears of insurrection, and (3) the growing frustration of poor whites, made frighteningly clear by Bacon's rebellion of 1676. That violent multiracial protest against Virginia's landed gentry prompted the elite to create a buffer zone between themselves and their less fortunate white kinsmen. Blackness conveniently became that zone, courtesy of the system of slave codes that both restricted the lives of bondsmen and gave poor whites something to be grateful for. These developments coincided with the colonists' growing disillusion with the mother country and their growing sense of independence.

THE ROOTS OF RESISTANCE

For the slaveholding class, validation was intimately bound to — in fact, impossible without — the consistent degradation of those they chose to enslave. Such degradation, heard in the court of public opinion and reinforced through daily plantation protocols, led to what might be called the founding fictions of American slave society: (1) whites were superior beings destined to rule over their lesser counterparts, and (2) blacks were unworthy creatures whose very unworthiness made them perfectly suited to a lifetime of forced servitude. "The idea of the superiority of whites was etched into the slave's consciousness by the lash and the ritual respect he was forced to give to every white man," noted John W. Blassingame in *The Slave Community.* At the same time, masters pretended that slaves were simple-minded and childlike because it helped "to relieve themselves of the anxiety of thinking about slaves as men." In the centuries that followed — long after the official end of slavery — whites of all classes came to rely on language (and especially the use of pejoratives like the N word) in their pursuit of such relief.

These early engagements should not be considered one-sided clashes between all-powerful racists and their cowering victims. Instead of giving in to efforts to dehumanize them, most slaves chose to fight back on the psychological level. Like Ignatius Sancho, they refused to see themselves as whites wished them to be. While some slaves undoubtedly succumbed to the spirit-numbing mind games inflicted upon them, others resisted, asserting themselves through a variety of tactics ranging from work slowdowns and subterfuge to stealthy acts of sabotage. Such responses, along with the nascent folk culture blacks developed in the slave quarters, were among the earliest and most effective forms of resistance. If freedom was not a realistic option for the overwhelming majority of slaves, some degree of self-determination — however fragile and precious — was.

This ongoing battle of wills between planters and their human property resulted in a relationship fraught with uncertainty. As the revolutionary fever slowly enveloped the colonies, this very uncertainty helped expose a vulnerable opening in white society, and some blacks — both free and enslaved — did not hesitate to press their advantage.

They were quick to call attention to the hypocrisy of would-be patriots who railed against the oppression imposed by the Crown while they were waited on by men and women in chains who fanned their brows and plowed their fields. Just as important, black people, after discovering the value of using the whites' impassioned language against them, launched the ongoing efforts at counter-narrative mentioned earlier. An example of this occurred in 1766, the same year in which Sancho objected to being called a "negur." Whites in Charleston protested the Stamp Act under the slogan "Liberty and stamp'd paper." Slaves in Charleston took note and launched a campaign of their own, parading about the town and chanting, "Liberty! Liberty!"

Four years later on March 5, a runaway slave named Crispus Attucks was the first to fall in the melee known as the Boston Massacre. Although John Adams tried to impugn his reputation, Attucks was celebrated by Paul Revere and other white patriots as a "new symbol of resistance." Perhaps some of his fellow blacks remembered his example when they petitioned the Massachusetts General Court in 1772, once again borrowing the fervent prose of the Revolution. Addressing the legislators as "men who have made such a noble stand against the designs of their *fellow-men* to enslave them," the petitioners demanded immediate emancipation. "In common with all other men we have a natural right to our freedoms," they declared. Rebuffed, they returned the following year, asking not only for manumission but also for some portion of uncultivated land on which they might work and live in peace.

In the chapters to come, we will examine the various ways in which modern black Americans have subverted the N word and other forms of racist language to assert their right to define themselves. Although their techniques span a range of widely different approaches, the roots of their methods extend to the earliest days of the Republic. For instance, long before the actor-rapper Mos Def could compose a song called "Mr. Nigga," in which he denounces whites who use racial slurs in private while "livin' off of slave traders' paper" and behaving as if "they think that illegal's a synonym for Negro," there was the black militiaman-poet Lemuel Haynes. His 1776 essay, "Liberty Further Extended," advanced a similar argument. "I think it not hyperbolical to affirm," he wrote, "that even an African, has Equally as good a right to his Liberty in common with Englishmen . . . consequently, the practice of slave-keeping, which so much abounds in this land is illicit."

Haynes's moving blend of passion and logic not only exemplifies the developing strain of black resistance to the majority cultures' systemic dehumanization of Negroes, it also anticipates the blacks' ongoing struggle to come up with a name for themselves. For Haynes and many of his peers, "African" — a far cry from "nigger" — was sufficient. His essay was just one of many similar efforts that showed how colonial blacks seized on literacy as a liberating tool and cleverly subverted the lofty sentiments and "learned discourse" of their oppressors.

Blacks did considerably more than write pamphlets and present petitions during the Revolution. When the actual fighting ended in 1781, twenty percent of Washington's troops were black, an estimated 5,000 in all.

The presence of such men interfered with the vision of the new nation taking shape in the imaginations of the Founding Fathers. The attainment of that vision required solving a question articulated early on by Patrick Henry: "Our country shall be peopled. Shall it be with Europeans or with Africans?" Benjamin Franklin had posed a similar inquiry in his *Observations Concerning the Increase of Mankind* (1751): "Why increase the Sons of Africa, by

Planting them in America, where we have so fair an Opportunity, by excluding all Blacks and Tawneys, of increasing the lovely White and Red?" Having so many sons of Africa in their midst was a necessary evil, it seemed, but to have so many wandering around unfettered and full of ideas about freedom and equality forced whites to wrestle with troubling existential puzzles. Seeking solace, some whites yielded to the diabolical temptations of simple race-based hatred. "To despise slaves as Negroes was redundant," wrote Winthrop Jordan, "but when Negroes were no longer slaves they became despicable only as Negroes."

To make matters worse for those who felt threatened by free blacks, the Revolution had "loosened the bonds of government everywhere," according to John Adams. Its ill and unintended effects included "Indians slighting their guardians and negroes growing insolent to their masters." Making the nation safe for white people could be more easily accomplished with the help of a whitewashed tale of its origins. Toward that end, another founding fiction emerged that also has contributed mightily to the enduring stereotype of the dangerous, incorrigible "nigger": a myth that the historian Roger Wilkins called "the story of the Great White Revolution carried out by Great White Men."

The mythologizing had begun while the war was still raging. Northern revolutionaries helped nurture the burgeoning idea of white superiority as part of a campaign to placate Southern slaveholders, who, Adams had complained in 1776, were reluctant to commit to a republican government. In 1779 South Carolina's council members rejected a plan to arm 3,000 black soldiers. Conveniently ignoring the heroics of black patriot-warriors, the South Carolinians contended that blacks were both untrustworthy and incompetent. Colonel Alexander Hamilton disagreed. Moving quickly to counter the notion that blacks were "too stupid to make soldiers," he wrote to John Jay, the president of the Continental Congress. "Their natural faculties are as good as ours," he observed. "The contempt we have been taught to entertain for the blacks, makes us fancy many things that are founded neither in reason nor experience." George Washington, ever the Southern slaveholder, was less concerned with blacks' combat skills than with the effect of their soldiering on their shackled kinsmen. "I am not clear that a discrimination will not render slavery more irksome to those who remain in it," was his response. "Most of the good and evil things of this life are judged of by comparison; and I fear comparison in this case will be productive of much discontent in those who are held in servitude." South Carolina's leaders agreed, maintaining that they'd rather lose than give guns to blacks. Charleston fell soon after, a reasonable consequence, giving British troops their most significant victory of the war and South Carolinians an experience they wouldn't soon forget.

Accompanying the perpetuation of the stereotype of black stupidity was the increased usage of such demeaning terms as "boy" and "darky," both of which entered the popular vernacular during the latter decades of the century. Crispus Attucks's martyrdom may have afforded him the chance to serve as a "new symbol of freedom," but not for long. Once celebrated by John Hancock as belonging "in the first rank of the men who dared," Attucks was seldom discussed or remembered in the days following the American victory. White men were clearly disconcerted by the potential legacy of such a patriot. Memories of brave black men willing to seize their own destinies could have an undesirable effect on black morale. Not surprisingly, Attucks's courageous deed lapsed into obscurity while the image of black men as too inept to fight gained currency.

Christopher Darden may very well have meant it when he denounced the N word as a term so despicable that it was beyond comparison. Or he may have been attempting solely to exclude testimony that was damaging to his case, a ploy that any lawyer worth his salt would have tried. Regardless of his motive, he touched a nerve that continues to throb in reaction to an insult older than the American justice system — indeed, older than the United States itself.

In Richmond, Philadelphia, Boston — anywhere the first generation of Americans gathered — the notion of black inferiority spread as rapidly as the spirit of independence that enlivened the new nation. Former Loyalists and Sons of Freedom alike realized they would have to forget their differences to work together for the good of the country, and their differences were plenty. They included disagreements over the morality of slavery and the proper treatment of blacks. There was much less dissent, however, regarding blacks' capabilities. Alexander Hamilton's belief in the potential of blacks was the exception that proved the rule. Over time, the degraded status of blacks, abetted by laws enacted to keep them down, became conveniently enforced through a variant of that same word that John Rolfe had scrawled in his Jamestown ledger.

Centuries later, "nigger" continues to arouse strong passions and deeply felt emotions, prompting provocative outpourings from poets, rappers, politicians, and dueling attorneys at a murder trial. As we shall see, its influence today also appears in deeply ironic and unpredictable forms, even on the very continent that those first twenty blacks once called home.

The founders would probably have laughed at the notion of black poets and artists, let alone attorneys in a court of law. No matter, for they had more pressing concerns, including how to entrench a system of white supremacy that would benefit them and their descendants in ways they could not have foreseen. Law and society were already on their side in this regard. Soon, they'd have "science" too.

2

Niggerology, Part 1

I advance it therefore as a suspicion only, that the blacks, whether originally a distinct race, or made distinct by time and circumstances, are inferior to the whites in endowments both of body and mind.

— Thomas Jefferson, *Notes on the State of Virginia*, 1785

TO JUSTIFY THEIR AVERSION to emancipation, both to themselves and to increasingly skeptical observers from foreign lands, slaveholders adhered to what Ira Berlin has called "the logic of subordination, generally finding the sources of their own domination in some rule of nature or law of God." Desperate to cloak their nakedly unreasonable system in the respectable garb of rationality, members of the propertied elite increasingly turned to the comforting pronouncements of scientific racism.

With his *Notes on the State of Virginia* — a seminal document in the American branch of this nefarious tradition — Thomas Jefferson gave himself and his peers just what they needed. First published in France, *Notes* reached American readers in 1785. It included a stunning section, ostensibly based on Jefferson's "observations" of Negroes, which suggested that blacks were little more than childlike, animalistic creatures doomed to lives of permanent subservience. His ludicrous, inflammatory absurdities, relayed in the careful prose of "learned discourse," set a poisonous precedent for the seemingly endless examples of racist pseudo-scholarship that would follow. Winthrop Jordan has called Jefferson's remarks on the Negro "the most influential utterances on the subject" until the mid-nineteenth century. Nearly sixty years after Jefferson, Josiah Nott, another "scholar" dedicated to proving Negro inferiority, memorably dubbed his brand of science "niggerology." In setting the stage for Nott and his cohorts, Jefferson's *Notes* made the self-styled philosopher-scientist the preeminent niggerologist of his time.

While Jefferson claimed to be conflicted about slavery, he evidently harbored few doubts regarding the apparently insurmountable inferiority of Negroes. Joseph Ellis has written that the sage of Monticello "was a staunch believer in white Anglo-Saxon supremacy, as were several other leading figures in the revolutionary generation." Yet none of his like-minded peers had dared to offer their potentially caustic summations in such carefully fashioned prose. Unlike George Washington, whom John Adams once described as having "the gift of silence," Jefferson could rarely resist sharing his thoughts with the world.

Notes was published in the United States the year before Robert Burns offered a poetic explanation of the Negro's plight in two lines of "The Ordination": "How graceless Ham leugh at his dad, / Which made Canaan a nigger." Burns echoes the long-held idea that blackness derived from a divine curse; the luckless wretches who bore its stamp were sentenced by the Creator to eternal servitude. Jefferson alludes to the concept when wondering if Negroes could be "nurtured" to a higher state of existence beyond what Nature appeared to ascribe to them. Both Burns's poem and Jefferson's *Notes* reflect the influence of Enlightenment thinking in Europe. Montesquieu's *Spirit of the Laws* exerted a recognizable influence on many of the leading intellectuals of the Revolutionary generation. Published in 1748, in addition to its author's disquisitions on types of government and principles of governing, *Spirit* suggests that man can improve his natural state by acquiring, among other things, knowledge and religion. In other words, basic human nature is universal but can be affected by environment and culture. Other voices of the Enlightenment argued that some "types" of mankind could not be improved. David Hume's essay "Of National Characters," also published in 1748, was amended five years later to include the author's contention that "negroes and in general all other species of men . . . are naturally inferior to the whites." Without challenging Montesquieu's notion of the "laws of human nature," Jefferson speculates that "time and circumstance" may be responsible for blacks' lowly status. (The other emerging theory behind blacks' alleged inferiority was that they were created in a different time and place from white men, a hypothesis to which we will return shortly.)

Jefferson entered the discussion just as scientists, influenced by Carolus Linnaeus's taxonomic system of the 1730s, had begun a quest to classify just about everything — including human beings. Almost inevitably, these efforts led to hierarchical categories not entirely dissimilar to those offered by a concomitant system of thought, the Great Chain of Being. Proponents of the Chain argued that Man belonged somewhere in the middle — above Beasts and below Angels. As quasi-science met quasi-philosophy, the ranking of living things (including men) was increasingly based on supposedly measurable anatomic differences. No matter the criteria, blacks usually suffered by comparison.

Jefferson was not only the author of the Declaration of Independence but also an international symbol of American enlightenment. Thus, his anti-Negro ramblings — the most intensive ever contrived during the post-Revolutionary era — established a model of rationalized racism that would inflict incalculable damage to blacks' quest for basic human rights.

"ANIMAL URGES"

According to Jefferson, blacks were "more ardent after their female: but love seems with them to be more an eager desire, than a tender delicate mixture of sentiment and sensation." He went on to argue that it was only natural for black men to prefer the superior beauty of white women, just as the "Oranootan" preferred "black women over those of his own species." Not everyone embraced Jefferson's bodacious claims. One of his fiercest critics was Gilbert Imlay, who in 1792 charged that Jefferson "suffered his imagination to be carried away" when predicting the amatory inclinations of apes. Such speculation, according to Imlay, was "paltry sophistry and nonsense!" Clement Clark Moore, writing in 1804, challenged Jefferson's scientific method: "Where Mr. Jefferson learnt that the orangoutang has less affection for his own females than for black women, he does not inform us."

Jefferson may have been familiar with William Smith's *New Voyage to Guinea,* which in 1744 told of apes frequently carrying off and sexually assaulting black women in the jungles of Africa. In 1799 Britain's Charles White, the last major niggerologist of the period, specifically referred to Jefferson's *Notes* to bolster his own "research" comparing black men with apes.

In each of these perverse fantasies, black men are portrayed as wild, simian creatures, whereas black women are described as uninhibited, sexually licentious creatures, perfectly suited as targets for rampant libidinous attacks. (Such characterization also justifies the rape of black women, for how could a gentleman planter possibly cause harm to a being who is designed by nature to want sex all the time, is accustomed to the brutal techniques of uncivilized black men, and has been known to satisfy orangutans? With such a rationale, one can argue that her mere presence is tantamount to "asking for it.")

Jefferson's and White's unseemly obsession with black sexuality coincided with the scientific community's fascination with comparative anatomy. White, for example, claimed to gauge blacks' intelligence by comparing the size of their skulls to those of whites. At the same time, white scientists' fixation with African penises, extant since at least the fifteenth century, peaked in grisly fashion. Charles White provided an indication of just how widespread this mania was and how it was gratified. In *An Account of the Regular Gradation in Man, and in Different Animals and Vegetables; and from the Former to the Latter* (1799), he enthused, "That the PENIS of an African is larger than that of an European has . . . been shewn in every anatomical school in London. Preparations of them are preserved in most anatomical museums; and I have one in mine."

One helplessly imagines a covetous spectator interrupting White's lecture to ask "Where can *I* get one of those?" The proclivity of slaveowners to dismember their captives, while perhaps not as fervent as that exhibited by lynchers in the nineteenth century, nonetheless ensured that sufficient specimens remained in supply to meet the appetites of dedicated collectors such as White. The result of these "studies" was to perpetuate the stereotype of the black man as a potential rapist, whose toxic sperm would infect white purity with the "blot of infection" that blackness was thought to carry.

Back in the late eighteenth century, white men's concerns were exacerbated by the swelling slave population. Viewed in conjunction with the related musings of Patrick Henry and Benjamin Franklin, it becomes clear that the fear of a black penis and the fear of a black planet have long been inextricably connected. Southern politicians of the nineteenth and twentieth centuries (as well as Republican strategists such as Lee Atwater, who harvested abundant political capital from exactly this sort of psychosexual paranoia) owed an enormous debt of gratitude to Thomas Jefferson.

"TRANSIENT GRIEFS"

Remarkably, Jefferson also fancied himself privy to blacks' innermost emotions. "Their griefs are transient," he wrote in *Notes*. "Those numberless afflictions, which render it doubtful whether heaven has given life to us in mercy or in wrath, are less felt, and sooner forgotten with them." Jefferson's counterintuitive attempt to establish his captives' lack of emotional depth offers proof of Roger Wilkins's observation that "to ease their guilt, whites invented and clung to the idea that blacks had no family feeling." Clearly, Jefferson was disturbed by the idea of slaves having emotions; that discomfort had to be part of his motive to dehumanize them so thoroughly in *Notes*, which appeared just as he was attempting to consolidate his various holdings and stem his financial difficulties. Part of that effort would involve getting rid of some 161 slaves over the next ten years, either by sale or by gift. Ellis suggests that Jefferson was able to perform such tasks by shielding himself from the "day-by-day realities of slave life." At Monticello he surrounded himself with pale-skinned house servants and avoided almost all contact with the adult slaves who worked in his fields. Despite this distance, he could write confidently not only of their work habits but also of their fears, dreams, desires, and regrets. Or their alleged lack of them.

Perhaps we can also blame Jefferson's distance from Mulberry Row (the slave quarters at Monticello) for his failure to consider that the slaves' apparent serenity was often, in the words of Paul Laurence Dunbar, "a mask that grins and lies." One former slave, Henry Watson, didn't publish his memoirs until 1848, but his explanation of slave "merriment" no doubt held true during the glory years of Jefferson's more attentive contemporaries: "the slaveholder watches every move of the slave, and if he is downcast or sad — in fact, if they are in any mood but laughing and singing, and manifesting symptoms of perfect content at heart — they are said to have the devil in them."

"PLAIN NARRATION"

Whereas Montesquieu described man as a being "hurried away by a thousand impetuous passions," Jefferson described blacks as "induced by the slightest amusements." For him, blacks' inclination toward distraction could be attributed to any number of inadequacies, from their tendency toward sensation rather than reflection, their "dull, tasteless, and anomalous" imaginations, or perhaps their "want of forethought." All of these shortcomings contributed to Jefferson's never having encountered a black who had "uttered a thought above the level of plain narration."

Jefferson's slaves included any number of highly skilled artisans, without whom the continuous construction at Monticello would not have progressed beyond his own presumably sharp, tasteful, and superior imagination; it is simply inconceivable that all of them were as inarticulate as Jefferson described. As the owner of what was probably the largest and most extensive private library in the United States, he must also have "encountered" narratives written by blacks, which began to appear around 1760. In fact, the writing by blacks during this period amounts to an eloquent counterargument to the allegations put forth by Jefferson and others, as forceful as those later advanced by Gilbert Imlay and Clement C. Moore. By the time *Notes* was published in the United States, James Gronniosaw, Briton Hammon, and Phillis Wheatley had already published works; Olaudah Equiano's memoir soon followed. If Jefferson saw any merit in their efforts, he was unwilling to admit it. He pronounced Wheatley's poems "beneath the dignity of criticism." Ignatius Sancho's work was far better in his view, although unequal to that of his white contemporaries — if, that is, it could even be proved that Sancho wrote it himself and "received amendment from no other hand."

FRIENDLY FIRE

Abolitionists weren't always much help at combating scientific racism, because all of them didn't necessarily disagree with its chief assertion. However, some did have their own ideas about its cause. Some anti-slavers, who conceded that blacks were inferior or "depraved," blamed their condition on the squalid environment in which the majority of them were forced to live. Therefore, their argument went, reform was not possible without emancipation. The environmental perspective had been introduced by John Woolman in Philadelphia in 1754, some twenty years before the meeting of the nation's first anti-slavery society was held there. In *Some Considerations on the Keeping of Negroes,* Woolman suggested that many of the shortcomings attributed to blacks stemmed directly from their enslavement. "If Oppression be so hard to bear, that a wise Man is made mad by it . . . then a Series of those Things, altering the Behaviour and Manners of a People, is what may reasonably be expected," he wrote. Woolman, a Quaker, implied that white men, too, would be inferior if they were enslaved.

Dr. Benjamin Rush, a prominent abolitionist in Philadelphia, echoed Woolman's contention in 1774, asserting that "Slavery is so foreign to the human mind, that the moral faculties, as well as those of the understanding are debased, and rendered torpid by it." Such sentiments, albeit well intentioned, did little to sway pro-slavers or anybody else. By 1800, the anti-slavery movement was all but dead.

But the image of Negroes as "brutish, ignorant, idle, crafty, treacherous, bloody, thievish, mistrustful, and superstitious" was alive and well. Jefferson's *Notes* had conveniently codified "truths" held to be self-evident by the majority of white Americans at the end of the eighteenth century. In sum, black men and women were best considered as lower primates, emotionally shallow, simple-minded, sexually licentious, and prone to laziness. Contempt for blacks was so widespread, wrote David Cooper in 1772, that children were encouraged "from the first dawn of reason, to consider people with a black skin on a footing with domestic animals, form'd to serve and obey."

A CODE OF CONDUCT

Washington and Jefferson were racists, but how racist was their language? As quintessential Southern men of their time, they behaved in public according to entrenched notions of honor, courtliness, and refinement. While violent language was considered beneath a gentleman, some forms of physical violence were not. In *Affairs of Honor*, Joanne B. Freeman identifies canings and nose-tweakings as acceptable components of the Revolutionary era's "grammar of combat." When flung at a gentleman, words such as "scoundrel," "rascal," and even "liar" were considered proper cause for retaliation.

In light of such customs, it is no surprise that during the constitutional convention "slavery" became in essence the "s" word, to be avoided out of respect for the delicate sensibilities of the distinguished members from the South. The delegates therefore engaged in shifty wordplay in the interests of civility, calling slaves "persons" or "persons held to Service or Labour." In what must be considered the very apogee of irony, the Atlantic slave trade was rechristened "migrations."

It is quite likely that Washington and Jefferson engaged in similar euphemisms at home, not out of respect to their captives, but in keeping with their concept of themselves as gentlemen of refinement. In correspondence, Washington referred to his slaves as "that species of property" (a phrase favored at the convention), "poor wretches" when he was feeling especially compassionate, and "those who are held in servitude" in missives of an official nature. At Monticello, Jefferson's elderly slaves were quaintly called "veteran aids," although the master was known to refer to adult black men as boys — a form of insult that gained in popularity during his time. It is reasonable to assume that the great lengths to which Jefferson shielded himself from the gritty reality of slave life included linguistic buffers as well. Crude terms such as "nigger" probably were not part of his vocabulary. Such coarseness was more appropriately left to the overseers and white men of the working class, whose tasks included the punishment and supervision of the idle wretches in the fields.

As the eighteenth century wound down, Jefferson's peers in the creative arts also condemned the character of the Negro, replacing him in the popular imagination with a grotesque caricature so lowly and egregious that its very presence demanded its ritualistic and cathartic abuse. Taking a cue from their more sober-minded peers who wrote essays and pamphlets, creative writers added their skewed perspectives to the prevalent image of the black American, collectively fashioning a debased character of the sort Henry Louis Gates Jr. has described as "an-Other Negro, a Negro who conformed to the deepest social fears and fantasies of the larger society."

Apparently what whites desired most in blacks was energetic servility combined with a willingness to laugh away life's troubles. After assessing such Revolutionary literature as John Leacock's "Fall of British Tyranny" (1776), J. Robinson's "Yorker's Stratagem" (1792), and John Murdock's "Triumph of Love" (1795), the brilliant critic Sterling Brown concluded, "The earliest plays, as [well as] the earliest novels, show the Negro character chiefly as comic servant and contented slave."

Of the Revolutionary writers, Jefferson deserves special attention for two reasons:

First, because his book endowed such fantasies with respectability and became a handy, influential primer for those who aspired to advance the cause of white supremacy. And its influence was far-reaching; Winthrop Jordan estimates that Jefferson's remarks "were more widely read, in all probability, than any others until the mid-nineteenth century."

Second, because Jefferson's influence continued to rise to unparalleled heights as the sun began to set on the Revolutionary era. Ironically, blacks had played a pivotal role in his long and eventful climb. He had relied heavily on the skills of black captives in the construction of Monticello, had depended on their monetary value as his "only salvation" when hopelessly mired in debt. Now, courtesy of the three-fifths compromise, they had helped him to carry the presidential election. At the turn of the century, the nation's foremost architect of Negro inferiority — the Revolutionary who had done more than any other to niggerize the popular conception of Africans in America — had become the most powerful man in the country.

PART II

The Progress of Prejudice
1800–1857

3

No Place to Be Somebody

> To use his own words, further, he said, "If you give a nigger an inch, he will take an ell. A nigger should know nothing but to obey his master — to do as he is told to do. Learning would *spoil* the best nigger in the world."
>
> — Frederick Douglass, *Narrative of the Life of Frederick Douglass*, 1845

THE FIRST HALF of the nineteenth century marked many significant changes in the new nation, including its dramatic western expansion thanks to Jefferson's brilliant purchase of the Louisiana Territory and the subsequent acquisition of lands from Mexico — all of which were complicated by the hardening of sentiment against the Negro in the North and a resolute adherence to slavery in the South.

Just as significant, the early 1800s marked the emergence of what can be accurately termed "a greatest generation": a relatively sizable body of free, knowledgeable, and daring blacks who began to circulate, communicate, and agitate on behalf of blacks everywhere. Alexander Crummell, Martin Delany, Sojourner Truth, Henry Highland Garnet, Harriet Tubman, Frederick Douglass, James McCune Smith, and John B. Russwurm were among the many who came to public attention during this period. By the turn of the century, Absalom Jones was an elder statesman among this group — but he was still active. In 1800 Jones, who had cofounded the first society of free blacks in 1787, led a group petitioning Congress to take action against the slave trade and commit to the gradual abolition of slavery. Although Jones's petition was never presented to the full Congress for consideration, it generated considerable turmoil during committee debates and, more important, it presaged an aggressive, increasingly militant philosophy among the new black intelligentsia that would reach its peak during the middle to late 1800s.

A year after Jones confronted Congress, President Jefferson shared his vision of the expanding nation in a letter to James Monroe. Jefferson had soured on the idea of using any part of the western territories as an "asylum" for blacks, and he now regarded Africa as the only feasible location for them. As for blacks mixing with whites in the new territories, he wrote that white Americans cannot "contemplate with satisfaction either blot or mixture on that surface." His vision of virtuous white "husbandmen" working their bountiful small farms in blissful independence never became a reality in the West, but Jefferson was dead-on in predicting continuing resistance to any "blots" or "mixtures" that blacks might contribute. His letter to Monroe adds a metaphorical gloss to the crystallization of black hostilities that took place during the 1820s and 1830s as free blacks became more numerous and more visible. These hostilities took the form of acts of physical violence — often perpetrated by rampaging mobs — and acts of legislative violence, as the Northern states began to curtail black rights. It all amounted to what George Fredrickson described as "an articulate and aggressive racism which excluded the Negro from the society of competing equals without deporting him, by the simple and brutal mechanism of formally defining him as subhuman." In short, the already flourishing myth of the lowly, animalistic "nigger" helped justify the new rules designed to contain him.

At the same time, vigilant legislators worked to keep blacks from seeking opportunity in the West. Federal law prevented them from access to the public domain, and four states (Indiana, Illinois, Iowa, and Oregon) made it illegal for them to even set foot in their respective territories. Through the ideology of manifest destiny, Eric Foner wrote, "territorial expansion came to be seen as proof of the innate superiority of the 'Anglo-Saxon race' (a mythical construct defined largely by its opposites: blacks, Indians, Hispanics, Catholics)."

ALLIES AND ADVERSARIES

Assertions from both Northern and Southern leaders further reinforced the idea of Negroes as a "degraded class," damaged beyond hope of redemption. George Fredrickson has written that during the 1830s, the doctrine of permanent black inferiority "became, for the first time, the basis of a world view, an explicit ideology around which the beneficiaries of white supremacy could organize themselves and their thoughts."

Blacks' principal allies in the struggle against this spreading ideology were the new generation of determined abolitionists that emerged during this period. Chief among them was William Lloyd Garrison, the fiery Massachusetts native who founded the nation's preeminent anti-slavery newspaper, *The Liberator*, in 1831. In 1833 he established the American Anti-Slavery Society, which was organized around the principles of nonviolence and passive resistance.

Garrison and his colleagues often engaged both the overt defenders of slavery and the less candid colonizationists in what George Fredrickson has described as a "propaganda war," but those exchanges were rarely over the alleged inferiority of Negroes. While pro-slavers had already assembled their arguments and organized them "in a rigid polemical pattern" (Fredrickson's phrase), abolitionists hurled only sporadic salvos in retaliation. The abolitionists' comparatively anemic response may be attributed to the likelihood that combating rumors of Negro inferiority wasn't a top priority. There may also have been lingering doubts in the abolitionist camp regarding blacks' capabilities, a possibility explored later in this chapter. The abolitionists had plenty of other things to contend with, including escalating violence. Northern mobs were venting their fury not only on hapless Negroes but on anti-slavery activists as well, crashing their meetings and wrecking their printing presses. Other groups found more creative ways to silence the abolitionists. The House of Representatives, for example, in 1836 resolved to ban further consideration of abolitionist petitions.

"NIGGER FREEDOM"

Conditions were not much better for blacks in the so-called free states. In New York and Pennsylvania, their voting rights were sharply curtailed. Of the states entering the Union after 1800, only Maine accorded suffrage to citizens other than white males. Blacks may not have been overly concerned with voting, however, as staying alive was a more pressing concern. John Russwurm wrote presciently in 1829, "If the free states have passed no law as yet forbidding the emigration of free persons of colour into their limits; it is no reason that they will not, as soon as they find themselves a little more burdened." In Pennsylvania, lawmakers discussed getting rid of the state's Negroes. White mobs ran wild in Philadelphia between 1832 and 1849, inflicting their unique brand of brotherly love on their dark-skinned neighbors in the form of five large riots. Elsewhere in the North, violence against Negroes became commonplace. Urban slums emerged: "New Guinea" in Cincinnati, "Little Africa" in New York, "Nigger Hill" in Boston. In the words of Leon Litwack, "The justification for [racial] discrimination in the North differed little from that used to defend slavery in the South: Negroes, it was held, constituted a depraved and inferior race which must be kept in its proper place in a white man's society."

Senator Robert Hayne of South Carolina attempted to expose the hypocrisy of the supposedly enlightened North during his 1830 debate with Senator Daniel Webster of New Hampshire. "Sir," he thundered, "there does not exist on the face of the earth, a population so poor, so wretched, so vile, so loathsome, so utterly destitute of all the comforts, conveniences, and decencies of life, as the unfortunate blacks of Philadelphia, and New York, and Boston. Liberty has been to them the greatest of calamities, the heaviest of curses."

Alexis de Tocqueville, who made his famous visit to the United States in May 1831, seemed to confirm Hayne's charges. In *Democracy in America* he found fault with Northern whites in particular: "The prejudice of race appears to me stronger in the States that abolished slavery than in those where slavery still exists, and nowhere does it show itself to be as intolerant as in the states that have never known slavery."

The Southern humorist William Thompson used racist language in his fictional *Major Jones's Sketches of Travel* (1848) to poke holes in the North's contrived liberalism. In one passage, a Georgian traveling in Philadelphia observes, "Nobody here that has any respect for themselves, treats a nigger as ther equal, except a few fannyticks, and they only do it to insult the feelins of others." Elsewhere, a character implies that Senator Hayne was right in regarding liberty for Negroes as "the heaviest of curses": "Thar they was, covered with rags and dirt, livin in houses and cellars, without hardly any furniture; and sum of 'em without dores or winders. . . . This, thinks I, is nigger freedom; this is the condition to which the filanthropists of the North wants to bring the happy black people of the South!"

While no self-respecting black thinkers considered downplaying the absolute necessity of freedom, neither did they hesitate to emphasize the limits of freedom without power. The colonization advocate Martin Delany, for instance, pulled no punches in his discussion of "free" blacks in the slave states: "the bondman is disfranchised, and for the most part so are we. . . . They are ruled and governed without representation, existing as mere nonentities among the citizens, and excrescences on the body politic — a mere dreg in community, and so are we."

Leon Litwack writes that in the North, "prevailing racial stereotypes, white vanity, and the widely held conviction that God had made the black man to perform disagreeable tasks combined to fix the Negro's economic status and bar him from most 'respectable' jobs." Those stereotypes prevailed even in Northern churches, where Negro worshipers were confined to "an 'African corner,' a

'Nigger Pew,' seats marked 'B.M.' (Black Members), or aloft in 'Nigger Heaven.'"

Emancipated blacks could find little or no relief in the North, the South was out of the question, and the West was mostly off-limits as well. As large as the country had become by the mid-nineteenth century, it still offered free Negroes few places to hide or to live in peace. Wherever they traveled, the prevalent image of the "degraded class" was sure to accompany them, that of indolent, depraved, licentious "niggers," capable of luring enslaved blacks from their fulfilling lives by their contaminating example while at the same time afflicting heedless whites with the infectious stain of intermixture.

FRIENDLY FIRE, REVISITED

Among the stellar black activists making their presence felt during this period, few spoke about black anguish as eloquently and movingly as Frederick Douglass. Soon after publishing *Narrative of the Life of Frederick Douglass: An American Slave* in 1845, he found eager audiences both at home and abroad, becoming the most influential black man in America. His leadership in the Negro convention movement and tireless lecturing added to his formidable persona. Douglass has been described as proudly bearing the title of Representative Colored Man of the United States, but it is more likely that most whites regarded him as the exception that proved the rule of Negro inferiority. Some in the abolitionist camp anticipated that Douglass's powerful intellect and spellbinding oratory might make whites skeptical of his origins. In 1841 an ally warned him, "People won't believe that you were ever a slave, Frederick, if you keep on in this way." Another added, "Better have a little of the plantation speech than not; it is not best that you seem to be learned."

The abolitionists' comments about Douglass's intellect and manner of speaking, although they reflect no little confusion about the capabilities of blacks, seem less curious when considered in context. George Fredrickson has explained that during the nineteenth century, "pseudoscientific racism or its equivalent tended . . . to increase its hold on the American mind and to infect even those whites who resisted its full implications." Douglass's allies must certainly be included among those who would seem to be, at least in theory, opposed to such stereotyping, yet their behavior frequently showed signs of its influence.

Owen Lovejoy, a congressman and a brother of the noted abolitionist Elijah, speaking in defense of Negroes, asked, "We may concede it as a matter of fact that [the Negro race] is inferior; but does it follow, therefore, that it is right to enslave a man simply because he is inferior?"

James W. Alvord, a fervent abolitionist, wrote to an ally about seeing a Negro girl sitting among white students at a school in Clifton, Connecticut. He supposed the girl's scent would offend the parents in attendance, although he "could not perceive the girls on either side were at all aware of her niggerly odour."

These and similar comments seem to confirm Litwack's observation that abolitionists might "refer to their African brethren — innocently or otherwise — as 'niggers' or emphasize some alleged physical or mental characteristic." Even William Lloyd Garrison, the Liberator himself, conceded that "the black color of the body, the wooly hair, the thick lips, and other peculiarities of the African" resulted in Negroes' being "branded by the hand of nature with a perpetual mark of disgrace."

At the same time, many abolitionists complicated the prevailing stereotypes by promoting the image of the Negro as a naturally meek, humble, and forgiving soul — ideal human qualities that could be further enhanced through emancipation and full exposure to the teachings of Christianity. Anti-slavery advocates were probably trying to alleviate white fears of black violence and to combat portrayals of Negroes as dangerous menaces to society, but their efforts often worked to assist the opposition. Both misrepresentations — black as beast, black as childlike idiot — were aspects of the "nigger" image heavily promoted during this era by the defenders of slavery. They argued that animalistic behavior was the natural lot of the slave, curable only through the humanizing influence of slavery, which was sure to bring out the lovable docility lurking beneath Negroes' brutish exteriors. These two extremes of niggerization created a nearly inescapable conundrum for enslaved blacks in the nineteenth century. In the words of W.E.B. Du Bois, "everything Negroes did was wrong. If they fought for freedom, they were beasts; if they did not fight, they were born slaves. If they cowered on the plantation, they loved slavery; if they ran away, they were loafers. If they sang, they were silly, if they scowled, they were impudent. . . . And they were funny, funny — ridiculous baboons, aping men!"

Free blacks faced a similar niggerizing trap. Litwack wrote that by the 1840s, "Northern whites had come to accept irresponsibility, ignorance, and submissiveness as peculiar Negro characteristics, as natural products of the Negroes' racial inferiority. Consequently, those who rose above depravity failed to fit the stereotype and somehow seemed abnormal, even menacing."

The niggerization of blacks was systematically enforced in Northern schools and households. The black abolitionist Hosea Easton reported that white children were "warned to behave or 'the old nigger will carry you off'"; naughty children were castigated as "worse than a little *nigger*." He described white teachers as punishing students by sending them to the "nigger-seat." All that niggerizing, according to Easton, had "a most disastrous effect upon the mind of the white community."

Those seeking more constructive responses about the status of free Negroes turned their attention to the Supreme Court in 1857. In 1846, a slave and his wife had petitioned for his freedom on the grounds that their twelve years' confinement in free territory violated the Missouri Compromise of 1821. Eleven years later, *Dred Scott v. Sanford* reached the nation's top court. Chief Justice Roger B. Taney ruled that Negro citizenship was "incompatible with the Constitution." Identifying blacks as members of "an inferior order," Taney asserted that they "had no rights which a white man was bound to respect." He also ruled that the Missouri Compromise was unconstitutional and that slavery could not be banned in the territories. This had dire implications, not only for those blacks still toiling on Southern plantations, but also for those who had been tentatively staking out independent lives. For the whites who had been in America for centuries and for the nearly five million Irish, German, and Scandinavian immigrants who had been streaming in since 1830, opportunity and wide open spaces loomed. Blacks, however, were running out of room.

TERMS OF ENDEARMENT?

In *Freedom's Journal*, the nation's first black newspaper, Samuel Cornish and John B. Russwurm lamented the tendency of some of their white allies to believe the worst about black people. They thought that "a simple representation of facts," offered by themselves and other black activists, would "arrest the progress of prejudice" and shield blacks against "the consequent evils." One of those evils was the adoption of racist epithets by blacks themselves. It was perhaps inevitable that enslaved Africans and their immediate descendants — who had English beaten into them — would find themselves as restricted by their oppressors' unfamiliar language as by the shackles and irons with which they were often punished. While the slaves' imaginations — as evidenced by the music and folklore they continued to create amid stifling circumstances — could often transcend their confinement, their language sometimes proved far more earthbound.

Litwack reported that travelers in the North remarked that "Negroes often reproached one another as 'dirty black naygurs,' an insult usually reserved for especially dark Negroes, lower-class blacks, or newly arrived southern immigrants." He includes an exchange between two black porters and a prospective customer in Philadelphia in 1846. One of them promotes his own talents at the expense of those of his competitor: "Neber mind him, Sa; he's only a nigga from Baltimore, just come to Philadelphy. I'se born her, Sa, and know de town like a book. Dat ere negga not seen good society yet — knows nuffin — habn't got de polish on." In such a context, the pejorative nature of the word is clear. Hosea Easton, writing in 1837, emphasized the lack of ambiguous intent on the part of anyone who uttered it. In *The Condition of the Colored People of the United States; and the Prejudice Exercised Towards Them,* he observed that "'nigger' is an opprobrious term, employed to impose contempt upon [blacks] as an inferior race."

The British actress Fanny Kemble reported encountering similar black-on-black usage during her visits to Georgia slave plantations in the late 1830s. In her view, "no contemptuous intonation ever equaled . . . the despotic insolence of this address of these poor wretches to each other." Her most wrenching example, however, did not involve usage between slaves. She described a female slave excitedly displaying her semiclad children to Kemble, who had just arrived as the mistress of a plantation. "Look, missis!" she called. "Little niggers for you and massa; plenty of little niggers for you and little missis!"

The historian Sterling Stuckey has suggested that Kemble failed to appreciate the subtle variations in the slaves' use of the N word. He identified a field holler that slave children in the nineteenth century sometimes sang to warn that patrollers were nearby:

> As I was goin cross de field
> A black snake bit me on my heel
>
> Run nigger run, de Patrol catch you
> Run nigger run, tis almos day.

Such songs, according to Stuckey, are an example of usage "with glowing affection." I am not entirely convinced, although I do agree that such usages are free of the despotic insolence that Kemble noted. The slaves' use of the N word, then, was less an indication of their acceptance of black inferiority than a reflection of their attempt to express themselves within a harshly restricted vocabulary imposed from without. Regardless of their intention, their usage, along with that of their free Northern brethren, was a lamentable development for both black and white abolitionists, who faced the daunting task of convincing the majority of Americans to accept their dark-skinned countrymen as peers who deserved freedom and humane treatment. The class lines developing among blacks were equally harmful since cooperation among them was critical if they were to acquire any real political and economic strength. "In their efforts to maintain racial supremacy and purity, the whites did not differentiate among the various classes of Negro society" at midcentury, according to Litwack. "Whites might distinguish 'good niggers' from 'uppity niggers' or express a preference for hiring mulattoes over blacks, but that was all."

Blacks who created distracting and unnecessary divisions — and called each other "nigger" — simply played into the hands of those who opposed their cause.

4

Niggerology, Part 2

The brain of the Negro is that of the imperfect brain of a seven month's infant in the womb of the White.

— Louis Agassiz, 1847

DURING A BRILLIANT, BLISTERING 1974 monologue about police brutality, the comic Richard Pryor marveled at the resiliency of the black psyche. "Often you wonder why a nigger don't go completely *mad*," he said. In contrast, American scientists in the latter half of the nineteenth century concluded that a great many blacks often did lose their minds. They believed that the nation's difficulties could usually be traced to the insane Negroes in their midst. What's more, they asserted, just about anything could cause blacks to become unbalanced; while it was true that their "condition of servitude" frequently drove slaves crazy, their free brethren were even more likely to become dangerously deranged. Niggerology, soon to become the favored term among the leading scientists of the period, achieved unprecedented popularity; like the N word, it became another convenient way to spread and reinforce notions of white supremacy.

The anti-Negro campaigns being waged in courtrooms, congressional committees, churches, and the popular media were also being conducted with gusto in the laboratories and lecture halls where the scientists and scholars of natural history plied their trade. The scientific establishment's low regard for blacks may be gauged by the considered opinions of the men frequently cited as the most accomplished naturalists of the nineteenth century.

Georges Cuvier, best known today for his dissection of Saartje Bartman (a.k.a. "The Hottentot Venus"), the South African woman whose genitals he displayed in the Museum of Mankind in Paris, was in his time recognized as Europe's premier zoologist. In 1812 he expressed his belief that Africans were "the most degraded of human races, whose form approaches that of the beast and whose intelligence is nowhere great enough to arrive at regular government." Charles Lyell, the "conventional founder of modern geology," determined that "the brain of the Bushman . . . leads toward the brain of the Simiade [monkey]. This implies a connexion between want of intelligence and structural assimilation." His work provided critical evidence that assisted the research of Charles Darwin, whose *Origin of Species* rocked the scientific and religious worlds in 1859. In a later work, *Descent of Man,* Darwin offered his thoughts on the likely expansion of the gap between men and monkeys. "The break will be then rendered wider," he predicted, "for it will intervene between man in a more civilized state, as we may hope, than the Caucasian, and some ape as low as a baboon, instead of at present between the negro or Australian and the gorilla." Darwin envisioned the eventual extinction of such "intermediate" species as chimpanzees and Negroes.

By the mid-1800s, American scientists began investigating the topic that had elicited these opinions from the eminent Europeans: the fascinating phenomenon of alleged Negro inferiority. It seems a natural development when one considers the extent to which mainstream American society was obsessed with the subject. The scientists were working in a milieu described by Stephen Jay Gould as divided into two schools, hardliners and soft-liners: "'hardliners' held that blacks were inferior and that their biological status justified enslavement and colonization. . . . 'soft-liners' . . . agreed that blacks were inferior, but held that a people's right to freedom did not depend upon their level of intelligence."

Enter Samuel George Morton, who in 1820 developed an interest in skulls. A newly minted graduate of the University of Pennsylvania Medical School, Morton began a lifelong affiliation with the Academy of Natural Sciences in Philadelphia that same year. After picking up a second degree in medicine at Edinburgh, he returned to Philadelphia in 1824 to start a private practice. He also began to collect skulls with renewed energy. In time his laboratory was nicknamed the American Golgotha, as his collection became the world's largest. In 1839 he published *Crania Americana,* which attempted to assess intelligence by measuring cranial capacities.

Borrowing Johann Friedrich Blumenbach's classification of five "races" — Caucasian, Mongolian, Malay, American, and Ethiopian — Morton ranked them according to brain power. Most advanced were — surprise! — the Caucasians, who possessed "the highest intellectual endowments." Least potent were — again, surprise! — the Ethiopians, whose skulls told Morton that they were "joyous, flexible, and indolent" but, alas, not very bright. Some Ethiopian tribes, in his estimation, represented "the lowest grade of humanity."

"IDIOTS AND INSANE PERSONS"

George Combe, a colleague of Morton's, had written an appendix to *Crania Americana* containing the unorthodox supposition that freedom might actually be good for Negroes' intelligence. It was a startling hypothesis, one that appeared to contradict Morton's observations, but Combe's analysis must have gone unnoticed in the hubbub surrounding the 1840 Census.

Released in 1841, it reported that Negroes had among them far more "idiots" and "insane persons" than the general population did. Further, there were far more crazy Negroes in the North. In Maine, for instance, every fourteenth Negro was nuts; in South Carolina, only 1 out of 4,310 was crazy. For most whites, unaware of Combe's essay, the reason for this disparity was obvious: Freedom drove blacks crazy.

Dr. Edward Jarvis gave voice to this conclusion, deducing that a life in bondage exerted "a wonderful influence upon the development of moral faculties and the intellectual powers." But in a stunning reversal, he discovered that the census was riddled with errors, including reports of insane Negroes in places where no Negroes were known to live. Thirteen months later, he published a refutation in the *American Journal of the Medical Sciences,* contending that the damage done by the census was exacerbated by the publication of its findings in Europe and "throughout the civilized world."

Jarvis called for an official correction. Secretary of State John C. Calhoun not only disapproved of a revision but also was fond of citing the census as proof of slavery's beneficent nature. In a letter to the British foreign secretary, Calhoun wrote that Negroes in the free states had "invariably sunk into vice and pauperism, accompanied by the bodily and mental afflictions incident thereto — deafness, blindness, insanity and idiocy — to a degree without example." In contrast, enslaved Negroes had "improved greatly in every respect — in number, comfort, intelligence, and morals."

In other discussions of slavery, Calhoun buttressed the statistics in the census with research from Samuel Morton, which the scientist had helpfully mailed. The facts, according to Calhoun, suggested that freedom for blacks would be "a curse instead of a blessing." He successfully resisted all efforts to revise the census. As late as 1870, the results of the 1840 Census were still considered the official record.

POLYGENISM

The same year that census takers were discovering black lunatics under every rock, Morton presented as a follow-up to *Crania Americana* a lecture further expressing his ideas about the size of black brains and their relation to white supremacy. He told his audience that the disparity between whites' and colored folks' brains stemmed from "those primeval attributes of mind, which for wise purposes, have given our race a decided and unquestionable superiority over all the nations of the earth." Because he had earlier surmised that "each Race was adapted from the beginning to its peculiar local destination" and because he obtained his data by measuring skulls, Morton emerged as a central figure in both of the dominant scientific interests of his time: craniometry and polygenism.

Before *Crania Americana,* the prevailing theory of racial difference held that humans descended from a common original pair. Such thinking enabled men of conscience to remain faithful to the Edenic beginning laid out in Genesis while owning slaves who had, for varying reasons, apparently become inferior over time. Morton, however, maintained that the races were created separately (polygenism, or many origins) and with unequal attributes. As Louis Menand explains, "polygenism is the more radical theory, because it supports the contention not just that black people and white people have evolved (or devolved) at different rates, but that they belong to entirely different species."

Morton, Josiah Nott, and the Swiss-born Louis Agassiz became the primary proponents of polygenesis. The founders of the new American school of anthropology, they also formed the unholy trinity of nineteenth-century niggerology.

Despite the intensely racist nature of their "research," the men seemed to be motivated at least as much by a strong resentment of religion's tenacious (albeit weakening) grip on science as by an overwhelming desire to defend slavery. (Nott once said that the purpose of his work was "to cut loose the natural history of mankind from the Bible.") Ephraim George Squier, a close friend, likeminded colleague, and "the first authoritative voice in American archaeology," offered a likely summation of the new American school's racial philosophy when he wrote to his parents that he had a "precious poor opinion of niggers, or any of the darker races," but he had "a still poorer one of slavery."

The anticlerical tone of the trio's work, up against the spirit of revival stemming from the Second Great Awakening, may explain why most of the criticism they attracted was in response to their challenging of scripture, not their racist conclusions. Their main opponent, a minister and amateur naturalist named John Bachman, challenged polygenism while asserting that "in intellectual power the African is an inferior variety of our species."

COMMENCED IN IGNORANCE

Nott first made a name for himself writing about "mulattoes" in 1843. In the *American Journal of the Medical Sciences,* he concluded that they were not the product of mixed races but of "two distinct species — as the mule from the ass." The article caught the attention of Morton, who in 1844 sent a laudatory letter to Mobile, Alabama, where Nott was practicing medicine. Nott replied in kind, cementing their friendship. That same year he delivered a talk in Mobile, which he would publish in 1845 as *Two Lectures on the Natural History of the Caucasian and Negro Races.* In the address (which he puckishly called his "lectures on niggerology"), he declared his faith in polygenism and cited Morton's work as proof.

Morton had published *Crania Aegyptica* in 1844. Among its many claims is Morton's deduction — from his measurement of Egyptian skulls — that Negroes were slaves in that ancient kingdom. His "discovery" heartened those white supremacists who argued that blacks had always been slaves and perhaps, through their bondage in the South, were simply fulfilling the Creator's design.

Nott's niggerology proceeded apace. In 1847 he published two articles in *De Bow's Review* that came perilously close to an outright endorsement of slavery despite his disavowals. That same year, he rebuked a visiting scientist, Charles Lyell, who dared to suspect that Negro inferiority could be corrected over time through exposure to white ways of living and thinking. In a letter to Morton, Nott recalled telling the geologist that Negroes were beyond rehabilitation, having already reached their "highest degree of civilization." Two years before Thomas Carlyle would memorably condemn race-based philanthropy as "benevolent twaddle," Nott dismissed "the angry and senseless discussions on negro emancipation" as having been "commenced in ignorance."

While Nott was publishing in *De Bow's Review,* Agassiz was holding forth on the size of Negroes' brains. He told a Charleston audience that "the brain of the Negro is that of the imperfect brain of a seven month's infant in the womb of the White," a choice morsel that was dutifully and admiringly reported to Morton. Agassiz was making a case for "the diversity of races," an indication of his move to the polygenist camp.

"THE NIGGER BUSINESS"

In 1849, the same year that a mob of whites waged a bloody terrorist campaign against blacks in his city, Morton published his *Catalog of Human Crania in the Collection of the Academy of Natural Sciences of Philadelphia.* Among other observations, it reiterated his earlier contention that the Negro "is the lowest form of humanity." His craniometry has since been shown to be riddled with flaws, including purely speculative racial attributions, fundamental mathematical errors, a failure to consider gender-related differences in skeletal dimension, and the deliberate deletion of measurements that contradicted his hypothesis. At the time, however, these findings were accepted without dispute and relied on as the basis of further research by scientists throughout the United States and Europe.

In July of the following year, Agassiz published the second of a three-part series of articles in the *Christian Examiner.* In "The Diversity of the Origin of the Human Races," he argued that "racial distinctions are primordial." The "different races do not rank upon one level in nature," he insisted. On the bottom level, of course, was "the submissive, obsequious, imitative negro." He advised whites, when dealing with blacks, to be "guided by a full consciousness of the real difference existing between us and them, and a desire to foster those dispositions that are eminently marked in them, rather than by treating them on terms of equality."

As in Morton's work, Agassiz's scientific method left more than a little to be desired. In the words of Stephen Jay Gould, "Agassiz never generated any data for polygeny. His conversion followed an immediate visceral judgment and some persistent persuasion by friends. His later support rested on nothing deeper in the realm of biological knowledge."

Agassiz's shortcomings and his embrace of white supremacy become all the more appalling when one considers his exalted status at Harvard's Lawrence Scientific School. His improbable odyssey illustrates one of the ways in which white supremacy became institutionalized at the highest level of American intellectual inquiry. A legitimate expert on the biology of fish who somehow became an authority on alleged Negro inferiority, Agassiz began teaching America's finest young minds in 1848.

In 1850 Nott was selling published versions of his lectures at a rapid clip. They were especially popular in the Deep South, where, he told his friend Ephraim Squier, "the public mind is at present excited about the nigger business." He was still continuing to argue that education was wasted on Negroes. In Charleston, he told a gathering of the American Association for the Advancement of Science that for blacks, further development just wasn't possible. He regarded the Liberian colony as "the last hope of the Negro as an independent race" but suspected that the effort was "a vain struggle against fixed laws of nature." Immediately following his address, Agassiz rose and gave some corroborating remarks.

BEST SELLERS

In the spring of 1851, Samuel G. Morton died. The *New York Tribune* wrote of the hard-working champion of white supremacy, "probably no scientific man in America enjoyed a higher reputation among scholars throughout the world." More to the point, the *Charleston Medical Journal*, the most prestigious publication of its kind in the South, wrote, "For the present, we can only say that we of the South should consider him as our benefactor, for aiding

most materially in giving to the negro his true position as an inferior race."

Josiah Nott had in mind an even more effusive tribute. Working
with the self-styled Egyptologist George Gliddon, he published
Types of Mankind in 1854 and dedicated it to Morton's memory.
The book is an eight-hundred-page compendium with contributions from Agassiz, Harry S. Patterson, and William Usher. Though
it was essentially a repackaging of prevailing arguments in favor of
polygenism and white supremacy, the first printing sold out immediately.

Nott's friend Ephraim Squier wrote an unsigned review in the
New York Herald, praising the book. He predicted it would "exercise
a great influence, and produce a profound and permanent impres-
sion on the public mind." Squier was right: *Types* went through ten
editions between 1854 and 1871 and became the leading American
text on human racial differences.

Once again, most of the unfavorable criticism objected to the
anti-scriptural tone of the book and declined to take note of its racism. A typical stance was presented by Nott's longtime nemesis,
John Bachman, who devoted much of his lengthy review in the
Charleston Medical Journal to disassociating himself from the taint
of abolitionism. He made it clear that a belief in the unity of mankind was not incompatible with a belief in Negro inferiority or a
healthy respect for the South's "domestic institutions."

A tireless worker, Nott took the time in 1856 to help bring out a
one-volume American edition of *The Moral and Intellectual Diversity of Races (Essai sur l'inégalité des races humaines)* by Count Joseph Arthur de Gobineau. Gobineau's book, "the bible of nineteenth-century racists," argued that "Negroes had an absolutely
fixed and unchangeable set of undesirable traits."

In 1857 Nott and Gliddon followed up with *Indigenous Races of
the Earth.* Nott wrote only one chapter but helped to assemble a
chart illustrating the geographical and intellectual proximity of
monkeys and Negroes, whom Chief Justice Taney would officially
degrade as members of "an inferior order" just a few months later.

In the year of the Dred Scott decision, the bookselling concession at a Nott lecture offered one-stop shopping for anyone with an interest in niggerology.

BLACK MEN, BLACK SHEEP, ETC.

"The grounds I have taken in my lecture were never for the mass," Nott wrote to a friend in 1845, "but they have been much talked of and read here and public opinion has come over to me as I was sure it would *in the South*." He probably underestimated the appetite for niggerology in the North, although he was perhaps correct in thinking that his pseudo-science may have been too highbrow for the typical racist. With his sharp entrepreneurial instincts, he most likely recognized, as did others, a potential market among whites who didn't make a habit of attending lectures at scientific academies and university lecture halls. Nonscientists and self-styled experts on Negro inferiority rushed to fill the demand.

It's difficult to say who was most absurd among the best-known popularizers of niggerology, but Peter A. Browne and Samuel A. Cartwright certainly deserve mention.

In the 1840s, Browne thought he'd go the craniometrists one better by giving lectures based on scientific comparisons of human hair. Using homemade instruments and units of comparison, he concluded that whereas white men's heads were topped with hair, black men's heads had wool closer to that found on a sheep. Therefore, he deduced, blacks and whites were two different species.

Many discussions have been published about the methods that slaves employed to sabotage the plantation process, including the breaking of tools and the deliberate mismanagement of tasks. Where others might have seen subversion or even the consequences of being "ruined by idleness," Cartwright saw disease. In 1851 he identified several ailments that slaves were likely to contract, including "rascality" and "dyesthesia," a disease of "inadequate breathing." A slave suffering from this condition "performs the task assigned to him in a headlong and careless manner, treading down with his feet or cutting with his hoe the plants he is put to cultivate — breaking the tools he works with, and spoiling everything he touches." The "cure" involved bathing, oiling, and beating the sufferer with a broad strap. My favorite of Cartwright's syndromes is "drapetomania." Like the patriots of the Revolutionary era, whom the British described as "liberty mad," slaves occasionally took sick with "drapetomania," or "the insane desire to run away." Slaves with this bizarre and inscrutable ailment had to be treated like children "to prevent and cure them from running away."

Cartwright was nine years away from unveiling his most fantastic theory, a highly imaginative reinterpretation of the biblical story of Genesis. In his version, Eve was not tempted by a serpent but instead was lured into sin by a Negro gardener. Cartwright cleared up this vast misunderstanding when he discovered that the Hebrew word for "snake" (*Nachash*) also meant "to be or become black." After that, it was just a matter of putting two and two together. The failure of Cartwright's Negro to tend the crops in the Garden of Eden may explain his descendants' subsequent "rascality" among the cotton and tobacco rows of dear old Dixie.

These views "were not the curious musings of an isolated crackpot" but were respected in the South as much as Nott's, according to George Fredrickson. They illustrate how the doctrine of Negro inferiority was spread in many directions. The highbrow rhetoric of the professorial class introduced niggerology to the top layers of society through the classrooms at ivy-bedecked institutions, lecture halls, and academies of science, from which its principles could funnel downward. At the same time, the extreme racism found in low-brow pamphlets appealed to the less learned even as its noxious fumes sent niggerology upward. Without such exchanges, the N word might have become just another short-lived insult, a quaint relic of a coarser age. Instead, "high" and "low" language combined to broaden its use while reinforcing false notions of blackness that would influence government policy and popular attitudes for decades to come.

5

Life Among the Lowly

> What de matter now, massa? Always want for to raise fuss wid old nigger. Was only funnin anyhow.
>
> — Edgar Allan Poe, "The Gold-Bug," 1843

"SURE A NAGUR has as much sowl as a white . . . come hither, ould man, and warm that shivering carcass of yeers by the blaze of this fire. I'm sure a Guinea nagur loves heat as much as a souldier loves his drop."

The "ould man" in question is Caesar Thompson, the costar and comic foil in *The Spy*, James Fenimore Cooper's tale of a Yankee peddler who doubles as an espionage agent for George Washington's Continental army. Published in 1821, it was Cooper's second novel and his first success. To him goes another far less distinctive first, one that passed without notice at the time: he created in Caesar what is quite likely "the first full-length portrait of the contented slave in American literature."

The gray-haired Caesar is shown to be tireless, superstitious, easily frightened, and loyal beyond reason to his master, Mr. Wharton. Cooper's description of his appearance contains hints of the qualities that nineteenth-century caricaturists would soon seize on and mercilessly exaggerate. We learn that Caesar possessed "abundantly capacious" nostrils and a mouth that was "capacious to a fault and was only tolerated on account of the double row of pearls it contained." His legs were warped and misshapen:

The calves were neither before nor behind, but rather on the outer side of the limb, inclining forward, and so close to the knee as to render the free use of that joint a subject of doubt . . . the leg was placed so near the center as to make it sometimes a matter of dispute whether he was walking backwards.

Cooper usually refers to Caesar as some variant of "the faithful old black" or "the African." Occasionally other characters rebuke or threaten him in a more colorful fashion. The epithets he is forced to endure include "blackie," "darkie," and "Mr. Blueskin." His obsequiousness seems to bring out the worst in the whites whom he must serve. A military officer tells him, "Harkee, blacky, if you quit the house again without my knowledge, I will shave off one of those ebony ears with this razor." But tolerance has its limits, even for such a faithful servant as Caesar. When a houseguest refers to the "niggers to the south," he can no longer hold his peace.

"No more negur than be yourself, Mister Birch," Caesar tells him before going on to assert that "a black man as good as white . . . so long he behave himself." He is more circumspect later in the novel when, just before he is invited to sit by the fire, his interrogator proudly tells him, "I am none of them who thinks niggurs haven't got souls."

Souls, sure, but brains are another matter. Caesar is easily frightened and distracted by visions of ghosts, unlike the sane, rational whites whose prejudices he must withstand. "It is in vain that philosophy and reason contend with our fears and early impressions," Cooper tells us, "but Caesar had neither to offer him their frail support."

The superstitious, contented slave was but one of the Negro stereotypes that early American novelists used with enthusiasm. Sterling Brown showed that while "some authors presented the Negro with dignity and sympathy . . . serious realism was still far off." He identified six other distinct types of black characters regularly found in this fiction: Wretched Freeman, Comic Negro, Brute Negro, Tragic Mulatto, Local Color Negro, and Exotic Primitive. One might also add Sable Temptress, an early example of which is Mari, a young slave who appears in another Cooper novel, *Satanstoe* (1845). The author describes her as a "buxom, glistening, smooth-faced, laughing, red-lipped, pearl-toothed, black-eyed hussy that seemed born for fun." It's no surprise that Cooper's description differs little from that offered by none other than Louis Agassiz some eighteen years later. Agassiz blamed Southern miscegenation on the sexual magnetism of dark-skinned slave women. According to the bizarre logic of niggerology, a female slave's sexual powers increased in direct proportion to the degree of melanin in her skin. A naïve young white gentleman could hardly be faulted if he found himself helpless to resist such allure. Once seduced, Agassiz said, he is led "gradually to seek more spicy partners, as I have heard the full blacks called by fast young men."

Cooper was hardly alone in the literary degradation of Negroes but, as the first major American novelist, must share some portion of blame. He probably would have defended himself against charges of niggerizing by saying he was simply giving the people what they wanted. A shrewd monitor of the marketplace, he modeled *The Spy* and his subsequent efforts after the Waverley novels of Sir Walter Scott. *Ivanhoe* and the other Scott romances tickled the imaginations of Southern men and women in particular, feeding their fantasies of gallant knights, damsels in distress, and a noble aristocracy built on caste, comportment, and plantation balls. Five million copies of Scott's novels were sold in the United States between 1813 and 1823, many of them in the South. Mark Twain later explained the author's popularity as "Sir Walter Scott disease." In *Life on the Mississippi* he wrote, "Scott had so large a hand in making Southern character, as it existed before the War, that he is a great measure responsible for the War."

Cooper exerted a similar influence in the shaping of the fictional Negro character, continuing to include blacks in subsequent novels such as *The Pioneers* (1823), *The Last of the Mohicans* (1826), and *The Red Rover* (1827), which features a memorable supporting character, a Brute Negro named Scipio Africa. So noble and physically powerful is this free sailor that his white crewmates feel compelled to testify to his exemplary strength after his death: "A Spanish windlass would not give a stronger screw than the knuckle of that nigger," one of them avers. Lest readers get too carried away by Scipio's virtues, "nigger" works handily to remind them of his debased status.

Other major American writers — the first group to successfully challenge the commercial and cultural domination of British and European novelists — followed Cooper's example, offering a generous sprinkling of "niggers" in their various works. Among them was Edgar Allan Poe, whose "Journal of Julius Rodman" (1840) features an "ugly old" slave named Toby who closely resembles our old friend Caesar Thompson. Toby has "swollen lips, large white protruding eyes, flat nose, long ears, double head, pot-belly and bow-legs."

In image and conduct he is kin to Jupiter, the old black servant in Poe's "Gold-Bug," who so enjoys being a slave that he could not be induced, "neither by threats nor by promises," to taste the fruits that freedom might yield. Jupiter refers to himself as a "nigger" throughout the brief story, and he repeatedly demonstrates that he cannot tell his left hand from his right. At one point the ever-submissive servant dares to talk back to his master; in pitifully broken English he says that he "needn't hollo at poor nigger dat style." Like Caesar Thompson, Jupiter has been burdened with a lofty name, as "if in mockery of his degraded state." Sterling Brown had such characters in mind when he wrote of the early American writers' dearly held "assumption that Negroes are especially designed as butts for rough practical jokes."

Among the white Americans writing fiction before the Civil War, Herman Melville may stand alone in his ability to fashion complex black characters. In various works such as *Moby-Dick* and especially *Benito Cereno*, he created Negroes who lived, struggled, and thought beyond the confines of stereotypes. However, most authors offered only evidence to support the observation of the critic Catherine Juanita Starke, who noted that white authors, "supported by the myth of white superiority and black inferiority . . . could, without compunction, depict blacks as accommodative chattels in literature."

"A FINE SET OF NIGGERS"

The plantation tradition in American literature can be seen as a logical outgrowth of readers' fascination with the novels of Walter Scott. Emphasizing courtly manners and building on the black stereotypes found in Cooper, Poe, Washington Irving, among others, novelists in this tradition offered a distinctly romantic view of the peculiar institution. To prove that slavery's alleged atrocities existed only in overwrought Yankee imaginations, these novelists presented bondage as a festive vacation, a joyful orgy of cornshucking, cotton-picking, and banjo-plucking, or, as Sterling Brown put it, "the grown-up slaves were contented, the pickaninnies were frolicking, the steamboat was hooting around the bend, God was in his heaven, and all was right with the world."

John Pendleton Kennedy's *Swallow Barn* (1832) marked the debut of the plantation tradition. The protagonist is a Northerner named Littleton who, after first expressing his disapproval of slaveholding, eventually concludes that it's not so bad after all. Most of the slaves that he encounters during a visit to the South recall the "merry-hearted, grinning, dancing, singing, affectionate kind of creatures" that Thomas Carlyle later described in his 1853 essay, "An Occasional Discourse on the Nigger Question." Littleton remarks, "I never meet a Negro man — unless he is quite old — that he is not whistling; and the women sing morning to night." Like Caesar Thompson, who had "neither philosophy nor reason" to govern his behavior, the blacks in *Swallow Barn* are incapable of rational thought. According to Littleton, the Negro "is in his moral constitution, a dependent upon the white race, dependent for guidance and direction ever to the procurement of his most indispensable necessaries." Kennedy's blacks differ little from the deformed, tragicomic gnomes found in Poe and Cooper. He describes elderly slaves as "wrinkled decrepit old men, with faces shortened as if with drawing string, noses that seemed to have run all to nostril, and with feet of the configuration of a mattock."

William Gilmore Simms, another prominent herald of the plantation tradition, rendered slavery in gentle, rose-colored tones in novels such as *Guy Rivers* (1834), *The Partisan* (1835), and *Richard Hurdis* (1838). *The Yemassee* (1832) includes among its characters a slave named Hector. He is so besotted with bondage that he refuses manumission when it is offered. He neatly combines several stereotypes in a brief speech to his master explaining why he is unfit for freedom. "'Tis onpossible, maussa," he says. "You make Hector free, he turn wuss more nor poor buckrah — he tief out of de shop — he git drunk and lie in de ditch."

In such novels black people frequently refer to themselves and one another as "niggers" in an improbable dialect that almost requires translation. Simms's *Forayers* (1855) features a massive slave named Abram Johnson who talks like so: "Wha da debbil dat! Who dat, I say, da hit maussa nigger wid hick'ry?" "Master" and "nigger" have the same ending, but poor Abram is too tongue-tied to manage it twice in the same sentence.

In Dion Boucicault's *Octoroon* (1859), blacks have grown so fond of slavery that whites needn't bother much anymore with such particulars as readying their chattel for the auction block — their faithful blacks will take care of such matters themselves. Consider Old Pete, who urges the other slaves — all of whom are to be sold down the river — to put on a good appearance for their master's sake: "Let every darkey look his best for de Judge's sake — so dem strangers from New Orleans shall say, dem's happy darkeys, dem's a fine set of niggers."

Novelists who described blacks in such terms added flesh to what had been mostly abstract conjurations of Negro inferiority; their vivid, "nigger"-laden descriptions filled a void in the popular imagination and inspired the demeaning images at the heart of the minstrel shows and racist cartoons that flourished in the middle and latter half of the nineteenth century.

TOMFOOLERY

Not every novelist defended slavery. The first anti-slavery novel arrived in 1836, four years after *Swallow Barn. The Slave or Memoirs of Archy Moore* was initially published anonymously. A revised edition, expanded and renamed *The White Slave,* came out in 1852; its author was identified as Richard Hildreth, a historian. Others soon followed, including *Jamie, The Fugitive* by Emily Catherine Pierson (1851) and *Thrice Through the Furnace* by Mrs. Sophia Little (1852). Whatever response they generated was soon overwhelmed in the uproar prompted by a book also published in 1852. The most influential reinforcement of the myth of Negro inferiority since Jefferson's *Notes on the State of Virginia,* it was *Uncle Tom's Cabin.*

Harriet Beecher Stowe's work was initially titled *Uncle Tom's Cabin, or The Man That Was a Thing* and appeared as a serial in the *National Era,* an abolitionist journal, in 1851. The following year the book appeared as *Uncle Tom's Cabin, or Life Among the Lowly.* Its reception was nothing less than sensational. It sold 10,000 copies in the first week alone and more than 300,000 in the first year. It quickly sold more than a million and a half copies in England and was translated into several foreign languages.

The title character, a Christlike figure who loves his tormentors and willingly suffers all manner of abuse, has over time become a symbol of black self-hatred and unreasonable acquiescence to racial oppression. Ironically, in some quarters his name is perhaps a more hateful epithet than "nigger." When he first appears in the novel, however, he is described in flattering terms: "He was a large, broad-chested, powerfully made man, of a full glossy black and a face whose truly African features were characterized by an expression of grave and steady good sense, united with much kindliness and benevolence." Although he does not appear cartoonish, like Jupiter and Hector before him, he shares their disenchantment with the idea of freedom. He refuses to run away when his first master plans to sell him, suggesting that any inclinations in that direction are undesirable character flaws. "Mas'r always found me on the spot," he explains. "He always will. I never broke trust, and I never will." He treats his second master with similar indulgence, expressing more concern for Augustine St. Clare's soul than for his own wife and children, still pining for him at the plantation where he formerly toiled. St. Clare's languid decadence has so perturbed faithful Tom that the dutiful servant is willing to die for his owner. "I's willin' to lay down my life, this blessed day, to see Mas'r a Christian," he fervently declares. Tom's tireless forbearance so enrages his third owner, the memorable Simon Legree, that he has Tom whipped to death. When the son of Tom's former master arrives to mourn the fallen slave, Legree becomes nearly apoplectic with disbelief. "What a fuss, for a dead nigger!" he exclaims.

Unsympathetic observers might have said something similar about the critical and popular response to the novel itself. Its admirers in the world of letters included George Sand, Charles Dickens, John Greenleaf Whittier, William Dean Howells, and Leo Tolstoy. The abolitionist camp was more reserved in its praise. Writing in *The Liberator*, William Lloyd Garrison praised Stowe's "rare descriptive powers . . . uncommon moral and philosophical acumen, great facility of thought and expression." But he questioned her interpretation of Scripture, especially with regard to nonviolent resistance. In a letter to *Frederick Douglass's Paper*, William G. Allen disagreed with Stowe's remarks in favor of colonization (as did Garrison) but generally praised the book. Uncle Tom's passivity did give Allen pause, however. "My non-resistance is that of the Douglass, Parker and Phillips school," he wrote. "I believe . . . that it is not light the slaveholder wants but fire, and he ought to have it. I do not advocate revenge, but simply, resistance to tyrants, if need be, to the death."

As expected, the Southern critics objected strenuously to *Uncle Tom's Cabin*. An unsigned, 10,000-word rebuttal in the *Southern Literary Messenger* condemned the novel's many shortcomings, among them an unorganized plot, a lack of veracity, and a disturbing tendency to forget the proper place of women in respectable society. Pro-slavery novelists also rushed into the fray, supplementing the many pamphlets, articles, and editorials used to shore up the splintery timbers of the plantation tradition. Sterling Brown estimates that at least fourteen pro-slavery novels appeared in the three years after the publication of *Uncle Tom's Cabin*.

Typical of them were *Aunt Phillis's Cabin* by Mary Eastman (1852) and Caroline Lee Hertz's *Planter's Northern Bride* (1854). Eastman's subtitle, *Or, Southern Life as It Is*, manages to take a swipe at both Stowe's novel and at *American Slavery as It Is* (1839), an abolitionist pamphlet by Theodore Weld that greatly influenced the writing of *Uncle Tom's Cabin*. Like William Lloyd Garrison, Eastman also had problems with Stowe's interpretations of Scripture. Garrison had asked, "when it is the whites who are trodden in the dust, does Christ justify them in taking up arms to vindicate their rights? And when it is the blacks who are thus treated, does Christ require them to be patient, harmless, long-suffering and forgiving? And are there two Christs?" Eastman did not ask questions; she provided answers. In her preface, for example, she explained that Christ "came on an errand of mercy to the world, and he was all powerful to accomplish the Divine intent; but, did he emancipate the slave? No; he came to redeem the world from the power of sin; his was no earthly mission; he did not interfere with the organization of society."

Caroline Lee Hertz, like Fanny Kemble, had married a Southern gentleman. Unlike the British actress, Hertz was moved to create a heroine who is quickly won over to the wonders of slaveholding. "Ooh," she coos to her valiant groom, "I never dreamed that slavery could present an aspect so tender and affectionate!" Building on the conventions established by *Swallow Barn* and other novels in the plantation tradition, Eastman and Hertz helped to advance a frontal assault on anti-slavery sensibilities.

Stowe didn't hesitate to defend herself. An author's note appended to the novel asserted that Stowe and her friends "have observed characters the counterpart of almost all that are here introduced; and many of the sayings are word for word as heard herself, or reported to her." In 1853 she published *A Key to Uncle Tom's Cabin*, a compilation of her principal sources, which was intended to counter arguments based on her having spent little time in the slaveholding South. She defended her title character's intense spiritual devotion by citing the example of Josiah Henson, a real former slave whose ghostwritten memoirs were published in 1849. Stowe contributed a preface to the revised edition, which appeared in 1858 as *Truth Stranger Than Fiction: Father Henson's Story of His Own Life*. "From that time to the present I have been called 'Uncle Tom,'" Henson later recalled, "and I feel proud of the title." However, as Darryl Pinckney has observed, "Stowe never answered clearly the question of whether or not Henson had been her primary model."

The most interesting of the fictional responses to *Uncle Tom* were written by men known primarily for their nonfiction contributions to the abolitionist struggle. Frederick Douglass's novella *The Heroic Slave* (1853) reads as a pointed rebuttal of the happy darkies that populate both the plantation follies of writers such as Kennedy and Eastman as well as Stowe's more earnest but equally myopic effort. Douglass uses a liberal portion of irony — a rare quality in this context — in his tale of Madison Washington, "one of the truest, manliest, and bravest" men in the history of Virginia. When we meet the hero, he is resolving to escape from slavery: "*Liberty* I will have, or die in the attempt to gain it." Madison is similar in stature to Uncle Tom, "tall, symmetrical, and strong," possessing "the strength of the lion" and "arms like polished iron." After running away from slavery, he sounds as if he's talking about Uncle Tom when he recalls seeing slaves "merrily passing away the time, as though their hearts knew no sorrow." He sees a "cowardly acquiescence in their own degradation."

Madison is recaptured when he returns to the plantation to rescue his wife and children. He escapes again with the help of a white ally named Listwell. Using files that Listwell provided, he severs his chains and leads a mutiny aboard a ship en route to New Orleans.

The events of the rebellion are narrated by Tom Grant, the first mate whose life Madison spared. Grant openly admires Madison. "As a general rule, they are ignorant," he says of blacks, "but . . . there are exceptions to this general rule."

Douglass took direct aim at the cult of white superiority, exposing the "general rule" of ignorance that seemed to guide white assessments of Negro potential. Both Listwell and Grant have what might be termed spiritual conversions after close encounters with Madison. "I felt myself in the presence of a superior man," Grant later confesses to a white audience, "one who, had he been a white man, I would have followed willingly and gladly in any honorable enterprise."

Wielding irony like a cutlass, Douglass skewered white attempts to link blacks to lower primates. After Madison and eighteen others overwhelm the captain, most of the cowardly white sailors climb up the rigging and refuse to come down. Grant recalls the terror-stricken sailors "clinging, like so many frightened monkeys." In exchange for his life, Grant agrees to steer the ship to Nassau, where a group of black soldiers in the British army allow the mutineers to go free. As much as *The Heroic Slave* rebuts the condescending pieties of *Uncle Tom's Cabin* and similar novels, it clearly is also intended as a cautionary tale, urging whites to come to their senses while they still had the opportunity. "It was a mystery to us *where* he got his knowledge of language," says Tom Grant, "but as little was said to him, none of us knew the extent of his intelligence and ability till it was too late."

Several unresolved questions remain about Martin Delany's *Blake,* which is often identified as the first black-nationalist novel written in the United States. We don't know exactly when Delany began to compose it, and it has never been published in its entirety (at least six chapters are believed to be missing). The tale of a slave rebel who hopes to foment a nationwide uprising, *Blake* builds on themes that had been present in Delany's writings for nearly a decade before the novel began to appear as a serial in January 1859. More certain is the novel's connection to *Uncle Tom's Cabin.* Long before the publication of *Blake*'s first chapters in *The Anglo-African Magazine*, Delany had established himself as one of *Uncle Tom*'s harshest critics. He published three strongly critical letters in 1853, taking Stowe to task for her denigration of dark-skinned blacks (a point echoed by many of the novel's later critics), for her careless treatment of slave dialect, and for the presumption and condescension barely concealed beneath her genteel advocacy. (Perhaps as motivation, Delany prefaced both parts of his novel with stanzas from Stowe's religious poetry.) Delany was clearly frustrated — if not infuriated — by the attention *Uncle Tom's Cabin* received. *Blake* can be read as his attempt to set the record straight.

Of the many issues that Delany raises, the most relevant here are his attempt to replace the image of the passive, inferior slave with a more defiant and "manly" one, his attitude toward the word "nigger," and his sustained attack on the use of Christianity to enforce submission among black captives.

Delany's hero, Henry Holland (he changes his surname to Blake in Part II), is the polar opposite of Stowe's Tom. He reacts angrily to news that his wife has been sold and scoffs when Mammy, a fellow slave, advises him to take comfort in religion. "Don't tell me about religion! What's religion to me? My wife is sold away from me by a man who is one of the leading members of the very church to which both she and I belong! Put my trust in the Lord! I have done so all my life nearly, and of what use is it to me? My wife is sold from me just the same as if I didn't."

Henry's fiery eloquence resembles that of Madison Washington, Douglass's protagonist. Neither hero's dialogue shows traces of the "plantation speech" that even white abolitionists regarded as evidence of Negro authenticity. Of Stowe's slave characters, only George Harris can speak the words as trippingly — and he has a mixed-race background. Delany drives his point home by stressing that Henry is "a black — a pure Negro — handsome, manly and intelligent."

The search for his wife becomes Henry's reason for running away and enables him to plant the seeds of rebellion as he travels from one plantation to another. Henry's bravery and willingness to wander far afield contradicts Stowe's assertion in *Uncle Tom's Cabin* that blacks "are not naturally daring and enterprising, but home-loving and affectionate." The slaves he meets are for the most part gentle dupes who have allowed the white man's religion to cloud their perceptions. Henry overcomes their doubts through eloquent persuasion and the power of his example. He possesses none of Uncle Tom's resilient piety and makes it clear that while he still believes in a higher power, he's prepared to believe on his own terms. "I do trust the Lord as much as ever," he tells Mammy, "but I now understand him better than I use to, that's all. I don't intend to be made a fool of any longer by false preaching."

Unlike Cooper's "faithful black" or Stowe's "faithful creature," the resourceful Henry is consistently described as "the intelligent slave." In a delightfully subversive touch, Delany provided an early example of liberation theology by using Christian language in the service of rebellion: he advises his accomplices to signal their approach by calling out, "Stand still and see the salvation." After leading his first party of escapees into Canada, Henry further distinguishes himself from Uncle Tom, who does little other than pray for and mourn his absent wife and children. In contrast, Henry immediately prepares to return to the United States to find and retrieve his spouse. With a divine providence on his side, he will prevail. He tells his fellow fugitives, "By the instincts of a husband, I'll have her if living! If dead, by impulses of a Heaven-inspired soul, I'll avenge her loss unto death!"

The white characters that Henry encounters routinely condemn blacks as "niggers" unworthy of respect or compassion. Dr. Donald, a white man who has married into an Indian tribe in Arkansas, doesn't hesitate to call Henry a "nigger" after a tense exchange. In the next chapter, a group of drunken white tavern-goers revel in the N word, bantering it about some seventeen times as they repeatedly wish for a "nigger" to be used as a test quarry for a pair of specially trained hunting dogs — or "nigger dogs," to be precise.

The widespread use of the N word as an opprobrious term is illustrated by the dialogue of two white immigrants whom Henry encounters in his travels. Delany provided both of them with a stream of nonsensical syllables, of which "nigger" is nearly the only word that can be deciphered. The first, a Dutchman who confronts Henry outside Washington, D.C., berates him without fear — "You nagher, you! dat ish not anzer mine question! I does ax you vat fahr you go to Charleston, and you anzer me dat!" — until Henry frightens him off by brandishing his gun.

A German named Slusher, whom he meets outside Detroit, is even less proficient in the language of his adopted land. "Gonvound dish bishnesh!" he exclaims. "Id alwaysh cosht more dan de ding ish wordt. Mine Got! afder dish I'll mindt mine own bishnesh. Iv tem Soudt Amerigans vill gheep niggersh de musht gedch dem demzelve. Mine ligger ish ghon, I losht mine resht, te niggersh rhun avay, an' I nod magk von zent!"

Delany seemed to be lampooning two things here: (1) the speed and alacrity with which the white immigrants adopted the racist beliefs and behavior of their fellow whites, and (2) the ludicrous gibberish often placed in the mouths of black characters by white novelists and purveyors of blackface minstrelsy, which was at its peak of popularity when *Blake* was written. His deft use of irony and pointed sarcasm can also be seen in the many parodies of minstrel lyrics that punctuate his prose. The black characters in *Blake* also use the N word but with considerably less frequency. Interestingly, they tend to use it mostly to speak ill of a black who is perceived to have sold out to white interests (a "rale wite folk's nigga") — an individual who in later works would most likely be called an Uncle Tom.

Delany's assessment of *Uncle Tom's Cabin* was considerably harsher than Douglass's. The latter remained circumspect, perhaps because he had already formulated his plan to enlist Stowe's help in raising funds for a school (a project that never got off the ground) — or perhaps he simply recognized that Stowe's intentions were good. Years after Douglass and Delany, black criticism of *Uncle Tom's Cabin* continued to balance its literary merits against the author's abolitionist sympathies. Sterling Brown, for example, noted in 1937 that "the rebellious and militant are generally shown to be of mixed blood . . . whereas the more African type is shown as docile." He went on to suggest the likelihood of subsequent novelists' echoing Stowe's prejudices, remarking, "some novelists depart from this pattern, but the pattern persists and has remained wrongly influential." Brown pulled back considerably after acknowledging the novel's flaws, generously concluding, "Mrs. Stowe showed that slavery was a great wrong, and that Negroes are human. Is it here that critics believe she lies?"

James Baldwin delivered a blistering denunciation of Stowe in a 1949 essay, "Everybody's Protest Novel." *Uncle Tom's Cabin* is "a very bad novel," according to Baldwin. He wondered why Stowe focused so much on violence and brutality while neglecting to explore "what it was, after all, that moved her people to such deeds." Because the only virtuous blacks other than Tom (and later Topsy) are mixed-race, Stowe has equated black with evil and white with grace, Baldwin argued. "Apart from her lively procession of field hands, house niggers, Chloe, Topsy, etc. . . . she has only three other Negroes in the book," he wrote. Baldwin was referring to George and Eliza Harris, both of whom were pale enough to pass for white, and their son, Harry. He reserved his greatest scorn for this trio, whose "quaintness" and "charm" reminded him of a "darky bootblack doing a buck and wing to the clatter of condescending coins."

The heat of Baldwin's words can be felt even when revisited in the twenty-first century. His vehemence is a testament to the deep cultural impact of *Uncle Tom's Cabin*, which Baldwin felt required comment nearly a hundred years after its publication. It's easy to dismiss past works when regarding them from a modern perspective. Still, the enduring ability of *Uncle Tom's Cabin* to stir debate merits its ongoing assessment. If nothing else, Stowe's novel demonstrates that the imaginary thread separating fervent believers in black inferiority from supporters of black emancipation was thin enough to slip through the eye of a needle with room to spare. The N word is spoken 109 times in *Uncle Tom's Cabin*, in nearly all instances by slaves or villainous whites. One could argue that Stowe used the epithet repeatedly as a way of emphasizing the racist tenor of her time. This defense would have more validity if not for the equally dehumanizing language of her ostensibly sympathetic narration. She preferred to call her black characters (and only her black characters) "creatures." Tom, for example, is successively described as "that good, faithful creature"; as part of a group of "poor, simple, dependent creatures"; and a "faithful, excellent, confiding creature." Such portrayals subtly imply that blacks are not sentient beings but unthinking animals, closer to beasts of burden than to white people on the evolutionary ladder.

The same is true of her pronouncements on Negro intelligence and behavior. However well intentioned, they exude the unmistakable stench of white superiority. They are particularly mind-boggling given Stowe's familiarity with Douglass, Henry Bibb, and other accomplished blacks. Those experiences notwithstanding, Stowe informs her readers that "the Negro mind, impassioned and imaginative, always attaches itself to hymns and expressions of a vivid and pictorial nature." Negroes with minds such as those she described don't sound much different from the slave characters in *Swallow Barn* who whistle or sing "morning to night." The author of *Swallow Barn*, whose hero believes that blacks when left alone exhibit "the helplessness of a child — without foresight, without thrift of any kind," should have found little to trouble him in Stowe's descriptions of Tom, who has "the soft, impressible nature of his kindly race, ever yearning toward the simple and childlike." Indeed, the notion of childlike simplicity rears its head with nauseating regularity in Stowe's novel. "There is no more use in making believe to be angry with a Negro than with a child," she told us. "Both instinctively see the true state of the case, through all attempts to affect the contrary." This is only slightly less insulting than the "findings" of Louis Agassiz, who had declared just a few years earlier that Negro minds compared unfavorably with those of white fetuses.

In Stowe's view, blacks' natural submissiveness blessed them with the potential to be exemplary Christians. For Stowe, African virtue was inseparable from primitiveness. The Negro, she imagined, may someday "show forth some of the latest and most magnificent revelations of human life. Certainly they will in their gentleness, their lowly docility of heart, their aptitude to repose on a superior mind and rest in a higher power, their childlike simplicity of affection, and facility of forgiveness." In the context of Stowe's faint "praise," Delany's criticism seems not only understandable but also a model of restraint.

By 1862 there was one copy of *Uncle Tom's Cabin* for every four or five readers in America. The unprecedented popularity of such a book — in which blacks are repeatedly described as "niggers" and "creatures" and shown to be incapable of any independent action besides praying — inevitably strengthened the myth of Negro inferiority. Ultimately, Stowe's well-intentioned but wrongheaded language was as damaging as the ideology she hoped to rebut.

6

Jim Crow and Company

Belobed Brack Brodren, — Me tend to dress my scorce to you dis nite on de all imported subject of Language, an de various tongues ob difern nations and niggars, libbin and dead, known and unknown.

— "Follitt's Black Lectures, No. 6," c. 1880s

IN HIS INTRODUCTION to the 1998 edition of *Uncle Tom's Cabin*, Darryl Pinckney reported that inadequate copyright laws stifled Stowe, leaving her "unable to protect herself against 'borrowing' of her character." As a result, staged adaptations "became a regular feature of big-city and small-town American entertainment." Producers of minstrel shows pounced on the prime material the novel offered, taking advantage of what can only be seen as a logical connection. Stowe's handling of certain scenes and characters shows that "adaptation" often worked both ways.

In a passage that drew James Baldwin's contempt, she introduces little Harry, the son of George and Eliza, in a scene right out of minstrelsy. After his master hails him as "Jim Crow," Harry enters with "an air of comic assurance" and proceeds to scamper after a handful of raisins tossed in his direction. Following additional prodding, "the boy commenced one of those wild, grotesque songs common among the Negroes, in a rich, clear voice, accompanying his singing with many revolutions of the hands, feet, and whole body, all in perfect time to the music."

Similarly, another slave, a fieldhand named Sam, resembles the gaudy dandies in minstrel shows who get laughs by mangling the language. Determined to dazzle his fellow captives, Sam prepares to "speechify these yer niggers." Hilariously and inadequately mimicking the speech of the whites with whom he comes in contact, Sam "performs" in the quarters, delivering soliloquies of "the most imperturbable earnestness and solemnity."

Topsy, an awkward sprite and wild child who may be Stowe's most disturbing creation, is introduced by her master as "rather a funny specimen in the Jim Crow line." Like little Harry, she is called on to perform — and she doesn't disappoint. Stowe provides a breathless play-by-play: "The black, glassy eyes glittered with a kind of wicked drollery, and the thing struck up, in a clear shrill voice, an odd Negro melody, to which she kept time with her hands and feet, spinning round, clapping her hands, knocking her knees together, in a wild, fantastic sort of time, and producing in her throat all those guttural sounds which distinguish the native music of her race."

Such obviously outsize characters all but beckoned to producers in search of lucrative vehicles. Even straightforward adaptations outside the sphere of minstrelsy imposed significant disservices, according to Sterling Brown. In adhering to Stowe's plot, "they glorified the Negro's submissiveness," he wrote, "and they fostered the error that the mixed blood characters, merely because they were nearer white, were more intelligent and militant, and therefore more tragic in their enslavement."

Less faithful renditions took liberties as their creators saw fit, over time affecting a dramatic change in presentations of the title character. "While Uncle Tom in Stowe's novel had been a strong and reasonably young man," Eric Lott has observed, "Uncle Tom in successive productions of the play grew older and older, no doubt owing to the influence of minstrelsy's pathetic elderly men such as Stephen Foster's 'Old Uncle Ned.'" Indeed, when images of Tom began to appear on whiskey bottles and other products toward the end of the century, the wizened Negro on the label often appeared to have shuffled right out of one of Foster's irreverent fantasies, such as:

> There was an old nigger,
> And his name was Uncle Ned,
> But he's dead long ago, long ago;
> He had no wool on the top of his head,
> In de place where de wool ought to grow.

"My Old Kentucky Home," one of the best-known selections in Foster's repertoire, was originally written to be sung by none other than Uncle Tom in a stage adaptation.

"NIGGER SHOWS"

Among the first white entertainers to blacken their faces in the dubious service of art was George Washington Dixon, who appeared in Negro drag during a circus in Albany, New York, in 1827. A year later, a twenty-year-old actor named Thomas Dartmouth Rice caught Dixon's act at the Chatham Theatre in New York City. He watched carefully while the veteran performer ran through his bill of fare, which included such tunes as "Coal Black Rose" and "Long Tail Blue":

> Some Niggers they have but one coat,
> But you see I've got two;
> I wears a jacket all the week,
> And Sunday my long tail blue.

Dixon earned a portion of minstrel immortality through his long association with Zip Coon, a character he created. Along with Jim Crow and Dan Tucker, Zip became one of the most memorable blackface personages. Dixon played him as a Northern black who'd become too big for his britches, spouting nonsensical syllables and lusting after white women in a misguided quest to become equal to whites. Overdressed in the manner of a dandy, Zip stood for the danger of miscegenation and functioned as a stereotype of the comic Negro, "addicted to the use of big words, to gaudy finery, to brawling with the razor, and to raiding chicken roosts."

"Dandy Jim of Caroline," another parody of the black urban up-start, was perhaps even more popular. Unlike Zip, Dandy Jim was performed by any number of minstrels, and variations of the same song were devoted to his exploits:

> Dar's dandy niggers in each place,
> Wid beef stake lips dat wink wid grace,
> But none among de gals can shine,
> Like dandy Jim ob Caroline

Echoes of Zip's and Dandy Jim's slick malapropisms, macho preening, bodacious wardrobe, and streetwise chatter resonate through a long line of black urban characters, including Sportin' Life (*Porgy and Bess*), Kingfish (*Amos 'n' Andy*), and Huggy Bear (*Starsky and Hutch*).

Soon after seeing Dixon, Tom Rice developed his own act. He called his solo revue of pseudo-Negro songs and sketches "Ethio-pian Opera." Rice, who became extremely influential, based his burlesques and parodies not on operas but on British plays and comic melodramas. Still, the label he chose seemed to have struck a sympathetic chord.

Mark Twain, recalling his introduction to minstrel performances during the 1840s, saw the connection as well. "If I could have the nigger show back again in its pristine purity and perfection I should have but little further use for opera," he enthused in his *Au-tobiography*.

Minstrelsy evolved into an ensemble effort in 1842, when Edwin P. Christy staged a group performance in Buffalo, New York. The following year, Dan Emmett formed a quartet, the Virginia Min-strels, and took the stage in New York City. Minstrel concerts were always flexible enough to accommodate improvisation and banter with audiences, but over time the basic structure became relatively uniform.

The Virginia Minstrels and other groups initially publicized their appearances as innovative performances derived from "fieldwork" conducted on the plantations of the South. Blackface comedy, according to such claims, was a faithful introduction to the "sports and pastimes of the Negro race." In reality, such fare was, in W. T. Lhamon's wonderful phrase, "straight-up faux anthropology, done as theatre." Minstrel show audiences, composed largely of immigrants and uneducated urban dwellers, were hardly in a position to judge the accuracy of the entertainers' alleged research and, as the genre matured, such claims — conceivably no longer necessary — became less frequent. As its practitioners abandoned all pretense of authenticity, Sterling Brown contended, the dialect of minstrelsy "became gibberish and the caricature a cartoon."

According to Shane White, the acceptance of gibberish as a reasonable parody of black speech "went hand in hand with another linguistic innovation, the use of the term 'nigger' in print. . . . the caricatured speech perpetuated through newspapers, handbills, and the like was insidiously effective in demeaning blacks."

Dan Emmett eventually took advantage of that trend by writing and performing drastically mangled "Negro Sermons," in which his colored preacher attempts to share the wisdom of the Bible with his addled parishioners. A sample: "Den yoa see de meanin of de 'postle when he say: de 'archiloozikus winky-wamity, an reelder-ackerus weltigooberous am too flamity bango, for de crackaboolity ob its own watchafalarity.'"

Minstrelsy's popularity peaked in the mid-1840s and early 1850s, coinciding with large waves of Irish and German immigration. Newcomers, almost exclusively working class, packed the theaters when minstrels performed. The Irish bore the brunt of the anti-immigrant sentiment during this period, often responding by venting their frustrations on blacks and abolitionists. Fearing the competition of Negroes for precious jobs in the skilled trades, Irishmen wasted little time endorsing the notion that black workers were fit for only menial occupations — if they were to be employed at all.

The Irish also expressed their resentment by rioting in the streets and participating in mob violence. In Pennsylvania, they clashed with blacks in 1832, 1842, 1849, and 1853; in bloody preludes to the Civil War, they terrorized blacks during the anti-abolitionist riots in New York in 1834 and during the Draft Riots of 1863.

In *North of Slavery*, Leon Litwack quoted a British traveler, who observed, "To be called an 'Irishman' is almost as great an insult as to be stigmatized as a 'nigger feller,' and in a street-row, both appellations are flung off among the combatants with great zest and vigour." Eric Lott has offered a similar observation: "Antebellum native whites widely equated immigrant Irish with blacks as an alien, subhuman, and brutal species." Especially enraged by such attempts to link them with blacks, Irishmen sought distance by voting for pro-slavery Democrats at the polls. They turned out in great numbers on election day in New York, filling the air with racist chants as they proceeded to the ballots. "Down with the Nagurs!" these brand-new Americans shouted. "Let them go back to Africa, where they belong." In a further display of unwitting (or witless) irony, some Irish leaders denounced abolitionist politics as "niggerology." And Josiah Nott thought only Southerners were all excited about the "nigger business."

Their contempt for Negroes in no way deterred Irishmen from trying on the cork and lampblack, however. Many of minstrelsy's most talented composers and performers during this era were Irish, including Emmett, the founder of the Virginia Minstrels and the composer of "Dixie," and Stephen Foster, who first gained public notice while writing songs for E. P. Christy's Minstrels.

JIM CROW'S JOURNEY

It began as a dance, performed to some variation of the following lyrics:

> Where you going, buzzard?
> Where you going, crow?

I'm going down to new ground
To knock Jim Crow.

Children in the Sea Islands of Georgia and the Carolinas learned it from their parents, a series of steps "imitating the motions of birds and hunters, and quite possibly magical in nature." The dance may have begun there among the Gullah people, whose singing, in the words of W.E.B. Du Bois, "stirred men with a mighty power." It had traveled up and down the Atlantic seaboard by the time T. D. Rice got wind of it around 1828. Anecdotes usually refer to an improbable encounter with a disheveled black laborer. In some accounts he is named Jim Crow; in most others his name is Cuff. He is usually dancing and singing on the Pittsburgh levee when Rice persuades "Cuff" to teach him the routine. Later that evening Rice, dressed in Cuff's rags, makes a triumphant appearance as a new character, Jim Crow. Rice polished his act in provincial theaters before launching it with a splash in New York City in 1832. Regardless of the actual circumstances surrounding his appropriation of the song and dance, the truth is he made it into something radically new. Reciting from scripts derived from British comedic staples and accenting his lines with gestures and movements allegedly taken from his direct observations of blacks, Rice was frequently praised by whites for the accuracy of his performances. Nevertheless, his character would not have been recognizably "black" without his makeup and affected dialect, and it's unlikely that those youngsters in the Sea Islands and elsewhere would have found anything familiar in his presentation.

Jim Crow made Rice a superstar. His shows were packed as working-class theatergoers rushed to see the man now billed as the nation's best "Ethiopian delineator." W. T. Lhamon wrote that Rice's revised chorus — *For I wheel about an' turn about, an' do just so, / An ebery time I turn about, I jump Jim Crow* — "sneaked onto the lips of all the Atlantic community in the antebellum years."

Of Rice's other innovations, the most notable was his peppering the song with a liberal distribution of "nigger," presumably in keeping with the tone and style of typical minstrel patter. "Delineators," as minstrels were sometimes called, often declared their fitness to perform their material by asserting their authenticity as "niggers" — in the same manner that modern rappers proudly (and loudly) lay claim to their status as "real niggas." For example, a minstrel might proclaim:

> I'm a full blooded niggar,
> Ob de real ole stock,
> And wid my head and shoulder
> I can split a horse block

Tireless and shrewd, Rice eventually took his niggerisms overseas, where he wowed the British. His creation did more than provide a little rhythm to enliven the white workers' lives; it gave their vocabularies a boost as well. According to the sociologist David Pilgrim, "by 1838, the term 'Jim Crow' was being used as a collective racial epithet for blacks, not as offensive as nigger, but as offensive as coon or darky. Obviously, the popularity of minstrel shows aided the spread of Jim Crow as a racial slur."

One can only imagine what it did for "nigger."

UNCLE TOM REDUX

It seems somehow fitting that Rice ended his career playing Uncle Tom. Continuing his polyglot approach and borrowing even more directly from British comedy, he wrote his own adaptations of Stowe's novels and performed in them until the late 1850s. He was really on his way out, however, as Uncle Tom was shuffling in, and his adaptations were simply a handful among a multitude. Owing to Stowe's aforementioned lack of copyright protection, soon after the novel was published the theatrical world was "crowded with offshoots, parodies, thefts, and rebuttals of every imaginable kind," including stage versions "written from antislavery, moderate and proslavery positions."

The range of perspectives yielded a certain peculiar flexibility where black characters were concerned, with most of them, in the words of Eric Lott, "veering between the devoted and the daft, one hardly better than the other."

> Come lay it out you niggers
> Come hoe it down with me,
> The way you'll heel and toe it out
> Will be a sight to see

The most popular stagings were produced by George Aiken and H. J. Conway, both of whom demonstrated the malleable politics of such shows. Just as T. D. Rice occasionally inserted lyrics in his Jim Crow patter that managed to be both racist and sympathetic (*I says, look here, white folk, / De country for me, / Is de country whar de people / Hab make poor nigga free*), Conway began his ostensibly anti-slavery version with blackface performers singing "Nigga in de Cornfield," the lyrics of which are quoted above. Despite the insertion of that song and other minstrel elements, the show was still perceived to be sufficiently abolitionist to provoke the ire of pro-slavery critics. Although it does use the N word frequently, Aiken's production was regarded as more progressive and does not contain the worst tendencies on display in Conway's staging.

"DEBASED MELODIES"

> Oh, I does hate a nigger,
> Tho' its colour ob my skin,
> But de blood ob dis nigger
> Am all white to de chin.

Notwithstanding the claims of the publicists and proponents of minstrelsy, the genre's nigger-happy lyrics demonstrated at best a tenuous connection to the developing folk art of blacks in America. As shown earlier, the lyrics of slaves and freedmen included the N word, but rarely (if ever) as widespread as those of minstrel composers.

Of course, the fans of minstrelsy would not be inclined to challenge the veracity of its songs. They "were almost entirely by white writers for white audiences," Sterling Brown pointed out, and as such they were warmly received. "The best-loved songs of the Midwest and western frontier, indeed, of all America during the expansive nineteenth century, came out of the 'nigger-minstrel' show," according to the cultural historian Alan Lomax. Many of those songs sprang from the capacious imagination of Stephen Foster. Widely regarded as one of the greatest talents to emerge from minstrelsy, Foster wrote several songs that became American standards, including such popular numbers as "The Camp Town Races" and "Oh, Susannah." His musical narratives of pastoral longing became a dominant influence on shows produced during the peak years of minstrelsy. Roughly ten years after the plantation tradition debuted in American literature, plantation follies took center stage in American theater.

Remarkably, those same angry workers who chased down real Negroes in the street and clubbed them to the ground wept over the sufferings of fake Negroes on minstrel stages. Even so, in retrospect it appears that minstrel composers were far more successful at generating comedy than at evoking pathos. They contributed mightily "toward fixing popular conceptions of the Negro," according to Brown, and frequently portrayed "an abject Negro who ridicules himself, with no sense of shame, just to make the white folks laugh."

Visual artists provided equally damaging accompaniment in the form of cover illustrations for pocket-sized songsters, or songbooks, produced to meet the demand for minstrel songs. Songsters rarely contained music; instead they offered page after page of racist lyrics. During minstrelsy's peak years, *Christy's Nigga Songster* and hundreds of others appeared annually under the endorsement of the genre's biggest stars. Racist cartoons, begun in earnest in Boston in 1815, began to gain widespread currency in the 1840s through the popularity of songsters and sheet music. The artwork often exaggerated the most extreme descriptions in the lyrics, portraying blacks as big-lipped, woolly-headed grotesques.

An appreciation of the published minstrel material required literacy and the ability to sight-read music, and the availability of these items suggests the expansion of blackface theater beyond its original working-class base. Eric Lott wrote, "Firth and Pond, Stephen Foster's New York publisher, employed twenty men to engrave and print its annual output of over two hundred pieces of music . . . the selling of which occupied another ten men and brought in a revenue of $70,000. In this form blackface minstrelsy entered the middle-class parlor." And racist language once frowned on by men who aspired to be gentlemen acquired a cloak of respectability.

PART III

Dreams Deferred

1858–1896

7

The World the War Made

I like niggers well enough as niggers, but when fools & idiots try & make niggers better than ourselves I have an opinion.
— General William T. Sherman, 1864

"WORDS ALONE DID NOT remake America, but they were mighty weapons in the myth-making that the Civil War inevitably produced," David W. Blight observed in his magisterial *Race and Reunion: The Civil War in American Memory*. Few folks alive during the dawn of that great conflict could have been more familiar with words as weapons than the four million black Americans still bound to the yoke of slavery. Having long endured the slings and arrows of outrageous insult, they quite likely welcomed the prospect of new words — like "free" and "equal," for example — that could transform their peculiar predicament. For nearly 250 years, the language surrounding their struggle had amounted to a glossary of disdain, full of adjectives (beastlike, depraved, inferior, childlike, menacing, lazy, small-brained) riding the back of a single noun that managed to encapsulate and illustrate the worst aspect of each modifier: "nigger." Despite consistent opposition from blacks, whites from all levels of society and in all manner of trades — from scientists to statesmen to unskilled laborers — continued to enthusiastically use a common vocabulary of contempt devised for the sole purpose of reminding blacks of their lowly, despised status. As white Northerners and white Southerners clashed over the future of America, black people wondered what it all meant for them.

They would find out that the words and the war that remade their country did little to improve their status or the labels by which they were known: they were "niggers" at the beginning and still "niggers" at the end.

"TOO MANY FREE NIGGERS"

On April 14, 1861, the Confederates fired on Fort Sumter, South Carolina. Almost immediately, blacks in Cincinnati formed a volunteer company called the Home Guards. But their services were declined. The city's chief of police told them, "We want you damn niggers to keep out of this; this is a white man's war." Secretary of War Simon Cameron chose more formal language when he rejected an overture from Jacob Dobson, a freeman who wanted to volunteer. "This Department has no intention at present to call into service of the Government any colored soldiers," he wrote. He was merely implementing the policies of his commander-in-chief, Abraham Lincoln, who had forbidden the enlistment of black soldiers. (Cameron came around before the president did, eventually recommending that Congress form an army of freed slaves.) While the president dithered, blacks fled their captivity by the thousands and found their way to the Union lines, where they presumed to find safe refuge. Until the passage — and intermittent enforcement — of the Confiscation Acts, however, Lincoln's troops could not be relied on to help. On occasion, Union soldiers "not only caught supposed fugitives but actually hunted up their masters and to them escorted the slaves," Penn Hallowell, an officer in the 20th Massachusetts, wrote to his brother Richard in 1861.

But the runaways kept coming, forcing the issue of emancipation. In 1861 the niggerologist Josiah Nott told a British newspaper that the possibility of manumission posed distressing problems for white Americans: "What is to be done with the slaves, and how the four millions of Negroes are to be prevented from becoming six, eight or ten millions." A letter from a Confederate soldier in 1862 expressed nearly identical sentiments: "I never want to see the day when a negro is put on an equality with a white person. There is too many free niggers . . . now to suit me, let alone having four millions."

Such fears didn't stop the Confederates from sending black soldiers into combat, an act that often brought out the worst impulses of the Union troops. A Union private wrote home in 1862: "I hear that the Rebels sent out a Regt. Of niggers to fight our men. . . . The soldiers are death on niggers now. If they catch a nigger in the woods, and there is no officer near, they hang them without any ceremony."

Lincoln's dithering included pursuing various colonization schemes, including asking for a constitutional amendment authorizing him to expatriate black Americans. The president occasionally waffled about his views on abolition, but he was much more consistent about his opinion of Negroes' inferiority. During one of his 1858 debates with Stephen Douglas, he had asserted his belief in irreconcilable "physical differences" between blacks and whites that would "forbid them living together on the footing of perfect equality." The historian Lerone Bennett Jr. has written that Lincoln used the N word "all the time, both in public and private." Bennett even quoted an eyewitness, who recalled that as president-elect, Lincoln "told the story of the Kentucky Justice of the Peace whose first case was a criminal prosecution for the abuse of slaves. Unable to find any precedent, he exclaimed angrily: 'I will be damned if I don't feel almost sorry for being elected when the niggers is the first thing I have to attend to.'"

Lincoln's officers were far less hesitant. They had already armed between three thousand and four thousand black men before the president decided in late 1862 that the time had come. Private Miles O'Riley of the 47th Regiment New York Volunteers is credited with writing the lyrics to "Sambo's Right to Be Kilt," offered in support of Lincoln's decision:

"Some tell me 'tis a burnin' shame / to make the naygers fight, / and that the trade of bein' kilt / Belongs but to the white." Such opinions are the sentiments of cowards, according to the song.

"The men who object to Sambo / Should take his place and fight; / and it's better to have a nayger's hue / than a liver that's wake and white."

The president's use of black troops brought him considerable ridicule during his 1864 reelection campaign. One anti-Lincoln ditty proclaimed:

Now listen to me, white folks, de truth I'm going to tell you:
Dat de white man isn't nowhere now, it's plain to men of sense;
For, it's nigger in de Senate-house, and nigger in de White House,
And nigger in de Custom house, and nigger on de fence.

"THE SHRINE OF THE GREAT NIGGER"

One Confederate soldier observed, "And I may as well remark upon the word 'nig' and 'nigger,' that I never heard this epithet applied to slaves in the South by any person of refinement and education." In fact, however, the reaction to black participation in the war spanned all classes and backgrounds, and much of it was expressed via the N word.

Private Henry Martyn Cross of the 48th Massachusetts Volunteers had once written disparagingly of "nigger regiments." But after witnessing the blacks' heroic performance in a Louisiana firefight on May 27, 1863, he wrote to his parents: "In *every respect* they are fully equal to any troops, and in many respects . . . *superior* to all. . . . If I ever get a commission, I hope that it will be in a 'nig. Regt.'" Corporal Felix Brannigan of the 74th New York Volunteers confided in a letter to his sister: "We don't want to fight side and side with the nigger. We think we are a too superior race for that." A Wisconsin cavalry officer on the Confederate side found his faith challenged. "I never believed in niggers before," he wrote, "but by Jasus, they are hell in fighting." Iowa's Governor Samuel J. Kirkwood wrote in 1862: "When this war is over & we have summed up the entire loss of life it has imposed, I shall not have any regrets if it is found that a part of the dead are *niggers* and that *all* are not white men."

Before the 54th Massachusetts Infantry Regiment's legendary attack on Fort Wagner, South Carolina, General Truman Seymour figured the Union should go ahead and "put those damn niggers from Massachusetts in the advance; we might as well get rid of them one time or another."

Seymour's ambivalence, not unusual for Union soldiers, illustrated the schism that often loomed between ardent Unionists and fervent abolitionists. Much of Lincoln's fence-sitting can be attributed to his reluctance to offend either side. The two groups clashed violently in Boston right up until the taking of Fort Sumter, which forced them into an uneasy alliance. A belief in a Union victory was different from a belief in freedom for blacks or in their equality. Private William C. H. Reeder of the 20th Indiana Volunteers was one of the soldiers who grew disenchanted with the conflict's increasingly abolitionist tone. "This war has turned out very Different from what I thought it would," he complained. "It is a War . . . to free the Nigars . . . and I do not propose to fight any more in such A cause."

Major Henry L. Abbott, a valiant Union warrior, thought so little of both emancipation and black people that he called the 54th Regiment "the shrine of the great nigger." (Abbott's friend Oliver Wendell Holmes Jr., a brave and much-wounded combatant, apparently had a modicum of compassion. Before mustering out in late 1864, he wrote to his mother: "Do you think I could get a place for my nagur boy if I brought him with me?")

General William T. Sherman had definite ideas about the "place" of Negroes. In September 1864 he wrote: "I don't see why we can't have some sense about negros as well as about horses mules, iron, copper &c. — but Say nigger in the U.S. and . . . the whole country goes Crazy. . . . I like niggers *well enough* as niggers, but when fools & idiots try & make niggers better than ourselves I have an opinion." Earlier in 1864, the Confederate general Nathan Bedford Forrest supervised the massacre of at least one hundred black soldiers believed to have raised their hands in surrender at Fort Pillow, Tennessee. Eyewitnesses told the investigating congressmen, Benjamin F. Wade and Daniel Gooch, that the rebels berated the black soldiers for "fighting against your master" and accosted white Union soldiers for fighting "side by side with niggers." The attitudes of high-ranking officers on both sides illustrate the degree to which the black soldier, in the words of the historian George Washington Williams, "had enemies in his rear and enemies in front."

Some observers had been more impressed by the 54th's performance than Major Abbott was. On August 23, 1863, General Ulysses S. Grant had written to President Lincoln: "I have given the subject of arming the Negro my hearty support. . . . By arming the Negro we have added a powerful ally." That same month, Lincoln wrote in a public letter: "there will be some black men who can remember that, with silent tongue and clenched teeth, and steady eye, and well-poised bayonet, they have helped mankind on to this great consummation."

Frederick Douglass, an outspoken critic of Lincoln who contributed mightily to the Union's recruitment efforts, urged his fellow blacks "to fly to arms, and smite with death the power that would bury the government and your liberty in the same hopeless grave."

But his image of swashbuckling avengers gained no ground against the prevailing notions about black men. The "image of innate black docility and inoffensiveness was, as it turned out, too deeply rooted to be demolished by the emergence of the Negro as a soldier," according to George Fredrickson. *The Final Report of the American Freedmen's Inquiry Commission* (1864) seems to bear this out. Robert Dale Owen, a coauthor of the report and an anti-slavery sympathizer, concluded: "The African race is . . . Genial, lively, docile, emotional, the affections rule; the social instincts maintain the ascendant except under cruel repression, its cheerfulness and love of mirth overflow with the exuberance of childhood. It is devotional by feeling. It is a knowing rather than a thinking race." Dr. Samuel Gridley Howe, another member of the commission (who had consulted with Louis Agassiz before writing his contribution), also took note of the Negro's alleged docility. "Africans have more of womanly virtues than fiercer people have," he concluded. "Indeed, it may be said that, among the races, Africa is like a gentle sister in a family of fierce brothers."

Somehow these happy-go-lucky girly boys helped turn the tide of the war and secure victory for the Union. More than one-third of the black soldiers gave their lives to the cause; 2,751 were killed in action, with some 67,000 more dead from wounds, disease, or accidents. Grant's biographer W. E. Woodward must have forgotten them when he concluded: "The American Negroes are the only people in the world, so far as I know, that ever became free without any effort of their own. . . . They had not started the war nor ended it. They twanged banjos around the railroad stations, sang melodious spirituals and believed that some Yankee would soon come along and give each of them forty acres and a mule."

"ATTACHED TO THE SOIL"

Whereas Lincoln's equivocating often frustrated Frederick Douglass and other black activists, no effort was required to figure out where his successor, Andrew Johnson, stood. As an ardent white supremacist, his views on Negroes were considerably harsher. He indicated his plans for Reconstruction on May 29, 1865, six weeks after Lincoln's murder. His first proclamation granted amnesty and restored property rights to nearly all the Rebels. He rejected outright a proposal from the Republican congressman Thaddeus Stevens, who called for confiscating the property of all former slaveholders who had owned more than two hundred slaves, dividing it into forty-acre plots for use by freedmen. (More progressive than either Lincoln or Johnson, Stevens was so identified with the fight for black equality that a Democratic newspaper denounced his 1858 congressional victory as a sign of "Niggerism Triumphant.")

While Stevens hoped to get hold of more Confederate acreage,

Johnson was determined to give it back. He gave in to the most duplicitous embrace of victimology in the short history of the United States. The South had been wronged. The South had been robbed. It wanted its land back. It wanted its "niggers" back. Johnson handed over both. In the words of W.E.B. Du Bois, "No sooner did the proclamations of general amnesty appear than the eight hundred thousand acres of abandoned lands in the hands of the Freedmen's Bureau melted quickly away."

Under Johnson's encouraging hand, infamous "Black Codes" curtailing black rights were enacted in Mississippi and South Carolina, soon followed by Virginia, Louisiana, and Texas. Although many subsequent codes didn't mention race, it was commonly understood whom the laws addressed. The regulations included prohibitions against hunting, fishing, gun ownership, and selling farm produce without written authorization from "masters." Mandatory labor contracts were imposed on men and women while court-ordered "apprenticeships" removed their children from homes and schools and forced them into service on plantations. The Thirteenth Amendment, abolishing slavery, had been approved by Congress in January, but the resurgent slavocracy was undeterred. One Southern planter enthused, "The nigger is going to be made a serf as sure as you live. It won't need any law for that. . . . They're attached to the soil and to their masters as much as ever."

The "legal" extremes of Presidential Reconstruction were enforced by the white Southerners' trademark terrorizing of their black neighbors. In Texas, where some blacks claimed that the rivers were frequently clogged with the floating bodies of dead freedmen, five hundred white men were indicted for the murder of blacks in 1865 and 1866, but none was convicted. During the same period the Ku Klux Klan was formed in Pulaski, Tennessee, and soon attracted former Rebel soldiers such as the notorious Nathan Bedford Forrest. The group had little difficulty fomenting the rage of traitors still burned by their defeat at the hands of the North. All too often, blacks became the targets of their anger. In *The Rise and Fall of Jim Crow*, Richard Wormser quoted one former Confederate who said, "I hope the day will come when we kill . . . kill them like dogs. I was never down on a nigger like I am now." Another said he killed blacks because he "wanted to thin out the niggers a little." It was not as effective as colonization at erasing the teeming four million but apparently a damn sight more fun.

"KEEPING THE NIGGER DOWN"

Johnson's policies were not at odds with the majority of Republicans. While they were not as obsessed with white supremacy as their Democratic rivals, they feared that being perceived as too supportive of blacks and other "extreme" causes would jeopardize their ability to reunite the country on their terms. Just five years before, thirty thousand protesters had marched against the Republicans in New York; their banners linked the party to "Free Love, Free Niggers, and Free Women." Despite the timidity of their colleagues, Thaddeus Stevens, Charles Sumner, and the other Radical Republicans managed to take control of Reconstruction in 1867.

Under their leadership, the Reconstruction Act divided the eleven Confederate states into five military districts, each overseen by a general who would supervise their readmission into the Union. Each state was required to ratify the Fourteenth Amendment (which guarantees citizens "equal protection under the law") and amend their own constitutions to award civil and political equality to blacks. Just as he had done with the Civil Rights Act of 1866 (intended to protect blacks from state-sponsored discrimination), Johnson tried to veto the act, but once again Congress overrode him. The president hoped to capitalize on the feelings against blacks and thus defeat his enemies in his own party. He knew that some Americans, like the fellow at one of his rallies, would applaud his efforts at "keeping the nigger down."

While Johnson pursued his white supremacist agenda, Josiah Nott moved to New York. He liked that city, he said, because it was "without morals, without political scruples, without religions and without *niggers*." The previous year he had published yet another pamphlet on black inferiority, *The Negro Race: Its Ethnology and History*. His "findings" proved useful to Representative James Brooks of New York, who referred to them while speaking out against the First Reconstruction Act. Science, according to Brooks, had established that "the negro is not the equal of the white man, much less his master," a fact easily proven "anatomically, physiologically and psychologically too, if necessary."

"I'M G'WINE TO VOTE AGIN THE NIGGER!"

The Democrats' successful racist gubernatorial campaign in Louisiana in 1864 can be seen as a model for the party's presidential effort in 1868. The Louisiana platform had declared: "We hold this to be a government of white people, made and to be perpetuated for the exclusive benefit of the white race. People of African descent cannot be considered as citizens of the United States . . . there can, in no event, be any equality between the white and other races." The national candidates in 1868, Horatio Seymour and Frank Blair, exploited whites' fears of Negro equality and the "amalgamation of the races." Blair, the vice-presidential nominee, challenged the Republicans' handling of Reconstruction throughout the campaign. He accused them of forcing the South to bow down to a "semi-barbarous race of blacks . . . who are polygamists," irresistibly compelled to "subject the white women to their unbridled lust."

Seymour and Blair lost the election to Ulysses S. Grant and Schuyler Colfax, but the character and tone of their campaign incited passions against blacks while foreshadowing Democratic efforts to come.

At the same time, blacks achieved both small and significant political gains. The Fourteenth Amendment was ratified in 1868. The Fifteenth Amendment, ensuring a citizen's right to vote regardless of "race, color, or previous condition of servitude," followed in 1870. The number of black elected officials continued to grow in the following decade. By 1873 seven blacks had seats in Congress; by 1875 that number had grown to eight. Also in 1875, a civil rights act was passed, banning discrimination in hotels, trains, and public spaces.

The Democrats kept fighting back. They continued to stir up white Southerners' most durable superstitions, all of which seemed to involve racial equality and the need to protect white women from rampaging black men, whose liberation led them inevitably to animalistic depravities. Poor whites were most susceptible to this kind of race-baiting. One such American expressed his political beliefs thusly: "I'm a Democrat, because my daddy was a Democrat, and I'm g'wine to vote agin the nigger!" These efforts were accompanied by a multiyear wave of terror. Dorothy Sterling has estimated that the Klan lynched twenty thousand of their fellow Americans between 1868 and 1871.

A series of political victories followed. In 1874 the Democrats won the House and increased their numbers in the Senate. They followed this congressional victory with takeovers of Virginia, Tennessee, Georgia, Texas, Arkansas, Florida, and Alabama, where whites murdered blacks at the polls. In Louisiana, the unsuccessful Democratic effort was conducted with the help of a new terrorist cell called the White League; its operating credo was "White supremacy, first, last and all the time." One member told a black man: "You niggers have had things your own way long enough and we white folks are going to have it our own way or kill all you Republican niggers." A Louisiana planter, a member of the refined class, was heard to remark: "Why is it that niggers keep on tryin to raise above their station in life? Some of them are scared to death of night riders visiting their home. Yet even the most scared of them takes an interest in politics and other matters that don't concern him."

The Democrats took the Magnolia State through the Mississippi Plan, which called for terrorizing blacks and shooting them "just the same as birds." Every Southern state except Louisiana and the Carolinas had fallen to the Democrats by 1876. The presidential election that year led to the Hayes-Tilden Compromise and the Republicans' concession of the South to the Democrats. Reconstruction ended on April 24, 1877, when President Rutherford B. Hayes withdrew the last federal troops from New Orleans.

David W. Blight has observed: "No true national consensus ever gathered around the cause of black liberty and equality except as it was necessary to restoring and reimagining the republic itself." According to W.E.B. Du Bois, as a result of the North's acquiescence, "the slave went free; stood a brief moment in the sun; then moved back again toward slavery."

Frederick Douglass expressed similar thoughts on April 16, 1883. During a speech in Washington, D.C., he soberly noted: "As the war for the Union recedes into the past, and the negro is no longer needed to assault forts and stop rebel bullets, he is in some sense of less importance. Peace with the old master class has been war for the negro. As the one has risen the other has fallen." Later that year, the Supreme Court added insult to injury when it repealed the Civil Rights Act of 1875, the last federal legislation of its kind until 1957. Black America's dogged trek through the last decades of the nineteenth century promised to be both lonely and dangerous.

"WHAT'S THAT NIGGER DOING ON THE STAGE?"

We have seen how racist language became the lingua franca of mainstream America: in the highest rungs of "refined" society, at the low levels of the unlettered and the poor, in the committee meetings and legislative sessions of the nation's policymakers. To gauge the effect of such language when wielded with maximum malevolence, it may be instructive to listen to one of its targets. Dorothy Bolden, who was a maid in Georgia during the 1880s, told an interviewer: "White folks didn't have no feelin' for you. They pretended they did. They had nannies to give their child comfort. That was my name: 'Nanny.' They would teach their children they was better than you. You was givin' them all that love and you'd hear them say, 'You're not supposed to love Nanny. Nanny's a nigger.' And they could say it so nasty. Til it would cut your heart out almost and you couldn't say a mumblin' word."

Bolden's plight would have been both familiar and disheartening to Frederick Douglass, who had devoted his entire career to helping his people overcome the niggerizing taint of inferiority. The former slave, whose tale of bondage and freedom had earned adulation and support the world over, died on February 20, 1895, just as Jim Crow was gaining momentum. That same year Ida B. Wells published *A Red Record*, her pioneering study of lynchings. Wells, a fearless and dedicated activist, was probably most qualified to assume Douglass's leadership role. But her womanhood worked against her, and that opportunity went to Booker T. Washington, who first gained widespread notice at the Atlanta Cotton Exposition seven months after Douglass died.

James Creelman, a reporter who witnessed Washington's appearance in Atlanta, offered this dispatch: "When among them a colored man appeared, a sudden chill fell on the whole assemblage. One after another asked, 'What's that nigger doing on the stage?'"

Creelman reported that by the time Washington finished his soon-to-be-famous offer of black capitulation, white women were tossing flowers on the stage. But James Kimble Vardaman, the future governor of Mississippi, was unimpressed. "The man who says the race problem in the South is settled is just about as capable of judging and understanding such matters as the average nigger is about understanding the philosophy of the Decalogue," he declared. "I am opposed to it, I am just as opposed to Booker T. Washington as a voter, with all his Anglo-Saxon refinements, as I am to the coconut-headed, chocolate-colored typical little coon, Andy Dotson, who blacks my shoes every evening. Neither is fit to perform the supreme function of citizenship."

Vardaman's refusal to see Washington as anything but just another "nigger" confirms the observation of the black educator Joseph C. Price, who had commented in 1890: "The Confederacy surrendered its sword at Appomattox, but did not there surrender its convictions." Activists and informed observers such as Price could have not been surprised in 1896 when the Supreme Court gave its blessing to racial segregation. *Plessy v. Ferguson* doomed black

Americans to an indefinite stretch of hard time, to be served from birth in segregated hospitals to burial in segregated cemeteries. The decision prescribed a life of enforced inferiority, an existence forever at the mercy of the white majority's unpredictable whims. It was a situation perhaps best described by a boastful white resident of New Orleans in 1888: "For the first time since the war, we've got the nigger where we want him."

8

Nigger Happy

You can't learn a nigger to argue.
— Huck Finn, 1885

IN AN ADDRESS to Mark Twain scholars and admirers in 1985, David Bradley referred to *Adventures of Huckleberry Finn* as "The First Nigger Novel." A gifted novelist and astute critic who found much to praise in the book, Bradley was probably just hoping to command his listeners' full attention; he knew that Twain's most celebrated novel was hardly the first work of fiction to qualify for such a designation. By the time it appeared in 1885, nigger-filled fiction was a firmly entrenched American tradition — so much so that it's more difficult to find works that didn't include demeaning portrayals of African Americans. A few of Twain's contemporaries — less gifted but high-minded novelists such as Albion Tourgée, George Washington Cable, and William Dean Howells — made admirable attempts to create sympathetic, credible black characters. Their efforts, however, were feeble in comparison to the dehumanizing sentiments of plantation fiction, which after the Civil War rode a resurgent wave of interest that crested from the mid-1880s to the end of the 1890s.

SENTIMENTAL JOURNEYS

For Sterling Brown, the new plantation tradition exceeded the antebellum version in terms of "realism and custom" but never showed black characters "in relation to themselves. They are confined to the two opposite grooves of loyalty or ingratitude." Tourgée, who was also a journalist and essayist, noted that black characters were generally limited to two forms, "the devoted slave who serves and sacrifices for his master and mistress" and "the poor 'nigger' to whom liberty has brought only misfortune."

Most prominent of the new "niggers" was a kindly codger named Uncle Remus. Joel Chandler Harris introduced his creation in his newspaper column in 1877, then gave him a wider and more lucrative forum in a book-length collection called *Uncle Remus: His Songs and Sayings.* A grinning, shuffling Negro full of fables starring Brer Rabbit and a host of wily critters, Uncle Remus is always quick to mourn the demise of the South's glorious past — and equally quick to condemn his colored brethren. He is "made to express admiration for white folks, to ridicule black education, and to praise the Old South and the old ways," Darryl Pinckney has written. "Uncle Remus, telling stories to entertain a white child, is a revision of Uncle Tom. . . . Tom sang hymns for Eva and told her stories, but there was never a twinkle in his eye."

The twinkle fades when Remus turns his gaze to his fellow freedmen. He frequently uses the N word to describe them and loves pointing out how they fail to measure up to white folks. "Put a spellin'-book in a nigger's han's, en right den en dar' you loozes a plow-hand," he contends. "What's a nigger gwineter larn outen books? I kin take a bar'l stave an' fling mo' sense inter a nigger in one minnit dan all de schoolhouses betwixt dis en de State er Midgigin."

Remus, like most of Harris's black creations, is less a well-rounded character than a transparent device for the author to express his white supremacist convictions. Ananias, another of Harris's Negroes, appears in *Balaam and His Master and Other Sketches and Stories* (1891). His assessment of blacks' abilities differs little from Uncle Remus's: "'Tain't wid niggers like it is wid white folks, suh. White folks know w'at ter do, kaze dey in de habits er doin' like dey wanter, but niggers, suh — niggers, dey is diffunt. Dey dunner w'at ter do." Harris's tales of happy "niggers" perfectly suited the appetites of a nation of hungry readers — who quickly gobbled them up. *Songs and Sayings* was the best-selling book of 1880.

Harris's chief rival was Thomas Nelson Page, whose stories appeared in such leading magazines as *Scribner's, Lippincott's, Century,* and *Harper's.* Page's best-selling collection, *In Ole Virginia,* was published in 1887. "In virtually every other story," wrote David W. Blight, "loyal slaves reminisce about the era of slavery — 'befo' de war' — before freedom left them lonely, bewildered, or ruined souls in a decaying landscape." Sterling Brown noted that, like Harris's work, the stories often featured "an old Negro, garrulous in praise of the old days, [who] tells a tale of handsome cavaliers and lovely ladies, with stress upon the love between master and slave." A representative line taken from "Marse Chan," a popular Page story that first appeared in *Century,* shows that his dialogue was nearly indistinguishable from that of Harris's fiction. "Dem wuz good ole times, marster," a nostalgic former slave reflects, "de bes' Sam ever see! . . . Niggers didn' hed nothin' 't all to do."

Like Josiah Nott before him, Page found that white Americans were all excited about "the nigger business" in the South, where *In Ole Virginia, Pastime Stories,* and his other books sold handsomely. Northerners took to him as well, and he gave readings all over the country.

The public's embrace of Harris and Page was an extension of its eager acceptance of Lost Cause mythology. That fantasy — which recast the South's grand betrayal as a glorious and misunderstood crusade — takes its name from Edward A. Pollard's *Lost Cause,* published in 1867. According to Pollard, the Civil War, while proving Southern gallantry, had failed to resolve the question of Negro equality. Comfortably indoctrinated, thousands of readers took what Blight has described as "sentimental, imaginative journeys Southward and into idealized war zones, guided and narrated by faithful slaves."

Those fanciful treks naturally precluded the unequivocal acknowledgment of black humanity. Whereas real blacks such as Harriet Tubman, Frederick Douglass, and Robert Smalls complicated such willfully distorted perspectives, cuddly mascots like Uncle Remus and Uncle Ananias consoled and affirmed. They served as nostalgic reminders of a glorious time when Southern princes reigned unchallenged and "niggers" knew their place.

"THE ADVENT OF THE NIGGER"

The decreased interest in Negro equality — and increased longing for the days of legally enforced black docility — after the demise of Reconstruction can be traced through the images of blacks in popular periodicals such as *Scribner's, Harper's,* and the *Atlantic Monthly* (the same magazines that promoted and published sentimental plantation fiction). Reflecting the sentiments of the time, most publications had showed a brief infatuation with the idea of freedmen as intelligent and unfairly oppressed, but by the end of the century they had returned to burdening newsstands with scornful and exaggerated black imagery. Readers had regular access to endless pages crammed to the margins with images of rampaging black primitives bent on destruction.

Before the war, a group of disgruntled black New Yorkers had asked: "What American artist has not caricatured us? What wit has not laughed at us in our wretchedness? Has not ridiculed and condemned us? Few, few, very few." An 1868 Thomas Nast cartoon in *Harper's Weekly* indicates that the group's despair was well founded and still relevant. Captioned "All the Difference in the World," Nast's engraving consists of two vertically aligned panels. In the upper panel, two white men are pictured shooing a black man away from the entrance to the Democratic Club. They are holding their noses beneath a line of text that reads: "The Odor of the Nigger (Republican) is Offensive." The bottom panel shows two black men with grotesque features enjoying the spoils of Democratic largesse. One of them sits and primps while a white statesman kneels and shines his shoes. The other struts, bug-eyed, with a white woman on each arm. Despite the pair's hugely swollen lips and absurd posturing, the cartoon seems intended to ridicule and expose the hypocrisies of the Democratic Party, not blacks. Even so, the intended irony behind the use of the N word — evident in retrospect — would likely have been lost on black readers in Nast's day. On a *Harper's* cover from October 1868, captioned "Why the Nigger Is Unfit to Vote," a slightly less offensive looking black man is shown outside the polls holding a Grant-Colfax ballot. In this example, like countless others in *Harper's* and elsewhere, the N word conveys casual disregard and appears completely devoid of irony.

Illustrations accompanying children's books, toys, household products, and sheet music frequently relied on grotesque renderings to heighten the insult. In *The Art and History of Black Memorabilia*, Larry Vincent Buster noted that during the latter half of the nineteenth century, the word "nigger" began to appear "repeatedly as a trade name for tobacco, oysters, stove polish, fruits, and vegetables." *The Ten Little Niggers*, a children's book published by the McLoughlin Brothers around 1875, features comparatively mild illustrations of red-lipped blacks cavorting in lurid, pajama-like clothing. Another version was published during the same period by M. A. Donohue & Company. Both books are based on variations of a nursery rhyme that mixes macabre fantasies of black mutilation with the durable hope that blacks left to their own devices will eventually destroy themselves.

Ten little nigger boys went out to dine;
One choked his little self, and then there were nine.

Nine little nigger boys sat up very late;
One overslept himself, and then there were eight.

Eight little nigger boys travelling in Devon;
One said he'd stay there, and then there were seven.

Seven little nigger boys chopping up sticks;
One chopped himself in half, and then there were six.

Six little nigger boys playing with a hive;
A bumble-bee stung one, and then there were five.

Five little nigger boys going in for law;
One got in chancery, and then there were four.

Four little nigger boys going out to sea;
A red herring swallowed one, and then there were three.

Three little nigger boys walking in the Zoo;
A big bear bugged one, and then there were two.

Two little nigger boys sitting in the sun;
One got frizzled up, and then there was one.

One little nigger boy living all alone;
He got married, and then there were none.

This rhyme probably inspired the McLoughlins to manufacture in 1874 a puzzle called "Chopped Up Niggers." Ditto for the Parker Brothers, who introduced "The Game of Ten Little Niggers" in 1895, a card game based on Old Maid. Less obvious is the source of a carnival and fair attraction frequently billed as "Dump the Nigger" (a.k.a. "Coon Dip"), a dunking booth where athletically inclined contestants, hailing from places like Nigger Run Fork, Virginia, or near Dead Nigger Creek in Texas, could aim for the target while stuffing their cheeks with Nigger Hair Tobacco, which went on the market in 1874. Interested Americans could supplement such diversions by building their very own collection of "nigger" toys. A Jolly Nigger Bank was patented in 1892, but the J. E. Stevens Company of Cromwell, Connecticut, was selling them as early as 1843. The bank was a mechanical device crafted to resemble a black man's head and upper torso. His large, red-lipped mouth is open to receive coins. A lever on his back allows fun-seekers to raise his arm to his mouth and make his yellow eyes roll dramatically. More than 160 years later, the Jolly Nigger Bank remains a hot item, popular among collectors and frequently listed for sale on the Internet. The filmmaker Spike Lee has said that he wrote the screenplay for *Bamboozled,* in which the bank plays a pivotal role, with his own Jolly Nigger sitting on his desk.

Jolly "niggers" were stalwart characters in minstrel shows, which remained popular after the war. The hundreds of revues touring the country reflected a significant change in the genre: the troupes after Reconstruction consisted mostly of black performers. The potential irony to be found in black performers imitating white performers (who weren't actually imitating but parodying black people) becomes as thick as the layers of burnt cork the new minstrels applied to their dark faces. Nathan Huggins has remarked that the audience of a minstrel show "had ingrained in its imagination a view of the Negro that was comic and pathetic. The theatrical darky was childlike; he could be duped into the most idiotic and foolish schemes; but like a child too, innocence would protect him and turn the tables on the schemers." The printed material connected with the shows — programs, posters, playbills — like the songsters of the antebellum era, used the N word liberally and were frequently festooned with garish, multicolored racist caricatures, effectively reinforcing the notion of blacks as subhuman grotesques whose only purposes in white society involved labor and entertainment.

Forming a brilliant — albeit woefully outnumbered — counterpoint to the onslaught of demeaning images were the paintings of Winslow Homer and Thomas Eakins, whose sensitive portraits of African Americans were as observant and sympathetic as they were skillfully rendered. But the gap between "high" and "low" culture, already growing before the war, continued to spread; most whites (especially in the North) continued to derive their knowledge of black Americans from hearsay and the harmful drivel of minstrelsy and popular magazines, not from galleries and art exhibitions. Few black men could have been more aware of this sad plight than Henry Ossawa Tanner, the talented African-American painter who studied with Eakins in 1880. While attending Eakins's class at the

Pennsylvania Academy of Fine Arts, Tanner was insulted, sneered at, and referred to as "the nigger." In *A History of African-American Artists,* Romare Bearden and Harry Henderson wrote: "One night Tanner and his easel were seized by his fellow students and dragged out onto Broad Street, where he was tied to his easel in a mock crucifixion and left, struggling to free himself." One of his assailants, Joseph Pennell, proudly recalled the incident years later, referring to it as 'the Advent of the Nigger.'"

Tanner quit Eakins's class and worked and saved to get to Paris; ten years later he made it. His experience recalls Albion Tourgée's critical observation that white American literature (and, by extension, society) "is very nearly silent" about "the Negro as a man, with hopes, fears, and aspirations like other men." His fateful choice also contains echoes of the old fight-or-flight arguments between Frederick Douglass and Martin Delany. Held face-down in a puddle of niggerness despite his fierce striving, Tanner decided to quit America altogether.

MISS WATSON'S NIGGER

Jim, the co-star of Huckleberry Finn's famous adventures, has similar designs. Introduced to readers as "Miss Watson's big nigger," he just wants to quit his mean-spirited owner. Pressed for cash, Miss Watson has decided to sell Jim down the river to New Orleans. A slave didn't have to have a wife and two kids, as Jim did, to conclude that death was preferable to such a fate. His flight from bondage in antebellum Missouri leads to his momentous alliance with Huck, who has chosen to escape from his abusive father and the well-meaning townspeople who aim to civilize him. Twain's novel had barely arrived in libraries before the pious minders of community virtue called for its removal, citing low-grade morality and "rough dialect" among its many flaws. Nary a peep arose about the very element that makes *Huck Finn* so volatile in the contentious present: While the book continues to garner high praise for its homespun poetry and gleeful lampooning of societal pretensions, it is often condemned for Twain's vigorous use — some 215 times — of the N word. In his introduction to the comprehensive edition, the Twain scholar Justin Kaplan notes that "nigger" has "more preemptive force today than it did in Mark Twain's time"; this makes sense, as its ubiquity ostensibly blinded most whites to its vituperative effect. Then, as now, some of them expressed confusion when blacks insisted that the white usage was derogatory; they saw no more harm in calling a black person a "nigger" than in calling a dog a mutt. (For a fascinating contemporary take on this view, see *The Two Towns of Jasper*, a 2002 documentary by Whitney Dow and Marco Williams.)

That Twain himself scorned such name-calling is now beyond dispute. Other writings, such as "Only a Nigger," an 1869 newspaper editorial credited to him; and his personal conduct, including his quiet benevolence toward the black law student Warner T. McGuinn, have more than settled this point. The editorial, like much of *Huck Finn*, is a savage skewering of white supremacist attitudes. Writing in the voice of a pro-lynching Southerner, Twain asked: "What are the lives of a few 'niggers' in comparison with the impetuous instincts of a proud and fiery race?"

Few of the instances that evoke the N word in *Huck Finn* seem out of the ordinary, given the time and place; on many occasions Twain puts his most racist venom in the mouths of his most ignorant characters, such as Pa Finn. More instructive, however, are the scenes in which members of the pampered, landowning elite (whom Huck calls "the quality") use language routinely ascribed to the unwashed and unlettered. In such settings, Twain slyly punctured the myth of white Southern female virtue, which was symptomatic of the "Walter Scott disease" that Twain had long despised.

After Huck reluctantly joins two con men — the King and the Duke — in their swindling of three grieving sisters, he has a telling interview with Joanna, the most civic-minded of the siblings. A humanitarian involved in charitable causes, she asks Huck (who is pretending to be British), "How's servants treated in England? Do they treat 'em better than we treat our niggers?" Joanna and her sisters are portrayed as naïve and trusting, but not so innocent that they don't know to draw the line at acknowledging their slaves' humanity. The same theme underscores Huck's oft-quoted conversation with Tom's aunt Sally, in which he relays the details of a steamboat mishap:

"'Good gracious! Anybody hurt?!'

"'No'm. Killed a nigger.'

"'Well, it's lucky; because sometimes people do get hurt.'"

By then Huck has already been convinced of Jim's humanity. Their common status as outcasts and their experiences on the run have cemented an unusual and, for Huck, instructive friendship. Increasingly impressed with Jim's dignity, resourcefulness, and sense of honor, Huck finds his instinctive contempt gradually evolving into grudging admiration. On more than one occasion he tells us that Jim had a wonderful or "uncommon level head, for a nigger."

In time he also realizes that Jim's pining for his family challenges what he's been taught about blacks' "transient griefs": "I do believe he cared just as much for his people as white folks do for their'n. It don't seem natural but I reckon it's so." At the same time, Twain positioned Huck's challenging new insights against the prejudices of his era. Huck ridicules Jim's superstitions, saying that "niggers is always talking about witches in the dark," while accommodating his own fear of spilled salt and of seeing the new moon over his left shoulder. Similarly, he reflects on a commonly held belief: "Give a nigger an inch and he'll take an ell," when Jim muses aloud about "stealing" his own children out of slavery. This thought occurs despite Pa Finn's double-talk about the difference between theft (when other folks do it) and "borrowing" (when he does it).

Twain claimed to have painstakingly researched black speech patterns before writing the book, although the evidence suggests that he relied as much on minstrelsy when fashioning Jim's dialogue and personality. As Stephen Railton has pointed out, Twain's comments on antebellum "nigger shows" (featuring white performers) indicate a belief in the shows' accuracy in depicting black behavior. Sterling Brown mostly approved of Twain's rendering of Jim, calling him "the best example of the average Negro slave" and "completely believable." Ralph Ellison, an outspoken admirer of Twain's, was effusive in his praise. In his view, Twain celebrated "the spoken idiom of Negro Americans" in the novel, especially "its flexibility, its musicality, its rhythms, freewheeling diction," and metaphors derived from black folklore. While Jim often conforms to minstrel-influenced concepts of black characterization, his friendship with Huck is nothing less than revolutionary. It is hampered somewhat, according to Ellison, by Twain's inability to see Jim as a man. He wrote, "Jim's friendship for Huck comes across as that of a boy for another boy rather than as the friendship of an adult for a junior; thus there is implicit in it not only a violation of the manners sanctioned by society for relations between Negroes and whites, there is a violation of our conception of adult maleness."

It is precisely with regard to "adult maleness" that I find Jim's characterization most troubling. I can't help wondering from what body of folklore or "spoken idiom" of Negroes Twain mined Jim's tender expressions of affection, such as "Lawsy, I's mighty glad to git you back again, honey." Nat, another black man whom Huck meets near the end of the novel (an especially ridiculous figure and the most embarrassing black character in the book), also spouts sweetly submissive words. When Tom Sawyer offers to make him a "witch pie" for use in combating evil spirits, Nat says, "Will ya do it, honey? — will ya? I'll wusshup de groun' und' yo' foot, I will!" When Jim is captured, Huck's recollection of the runaway's tender qualities ("how he would always call me honey, and pet me") nearly moves him to tears. Ellison is right in implying that Jim would have become a father figure for Huck if he had been white; instead, the boy regards him, albeit affectionately, as a loving and faithful mascot. In this respect, Jim fits into both categories that Albion Tourgée described: he is the "devoted slave who serves and sacrifices for his master and mistress" and the poor "nigger" whose liberty — such as it was — "brought only misfortune." Here Twain's rendering of him seems derived, not from the wayward portrayals of minstrelsy (or the homoerotic impulses of white men, as Leslie Fiedler has suggested), but from that enduring, inscrutable view of black men as feminine, docile "creatures" in whom "the affections rule" and who possess more of "the womanly virtues." Niggerologists had long promoted this view, and sympathizers with the black cause frequently offered the same bizarre refrain. Twain's portrayal of Jim adheres closely to a view advanced by Theodore Tilton, who, like Twain, was a newspaper editor and held progressive views regarding race relations. In 1863 Tilton had written in an influential editorial: "It is sometimes said . . . that the negro race is the feminine race of the world. This is not only because of his social and affectionate nature, but because he possesses that strange moral, instinctive insight that belongs more to women than to men."

That opinion, garbed in the legitimizing language of the laboratory — and put forth by both opponents and advocates of black equality — has proved incredibly hard to shake. Echoing Louis Agassiz and Samuel Gridley Howe, among others, Ernest Burgess wrote in his *Introduction to the Science of Sociology*: "the Negro is by natural disposition neither an intellectual nor an idealist. . . . He is primarily an artist, loving life for its own sake. His métier is expression rather than action. He is, so to speak, the lady among the races." Published in 1924, Burgess's textbook was used at some black colleges as late as the 1950s.

For many African Americans, the 215 "niggers" in *Huckleberry Finn* make the book difficult to stomach and absolutely unacceptable as assigned reading in school. Of the American Library Association's top 100 list of books most frequently challenged between 1990 and 1999, it ranked fifth. Hardly a year passes without an effort by blacks in some school district to have the book removed from reading lists. In 1998 the Pennsylvania Branch of the NAACP's effort to ban the book hinged on one of the unsteadiest of legal concepts: because its "nigger"-heavy text constituted "hate speech."

I am sympathetic toward those who are made uneasy by the language in *Huck Finn,* but I believe its merits as literature and as a teaching tool outweigh its shortcomings. I do think educators would do better to hold off teaching the novel until high school, and they should provide an alternative wherever possible for students whose parents find it undesirable. Replacing "nigger" with "slave" or "Negro," as some critics have suggested, would not only undermine Twain's attempted fidelity to the customs and attitudes of mid-nineteenth-century Missouri but also dilute the impact of his scathing sendup of white hypocrisy. The Twain scholar Shelley Fisher Fishkin said it best: "If one is not willing to show racists, how can one effectively satirize racism?" Teaching methods that fail to illuminate the ironic intent of the novel or place it in its proper historical context reflect badly on the state of modern pedagogy, not on Twain or his creation.

"HOODOO NONSENSE"

Stage and film adaptations of *Huck Finn* have caused similar conflict. Black actors portraying Jim have been accused of selling out or Uncle Tomming (how's that for irony?). Meschach Taylor, who assayed the role during a 1985 production at the Goodman Theatre in Chicago, offered an eloquent defense of his decision on *Nightline* in April of that year. "First of all, let me say that I feel that the word 'nigger' is an offensive word," he began. "I do feel that slavery was offensive as well. I think that if we're going to be true to the time, however, that we must speak the way the people spoke during that time. And I think it's important for people to understand exactly what the history of racism in this country is." Disney spared Courtney B. Vance from having to offer any such testimony regarding its 1993 adaptation by dispensing with the N word altogether.

Almost inevitably, "niggers" spat from the mouths of white characters land with explosive results while the same epithet uttered by black characters (and in black contexts) often passes without comment. For instance, during early test screenings of *Ride with the Devil*, a fine Civil War film directed by Ang Lee, black viewers reportedly walked out in the first hour. Both James Schamus, the film's writer-producer, and the charismatic actor Jeffrey Wright, who stars as a black Confederate scout, apparently believed some of those who left were reacting to the use of the N word. What's more, Wright reportedly told interviewers that the Motion Pictures Association of America wouldn't allow the film's producers to use "nigger" in the trailer. "I had to go back and 'loop' a new word," he said. "I used 'nigra.' Or slave." So flustered was he by the experience that the usually articulate Wright offered a somewhat inchoate and inaccurate response to the criticism he perceived. "The word is from the word Niger," he said. "The Niger River. It was Anglicized and corrupted by white racists. It was then co-opted by black folks as a term of endearment sometimes. So simply because some white racist uses it as a pejorative doesn't mean it's pejorative. Scientifically, if you want to go back, we're all descended from Africa, we're all niggers. So dig it."

SPEAKING FOR THEMSELVES

Huck Finn would perhaps be better understood if it were taught in conjunction with works that black authors published during the same period. Harriet E. Wilson's *Our Nig; or, Sketches from the Life of a Free Black* certainly qualifies as a companion text. First published in 1859, it is the fictional memoir of Wilson's arduous tenure as a nominally free indentured servant during the decades before the Civil War. While Twain's Huck was traveling with Jim through the Mississippi Valley, Wilson's Frado was toiling in New Hampshire under the thumb of an abusive white woman.

Not counting references to "Nig," which some of Frado's employers prefer to call her, the N word is used twenty-one times. In his introduction to the 1983 reissue of the novel, Henry Louis Gates Jr. noted: "The boldness and cleverness in the ironic use of 'Nig' as title and pseudonym is, to say the least, impressive, standing certainly as one of the black tradition's earliest recorded usages. . . .

"The book's title derives from the term of abuse that the heroine's antagonists 'rename her,' calling her 'Our Nig,' or simply 'Nig.' . . . Transformed into an *object* of abuse and scorn by her enemies, the 'object,' the heroine of *Our Nig* reverses this relationship by re-naming herself not Our Nig but 'Our Nig,' thereby transforming herself into a *subject*," Gates observed. Devoting attention to these small acts of resistance may balance their lack in *Huck Finn* and help alleviate concerns that Twain's work overemphasizes the help-lessness and victimhood of slaves.

"Nigger" is first spoken in Wilson's novel by Frado's father, Jim, who jokingly calls his friend Peter a "sly nigger" for sneaking up on him. "Git out, Pete," he says, "and when you come in dis shop again, let a nigger know it. Don't steal in like a thief." Jim's usage shows no hint of self-denigration and recalls Sterling Stuckey's discussion of ironic usage among slave-era blacks. This is the only time blacks use the N word in the novel.

After the sudden death of Frado's father, her mother abandons her at the Bellmont household, where she is taken in as a ser-vant and treated as a slave. The mother and eldest daughter in the household despise Frado and insist on calling her "Nig" and "Nigger." The N word is among Mrs. Bellmont's favorites. She iden-tifies Frado's substandard attic bedroom as "good enough for a nigger." She habitually refers to Frado as "that little nigger" or "that black nigger" and maintains that "religion was not meant for niggers." She frequently abuses her young servant with a rawhide whip while contending that "niggers are just like black snakes; you *can't* kill them."

Aunt Abby, Mr. Bellmont's sister, and his son James are both kindly and sympathetic. They allow Frado to listen while they "dis-cuss the prevalent opinion of the public, that people of color are re-ally inferior; incapable of cultivation and refinement." James recalls overhearing Frado's lament: "Work as long as I can stand, and then fall down and lay there till I can get up. No mother, father, brother or sister to care for me, and then it is, You lazy nigger, lazy nigger — all because I am black." Frado often wishes for death in the manner of a typical heroine of a sentimental novel.

Freed of the Bellmonts after more than a decade of labor, the adult Frado's adventures in Massachusetts include being "watched by kidnappers, maltreated by professed abolitionists, who didn't want slaves at the South, nor niggers in their own houses, North."

Wilson's tale would be no less harrowing without her ironic use of 'Nig,' but the usage does underscore, however subtly, one of her central premises: that life in the "enlightened" North is hardly as wonderful as abolitionists often supposed and suggested. Indeed, Wilson implied that Southern blacks would find themselves no less niggerized if transplanted to the North. At the same time, her Preface expresses her fear that disclosing Northern inequities might aid advocates of slavery, so she makes it clear that her cruel mistress "was wholly imbued with *southern* principles."

Harriet Jacobs published *Incidents in the Life of a Slave Girl* in 1861 under the pseudonym Linda Brent. Her memoir relates her experiences as a slave in North Carolina; it is frequently noted for its stark recollection of her seven-year refuge in a cold, drafty, and mostly dark attic. There she hid from her owner, the cruel "Dr. Flint," who wanted to force her into a sexual relationship.

The N word is used approximately twenty-seven times in *Incidents*, with black characters uttering it on only two occasions. Unlike Huck's friend Jim, both use it in an ironic fashion. A house slave named Betty, who helps Jacobs to stay hidden, chuckles at her own ability to outwit her friend's white pursuers. "Dis nigger's too cute for 'em dis time," she boasts. Betty also uses the N word to denounce a fellow slave whom she distrusts. "Dat nigger allers got de debble in her," she argues.

After Jacobs flees to New York, she warns a fellow runaway about the new Fugitive Slave Law. But Luke is not concerned because he believes he is too clever for any slave catchers. To prove his point, he tells Jacobs what he did after his master died: "I knowed de debbil would hab him, an couldn't vant him to bring his money 'long too. So I tuk some of his bills, and put 'em in de pocket of his ole trousers. An ven he was buried, dis nigger ask fur dem ole trousers, an dey gub' 'em to me. You see I didn't *steal* it; dey *gub* it to me."

Whereas sympathetic characters in *Our Nig* refrain from calling the heroine anything but Frado, relatively softhearted figures in the memoir talk no differently from the cruel ones. A slave trader who has discovered he has no stomach for his business still has the guts to use the language of contempt: "This trading in niggers is a bad business for a fellow that's got any heart."

The heroines of both books have occasion to reflect on the prevailing opinions of Negro inferiority. Whereas Frado's reaction to white supremacy seldom rises above the typical melodrama of a sentimental novel, Jacobs was moved to eloquent outrage. "I admit that the black man *is* inferior," she wrote. "But what is it that makes him so? It is the ignorance in which white men compel him to live; it is the torturing whip that lashes manhood out of him; it is the fierce bloodhounds of the South, and the scarcely less cruel human bloodhounds of the North, who enforce the Fugitive Slave Law. *They* do the work."

While Twain, Wilson, and Jacobs presented far more nuanced portrayals of black humanity, niggerologists such as Josiah Nott, Hinton Rowan Helper (*Nojoque*), and John Van Evrie (*White Supremacy and Negro Subordination*) continued to publish a harshly contrarian view. By the turn of the century, however, eloquent opposition emerged in the form of Franz Boas. In 1894 the soon-to-be-eminent anthropologist delivered a talk before the American Association for the Advancement of Science in which he denounced as useless the entire century's body of race-based research. His address, published in 1911 as *The Mind of Primitive Man*, charged that the writings of Nott and his colleague George Gliddon "either do not sufficiently take into account the social conditions of race . . . or were dictated by scientific or humanitarian bias or by the desire to justify the institution of slavery." It would take a good while before such radical views could take hold, however, and the demise of slavery failed to diminish the public's appetite for niggerology. Two years after Boas's talk (and the same year as *Plessy v. Ferguson*), the American Economic Association published Frederick Hoffman's *Race Traits and Tendencies of the American Negro*, which, according to Mark Bauerlein, described "black lust" as "a venereal impulse surfacing with ever greater frequency as the regime of slavery faded into the distant past." According to Hoffman, Negroes showed "the least power of resistance in the struggle for life" and were likely to become extinct before too long.

Taken collectively, the images and stereotypes clinging to black identity in the decades after Reconstruction form what Gunnar Myrdal called a set of "false beliefs with a purpose." His phrase neatly describes the majority of whites' attitudes toward blacks as the nineteenth century drew to a close. False beliefs would be reinforced in the decades to come by popular historians such as Myrta Lockett Avary, filmmakers such as D. W. Griffith, and novelists such as Thomas Dixon; these and other luminaries of America's surging popular culture followed the smoldering tracks of scientific racists and carried the myth of the nigger — and all its astonishing, contradictory qualities — lumbering into the modern age.

PART IV

Separate and Unequal
1897–1954

9

Different Times

The busy city dinned about us; they did not say much, those pale-faced hurrying men and women; they did not say much, — they only glanced and said, "Niggers!"

— W.E.B. Du Bois, *The Souls of Black Folk*, 1903

FROM A HISTORICAL VANTAGE point, the distance between *Plessy v. Ferguson* and *Brown v. Board of Education* seems quite short. To the African Americans who struggled and endured during that span, however, the idea of a desegregated society must often have seemed like a far-off dream. Many events and developments helped bring about the beginning of the end of Jim Crow, not least among them the activism of black Americans and their courageous white allies. At least as important, though, was the realization of powerful whites in government and industry that the United States could never be recognized as a paragon of civil liberty and democratic fortitude as long as it maintained its embarrassing attachment to outdated racial attitudes. Along with its growing domination of world culture and economy, the country's efforts to overcome its worst impulses would define the modern American era — an endeavor Du Bois had in mind when he memorably predicted that the problem of the twentieth century would be the problem of the color line.

DEGENERACY AND VOODOOISM

The modern era meant a full-fledged commitment to the wonders of machines. American manufacturers quickly climbed to global dominance, outstripping such European stalwarts as Great Britain, France, and Germany. Answering the siren call of the factories springing up in the New World, tired, huddled masses of Europeans rushed to tend the great grinding gears that made the new economy go. Between 1860 and 1915, nearly 30 million immigrants arrived from Europe.

The outbreak of World War I increased the northward flow of African Americans, who had already begun to flee the South. Between 1910 and 1920, more than 500,000 blacks made the journey, most of them intent on finding industrial jobs. Their migration made new urban meccas of such places as Harlem and the South Side of Chicago.

Few in the South were sad to see them leave. *Plessy v. Ferguson* failed to placate whites, who in the three decades since the end of the Civil War still believed that blacks were unfit for freedom. Furthermore, their presence as free individuals was a hindrance to anyone who longed to see the former Confederate states return to full strength. Georgia's state representative Thomas Hardwick, writing to his fellow Southerner Tom Watson in 1905, declared, "Until the South is finally rid of the Negro even as a political potentiality she will never again have either freedom of thought or independence of action." If blacks could no longer be confined in chains and treated like animals, they could at least be kept in their place. As far as most whites were concerned, that place was a peculiar limbo suspended beneath full citizenship and just above the tier occupied by dogs, donkeys, and horses. In 1903 Du Bois described it as "the thought of the older South — the sincere and passionate belief that somewhere between men and cattle, God created a tertium quid, and called it a Negro — a clownish, simple creature, at times even lovable within its limitations."

Thus blacks entered the twentieth century much as they had the three previous centuries: combating the niggerizing stereotypes that had been passed down through generations of whites who insisted on embracing them as gospel truths. Like Agassiz and the other "scholars" who preceded them, white academicians continued to produce dubious findings designed to keep blacks down. During the first two years of the new century, the political scientists John W. Burgess of Columbia and Woodrow Wilson of Princeton each published essays suggesting that blacks were not ready for full membership in American society. Typical of most Southern proponents of a belief in Negro "degeneracy," Wilson wrote that blacks were "excited by a freedom they did not understand" and were not equipped to handle the demands and privileges of citizenship. The United States was a modern place, hardly the place for primitives. Echoing Wilson and Burgess, in *Dixie After the War* Myrta Lockett Avary contended: "with freedom, the negro *en masse*, relapsed promptly into the voodooism of Africa." Avary's conclusions agreed with those of William B. Smith, a Tulane University professor who argued in *The Color Line* that blacks would soon be extinct. Neither would likely have found fault with Senator "Pitchfork" Ben Tillman, a leader of the defiant South, who offered his own brand of anthropology on the Senate floor: "We took them as barbarians, fresh from Africa . . . We gave them what little knowledge of civilization they have today."

This resurgent stereotype of Negroes as wild savages with animalistic impulses that only slavery could tame was given dramatic impetus in 1900, when Charles Carroll published *The Negro A Beast*. Picking up on Samuel Cartwright's evocation of the black yardman lurking around the Garden of Eden, Carroll argued that the Negro was literally an ape (created on the sixth day with the other animals) and the "tempter of Eve." Three years later, Dr. William Lee Howard wrote an article blaming an alleged increase of rapes of white women on "African" men, whose "birthright was . . . sexual madness and excess." In "Some Racial Peculiarities of the Negro Brain," an article in the *American Journal of Anatomy* in 1906, Robert Bennett Bean suggested that blacks' menacing tendencies likely derived from their lack of such "higher" mental faculties as "self-control, will power, ethical and aesthetic senses and reason." All of these arguments built on those of Frederick Hoffman. In *Race Traits and Tendencies of the American Negro* (1896), he explained black sexual hunger as an appetite that threatened to grow to horrible proportions as blacks became accustomed to freedom. The widespread and aggressive stereotyping of black men as monstrous rapists (cloaked in the language of biological determinism, not unlike contemporary discussions of a "criminal gene"), doubtless contributed to the frenzied lynching rituals that restless whites pursued during the early twentieth century.

"WE'RE AFTER NIGGERS"

In his monumental study of lynching, *At the Hands of Persons Unknown,* Philip Dray suggested that the most intense period of such killings took place from "about 1890 to the Red Summer of 1919," which roughly correlates with a series of major white riots stretching from 1898 to 1921. The first such riot of the twentieth century took place in Atlanta in 1906. The thirst for black blood was of nearly epidemic proportions in the South, stirred up by such leaders as Senator Tillman of South Carolina, perhaps the most quotable racist of the period. A typical Tillman speech could be relied on to demonstrate white supremacists' enduring fondness for and dependence on the N word. After Booker T. Washington's much-discussed meeting with President Theodore Roosevelt in the White House, Tillman had memorably declared that the event would "necessitate our killing a thousand niggers in the South before they will learn their place again."

The "uppityness" that Tillman and his fellow Southerners imagined most often took the form of sexual aggression, at least as it pertained to black men. By September 1906, Atlantans had been served a summer's worth of daily newspaper reports of Negro beasts marauding through the city and committing "outrages" against white women. Sometimes these articles acquired the flavor of science fiction. A little more than two weeks before the riot, the *Constitution* ran the following headline: NEGRO, SEEN IN DREAM, CAUSES DEATH OF GIRL. According to Dray, newspapers "included a dozen reported assaults through the month of September, and then four fresh ones on Friday the twenty-first and Saturday the twenty-second. Most of these were either wholly concocted or else were minor incidents blown out of proportion."

Incited by such reports, more than two thousand whites — many of them drunk — assembled in the streets of Atlanta to hunt for "black brutes." In *Negrophobia: A Race Riot in Atlanta, 1906,* Mark Bauerlein described war cries echoing "from party to party: 'Kill every damn nigger in town!' 'Lynch the niggers!' 'Bring back the Klan!'" When Mayor James Woodward stepped forward and tried to dissuade the crowd, he was shouted down. "Oh, go home yourself," he was told. "We're after niggers."

The mob eventually swelled to more than ten thousand men. Armed with clubs and knives, they destroyed buildings, broke glass, set fire to streetcars, and assaulted every black person unlucky enough to be caught on the street. The *Atlanta Evening News* called the rampage a "mad 'nigger chase.'" Dray put the total at "thirty killed, hundreds injured, [and] thousands forced to abandon their homes and places of work."

John Temple Graves, the editor of the *Atlanta Georgian,* blamed the entire spectacle on "the cumulative provocation of a series of assaults by Negroes upon white women, which, in number, in atrocity and in unspeakable audacity, are without parallel in the history of crime among Southern Negroes."

"KILL THE NIGGERS"

The Springfield, Illinois, riot of 1908 resulted in two blacks lynched, four whites killed, and hundreds wounded. Although it began when a crowd of whites went wild after failing to remove two black suspects from police custody, a newspaper placed the blame squarely on the blacks. Besides riots, it said, there was "no other remedy" for combating black "misconduct, general inferiority" and "unfitness for free institutions." Later, a sign posted outside Springfield illustrates how the N word continued to serve as a convenient shorthand for racist and violent sentiment: ALL NIGGERS ARE WARNED OUT OF TOWN BY MONDAY 12 P.M. SHARP.

The NAACP counted more than seventy lynchings during 1913, the year Woodrow Wilson took office as president. Wilson, the scholar who had deemed blacks unfit for freedom and education, also found them largely unfit for government service. After moving into the White House, he allowed his staffers to segregate federal employees (there were nineteen thousand black workers at the time, many of whom had been allowed to work closely with whites) and send packing black officeholders who had been appointed by his predecessors Roosevelt and Taft. As the journalist Charles Paul Freund has shown, Wilson's Jim Crow regime was "an available model" for the Dixiecrat segregationists who came later. Freund reported, "Wilson allowed various officials to segregate the toilets, cafeterias, and work areas of their departments. . . . In extreme cases, federal officials built separate structures to house black workers. Most diplomats were replaced by whites; numerous black federal officials in the South were removed from their posts; the local Washington police force and fire department stopped hiring blacks."

Du Bois and other black leaders loudly protested Wilson's changes. Perhaps the most vocal was William Monroe Trotter, an outspoken black activist who had clashed with Du Bois and others over the founding of the NAACP in 1909. Trotter sparred with Wilson while part of a delegation to the White House in 1914. He challenged Wilson's defense of segregation in government offices, prompting the president to interrupt and rebuke Trotter's "tone." Trotter didn't back down, provoking the ire of the Southern press. One Mississippi paper harshly condemned "the recent episode in which a Nigger leader of a delegation of Niggers practically insulted the President of the United States."

The next major riot took place in East St. Louis, Illinois, in 1917.

After blacks mistakenly fired on an unmarked police car and killed two white detectives, simmering tensions around housing and jobs boiled over into violence. Whites vented their unrestrained fury on men, women, and children, terrorizing the community. Thirty-nine blacks and eight whites were killed while thousands more were left homeless. Hundreds of buildings were reduced to rubble.

Daisy Westbrook, a black woman who survived the riot, relayed the details in a letter to a friend. "They shot & yelled something awful," she wrote of the mob. "Finally they reached our house. At first, they did not bother us (we watched from the basement window), they remarked that 'white people live in that house, that is not a nigger house.' Later, someone must have tipped them that it was a 'nigger' house, because, after leaving us for about 20 min. they returned and started shooting in the house throwing bricks & yelling like mad 'kill the niggers,' burn that house.'"

The house was destroyed, and Westbrook and her family "lost everything but what we had on and that was very little."

The East St. Louis conflagration was a bloody prelude to 1919, part of which James Weldon Johnson famously labeled the Red Summer. White riots erupted in twenty-six cities that season, and seventy-six lynchings were recorded. The most notorious conflict took place in Chicago, resulting in 23 blacks and 15 whites killed, 537 wounded, and 1,000 families left homeless. Philip Dray estimated that lynch mobs killed blacks "at the rate of one every five days" that year.

While racial violence slowed somewhat for a time, it by no means stopped. In Tulsa, Oklahoma, ten thousand whites went wild on May 31, 1921, after the alleged rape of a white woman by a black man. They burned forty-four blocks of black-owned property — destroying the prosperous community of Greenwood — and killed as many as three hundred blacks, many of whom were believed to have been secretly buried in mass graves. In the *New York Times*, Brent Staples reported that the *Tulsa Tribune* "primed its city for the riot with months of race baiting during which it referred to Greenwood as 'niggertown.'"

The Ku Klux Klan, rising again, was on its way to four million members. Walter White, the NAACP's fearless investigator, discovered firsthand that the Klan had played a part in the Tulsa mayhem. Coming to town in the guise of a white newspaperman, White heard a monologue that would have made Senator Tillman grin. "There's an organization in the South that doesn't love niggers," a hostile stranger said to him. "It has branches everywhere. You needn't ask me the name — I can't tell you. But it has come back into existence to fight this damned nigger Advancement Association. We watch every movement of the officers of this nigger society and we're out to get them for putting notions of equality into the heads of our niggers down South here."

Two years later, whites leveled the black community in Rosewood, Florida. Whites lynched at least fifty blacks each year from 1920 to 1922, when the latest of several attempts at passing a federal law against lynching was debated in Congress. In one telling exchange, someone shouted to the boisterous blacks watching the proceedings, "Sit down, niggers." To which they replied, "We are not niggers, you liars."

Their retort was unusual for its time, especially for Southern blacks. So accustomed were they to being called niggers that they seldom bothered to protest. As they had in other contexts, they often used the epithet themselves. Ira Tucker Jr., the longtime lead singer of the Dixie Hummingbirds gospel group, touched on this practice as he recalled his 1920s childhood in South Carolina: "They had names for the neighborhoods in Spartanburg like John's Alley, Jim's Alley, Highland, Baptist Side, Niggertown. And *everybody* said these names, whites and blacks. 'Yeah, let's go down to Niggertown, man.' You know, it was just a word. I didn't even think about it. 'I have to go to Niggertown, man.' Different times."

Annual recordings of lynchings declined to single-digit totals by the mid-1930s, although, as Dray persuasively argues, racial murder continued in less overt ways into the 1960s, with intermittent instances occurring as recently as 1998. Like lynching, the verbal denunciation of blacks also acquired subtler and disingenuous methods. Whereas Senator Tillman and his like-minded colleagues could freely chastise "niggers" during congressional debate, some of their philosophical heirs hid their venom behind devious "mispronunciations" and kinder, gentler racial slurs. For instance, in 1948 Governor Strom Thurmond of South Carolina could ensure his supporters: "I want to tell you, ladies and gentlemen, that there's not enough troops in the army to force the southern people to break down segregation and admit the nigger race into our theaters, into our swimming pools, into our homes, and into our churches." Thurmond, who went on to become the longest-serving U.S. senator in history, and other Southerners often maintained that they referred to blacks by saying "nigra," their attempt to pronounce "negro." However, Thurmond's famous 1948 speech was captured on tape, and although his description of blacks therein is usually transcribed as "nigra," it sounds very much like "nigger." Those who insisted that a distinction could be made between "nigra" and "nigger" were about as convincing as contemporary speakers who attempt to make a distinction between "nigga" — that old favorite of white blackface performers — and "nigger."

Dixiecrats such as Thurmond didn't appear to know it at the time, but their brand of boisterous racism was already giving way to a modern, triumphant liberalism. Perhaps nothing signaled that shift as dramatically as the *Brown* decision. Just six years after Thurmond's defiant proclamation, the Supreme Court struck down legally enforced segregation once and for all.

10

From House Niggers to Niggerati

The word nigger, you see, sums up for us who are colored all the bitter years of insult and struggle in America.

— Langston Hughes, *The Big Sea*, 1940

REMEMBER CAESAR THOMPSON? He was that comical slave in *The Spy*, James Fenimore Cooper's 1821 novel. Cooper introduced Caesar as a man with "abundantly capacious nostrils" and a huge mouth that was "only tolerated on account of the double row of pearls it contained." His legs were so disjointed that it was "sometimes a matter of dispute whether he was walking backwards."

Of Caesar's many literary descendants, few resemble him as closely as Aleck, one of the hapless Negroes prominently featured in *The Clansman* (1905), a notorious novel by Thomas Dixon Jr. Like Caesar, Aleck has a broad nose. But, Dixon tells us, "the one perfect thing about him was the size and setting of his mouth — he was a born African orator, undoubtedly descended from a long line of savage spell-binders, whose eloquence in the palaver houses of the jungle had made them native leaders. His thin spindle-shanks supported an oblong, protruding stomach, resembling an elderly monkey's, which seemed so heavy it swayed his back to carry it."

It's true that less than a century stretched between the two novels, yet it's still reasonable to despair at how little the image of blacks changed in that time. By the early 1900s, writers far more gifted and sensitive than Dixon had begun to portray black characters in their fiction, including Mark Twain and Theodore Dreiser. Dixon is of particular interest here, however, not simply because his insipid melodrama and his stage adaptation of it were both extremely popular, but because the film version of *The Clansman* — renamed *The Birth of a Nation* — became one of the most potent niggerizing forces ever unleashed in American popular culture. Dixon immodestly described his barely readable ode to the Ku Klux Klan as a faithful chronicle of "one of the most dramatic chapters in the history of the Aryan race." Considering the glorious mandate Dixon assigned himself, it's not surprising that Aleck is so harshly drawn.

Dixon's story revolves around the Confederate hero Ben Cameron, his lover Elsie Stoneman, her brother Phil, and her father Austin, who is very loosely based on Thaddeus Stevens. In a Reconstruction-ravaged Piedmont, South Carolina, overrun by mad Negroes, Ben leads the Klan on a glorious quest to reclaim the smoldering Southland for the white folks to whom it properly belongs. The N word appears only twenty times in the novel, but it is hardly needed, so enthusiastic is Dixon's evocation of a tormented South where "droves of brutal negroes roam at large, stealing, murdering, and threatening blacker crimes." While Dixon allows mulattoes to possess somewhat pleasing features — the result of their "Aryan" characteristics overcoming their "jungle" heritage — "pure" Negroes bear the brunt of the author's racist renderings. Austin Stoneman, the Speaker of the House who aims to confiscate Confederate property and hand it over to former slaves, has two such unlucky attendants, whose "kinky heads, black skin, thick lips, white teeth, and flat noses" come "wrapped in the night of four thousand years of barbarism."

That pair seems positively portrayed in comparison to Gus, the slave-turned-trooper whose sole function is to represent the unbridled lust of the ex-bondsman. "He had the short, heavy-set neck of the lower order of animals," Dixon tells us. "His skin was coal black . . . his nose was flat, and its enormous nostrils seemed in perpetual dilation. The sinister bead eyes, with brown splotches in their whites, were set wide apart and gleamed ape-like under his scant brows. His enormous cheekbones and jaws seemed to protrude beyond the ears and almost hide them."

Gus's impudence arouses the ire of both Phil, a former Yankee soldier, and Ben, who humiliates Gus and clubs him on the head with a fence post. With Ben's encouragement, Phil adopts the unofficial creed of the Lost Cause, part of which elevates the virtues of the Southern belle: "in spite of war and poverty, troubles present, and troubles to come, the young Southern woman was the divinity that claimed and received the chief worship of man." Ben, too, fervently expresses his reverence for the "girls of the South who came out of the war clad in the pathos of poverty, smiling bravely through the shadows, bearing themselves as queens though they wore the dress of the shepherdess."

Among the characters who use racist language in *The Clansman*, the "queens" distinguish themselves by their peculiar invocations of the N word. For example, Marion, a virtuous young maiden doomed to fall prey to Gus's all-consuming hunger, claims that the wrens singing in the shrubbery are actually warbling, "Free-nigger! Free-nigger!" Marion later explains to the Northern-born Elsie that "nigger dog" is the proper designation for a pet that "belongs to some colored people." The curious exchange between the two maidens illustrates how Dixon resorted to both overt and subtle language to drive home his notion that blacks were closer to the lower animals than to white people. Gus, with his "beady, yellow-splotched eyes" that gleamed "like a gorilla's," is lynched after assaulting Marion, but it's Aleck who receives a fate perhaps worse than death. To use modern parlance, he is deprogrammed by the Klan, convinced to give up his sheriff's badge, and acknowledge that he "ain't nuttin' but er plain nigger."

Walter Scott–style chivalry forced through a wringer of bad prose and draped in a sheet, *The Clansman* was a crude revenge fantasy perfectly suited for Americans eager to get on with national reconciliation. (Like Josiah Nott before him, Dixon learned to count on the avid attention of Northern audiences, who remained at least as excited about "the nigger business" as their Southern peers. The stage version actually made more money in the North than it earned down in Dixie.) In addition to serving as the basis of *The Birth of a Nation, The Clansman* heavily influenced the most popular novel ever to emerge from the moonlight-and-magnolias school, Margaret Mitchell's *Gone With the Wind.*

"YOU LOOK LIKE A NIGGER"

Mitchell won the Pulitzer Prize for her interminable novel, which was published in 1936. In it she tells the story of Scarlett O'Hara, a headstrong young Southern woman who survives the Civil War and other calamities, builds a sizable fortune, and saves Tara, the beloved plantation on which she grew up. Although Mitchell disavowed any connection to the plantation tradition of Southern fiction, her novel both revised and extended the genre, combining much that is found in such books — especially their caricatures of Negroes — with the extremely skewed view of Reconstruction found in Dixon's work. *The Clansman* wasn't really out of the plantation tradition — it is perhaps best described as a mutant offshoot — although Dixon adopted the subgenre's softhearted portrayal of virtuous maidens, who, except for a few, were incapable of doing much other than fluttering their lashes and running from lusty Negroes. Mitchell's heroine, the duplicitous and indefatigable Scarlett, knows that she can perform most tasks better than men and only deigns to flutter her lashes when it will induce dimwitted males to do her bidding. But Scarlett's maturation comes at the expense of the black characters in *Gone With the Wind,* and this is where Mitchell showed a close kinship with Dixon, whose work she often praised.

Just as Ben's emergence as a leader of the new South is signified by his pummeling of Gus with a fence post, Scarlett's emotional development is marked by her slapping of Prissy, her seemingly simple-minded servant. When Prissy, who always seems to know more than she lets on, confesses to knowing "nuthin' 'bout bringin' babies," Scarlett slaps the girl's "black cheek with all the force in her tired arm." Her violent response further signals her abandonment of her mother's stultifying customs and elaborate, genteel code of etiquette, a shift that will be reinforced in equally dramatic terms in a subsequent confrontation with the hapless Prissy.

Up to this point in the novel, Scarlett has been one of the few characters to avoid using the N word, which appears approximately 95 times in the book's 1,037 pages. Most often it falls from the lips of slaves and poor whites, neither of whom are expected to know much about manners and the polite language favored by "quality" people. But slapping Prissy has freed Scarlett from the restrictions of tradition, which allows her to denounce Prissy as "a fool nigger" before promising to "wear this whip out" on her. Scarlett is aware that she has crossed a line, but the knowledge of having done so merely strengthens her defiance: "There she thought, I've said 'nigger' and Mother wouldn't like that at all."

Scarlett continues to see her survival as at least partially dependent on her ability to call a Negro a "nigger" when the occasion calls for it. She commits herself to talking as briefly as possible with her servants, "dispensing with the usual forms of courtesy her mother had always taught her to use with negroes."

She also begins to speak freely in conversations with white men, another change that her mother would not have approved of. Often this outspokenness takes the form of denouncing blacks, or "niggers," as Scarlett has grown accustomed to calling them. "Free issue niggers are something else," she tells her second husband, "and a good whipping would do some of them a lot of good." When she discovers that emancipated blacks expect to be paid for their labors at her sawmill — and don't take kindly to whippings — she decides to employ convicts instead. "She would never fool with free niggers again," Mitchell wrote. "How could anyone get any work done with free niggers quitting all the time?"

When Scarlett and Melanie Wilkes succeed in putting out a fire at Tara, their bravery improves the often troubled relationship between the women and increases Scarlett's grudging respect for her sister-in-law. It is another memorable turning point in Scarlett's life, and once again she christens it with the N word. Regaining consciousness and gazing into Melanie's soot-blackened face, she remarks, "You look like a nigger." "And you look like the end-man in a minstrel show" is Melanie's sweet reply. From such intimate exchanges are beautiful friendships born.

NIGGERS WITH GUNS?

In the fictional Reconstruction of both Dixon and Mitchell, Negroes are not only unreliable but also threatening. Dixon wrote of "gangs of drunken negroes . . . [who] paraded the streets at night firing their muskets unchallenged and unmolested" and "desperadoes" who have come to Piedmont to teach the black hordes "insolence and crime." In Dixon's fictional state legislature, the black majority introduces a series of bills aimed at transferring "the intelligence and wealth of this mighty state . . . to the Negro race." (Interestingly, one piece of legislation seeks "to prevent any person calling another a 'nigger,'" evidence that Dixon was fully aware of white supremacy's dependence on the word.)

In *Gone With the Wind*, blacks' "insolence" takes the form of "niggers pushin' white folks off the sidewalks," a reflection of the uppityness they've gained from emancipation. Will Benteen, the yeoman farmer who eventually marries Scarlett's sister, complains to Scarlett, "Those niggers can do anything against us and the Freedmen's Bureau and the soldiers will back them up with guns and we can't vote or do nothin' about it." Neither Dixon nor Mitchell can resist working in the stereotype of the smelly Negro (what Jefferson called blacks' "strong and disagreeable odour") when the opportunity presents itself. Scarlett experiences one of her many epiphanies while stumbling half-starved among the "faint nigger smell" of the slave cabins, later recalled as a "niggery" scent. Dixon, noting the stench whenever blacks gather in *The Clansman*, suggested that "A new mob of onion-laden breath, mixed with perspiring African odour, has become the symbol of American Democracy."

One of Dixon's heroes, the dashing Dr. Cameron (who can subdue black Union soldiers simply by staring into their eyes), observes with barely contained fury, "The bayonet is now in the hands of a brutal Negro militia," all of whom, he says, have "the intelligence of children and the instincts of savages." Mitchell, whose passages celebrating the noble knights of the Klan closely echo Dixon's, noted "the astonishing spectacle of half a nation attempting, at the point of bayonet, to force upon the other half the rule of negroes, many of them scarcely one generation out of the African jungles." *The Clansman* takes place in 1867, by which time the federal government had removed all of its black U.S. Army troops from the Southern states. If there were any bayonets to be found, they weren't in black hands.

"AH'S A HOUSE NIGGER"

Characters in both books imply that Negroes have unwittingly exchanged a mutually beneficial relationship for a far harsher kind of slavery; they are now merely dialect-spouting puppets of their Yankee masters. To Scarlett O'Hara, the reason for this unfortunate switch is clear: "How stupid negroes were! They never thought of anything unless they were told."

But in Mitchell's war-wrecked Atlanta, only the "mean niggers" need to be told that Reconstruction was a bargain with the devil. Experience is enough to convince others of the error of their ways. The Negroes in *Gone With the Wind* who no longer "b'long" to quality white folks are frequently portrayed as barely surviving, "far better off under slavery than they were now under freedom," in the words of Frank Kennedy, Scarlett's second husband. Mitchell wrote of "aged country darkies" abandoned by their children, sitting on the curb and pleading with white women as they pass by: "Mistis, please Ma'm, write mah old Marster down in Fayette County dat

Ah's up hyah. He'll come tek dis ole nigger home agin. 'Fo Gawd, Ah done got nuff of dis freedom!"

Silas Lynch, the menacing mixed-race lieutenant governor in *The Clansman*, claims to encounter such Negroes regularly. "We find some so attached to their former masters that reason is impossible with them," he complains. "Even threats and the promise of forty acres of land have no influence." He could very well be describing the Negroes who are attached to Scarlett O'Hara. Led by Mammy, the unofficial plantation manager and Scarlett's surrogate mother, the blacks of Tara sweat and bleed for the white folks who, when feeling kind, refer to them as family. They also use the N word forty-six times, most often when distinguishing themselves from the unfortunate wretches who spent all of slavery toiling in the cotton. "I ain't a yard nigger," Prissy protests when Scarlett orders her to tie a cow to their wagon. "Ah's a house nigger." Pork, the long-time faithful valet to Scarlett's father, becomes indignant when his mistress tells him to go into the swamp and look for an escaped pig. "Miss Scarlett," he says, "dat a fe'el han's bizness. Ah's allus been a house nigger." Not much later, Mammy declares that she's a house nigger and has "never even been a yard nigger."

They don't care much for poor whites either, whom Mammy dismisses as "white trash." "Dey is de shiflesses, mos' ungrateful passel of no-counts livin'," she says of one local family. "Did dey be wuth shootin' dey'd have niggers ter wait on dem." Following emancipation, house servants reserved their harshest scorn for "free-issue niggers," who had no connection to quality white folks. When Mammy spits that epithet at a hack driver in Atlanta, he responds, "Ah ain' no free issue nigger. Ah b'longs ter Ole Miss Talbot." Clearly it's the "free issue" part that he finds insulting.

Mitchell suggested that blacks' use of the N word among themselves is so frequent and so casual that it only stings when it arises in unexpected circumstances. Elderly Uncle Peter, perhaps the most pretentious of the house servants who proudly serve Scarlett's family, is completely traumatized when a snotty Yankee woman insults him. Incredibly, "he had never had the term 'nigger' applied to him by a white person in all his life," Mitchell wrote. "By other negroes, yes. But never by a white person."

That white people, from whom he had received only love and affection, could intentionally hurt his feelings is the worst hurt that Peter, a former slave, has ever known. The source of the insult — a rude Northerner — only reinforces the notion that Southerners are the only whites who know how to treat Negroes properly, and that the smart "niggers" are the ones clever enough to recognize this fact. Uncle Peter's confrontation is one of many designed to reinforce that old plantation-tradition idea that the Yankees must go home if Southern blacks and whites are ever to reestablish the harmonious alliance they enjoyed before the war.

Mitchell's obvious comfort with the N word and her audiences' largely uncritical acceptance of it provides some indication of the extent to which antebellum racist descriptions of black people — and their attendant stereotypes — influenced early-twentieth-century popular culture. *Scarlett*, a sequel to *Gone With the Wind* written by Alexandra Ripley in 1991, and *The Wind Done Gone*, a parody written by Alice Randall in 2001, reflect the degree to which the popular acceptance of racist language has changed since Mitchell's novel was published. "Nigger" appears just twice in *Scarlett* and on both occasions is spoken by whites. Ripley also softened Mitchell's descriptions of blacks, removing the Dixonesque flourishes that insisted on linking Negroes to a quasi-simian jungle past. Whereas Mitchell wrote of Mammy's "kind black face sad with the uncomprehending sadness of a monkey's face," Ripley rhapsodically recalls Mammy as being "strong and fleshy, with warm brown skin."

The epithet is spoken approximately seventeen times in *The Wind Done Gone*. Cynara, its black heroine and ostensibly Scarlett's half-sister, uses the word eleven times. For her, as for many blacks, it seems to hold multiple meanings. At times it serves as a positive synonym for blackness, such as when Cynara reflects, "Almost everything best about me is niggerish ways." In other instances it functions as a traditional pejorative, as in Cynara's curious observation:

"One way of looking at it, all women are niggers. For sure, every woman I ever knew was a nigger — whether she knew it or not."

It is tempting to derive a wholesale indictment of white American society from the public's enthusiastic embrace of a novel so heavily peppered with "niggers," "darkies," and other hopelessly inept caricatures of black humanity. The fact remains, however, that some of Mitchell's literary contemporaries, such as Lillian Smith and Paul Green, were creating far more accurate and sympathetic portrayals of African Americans in their fiction — and found a willing audience. But Mitchell's blockbuster success and critical recognition for an overlong, patently racist paean to the glorious Confederacy is a troubling phenomenon nonetheless. As Grace Elizabeth Hale has noted in *Making Whiteness*, Mitchell's spectacular debut "proved how much white southern interpretations of [Reconstruction] had become the national standard." Americans grabbed fifty thousand copies of *Gone With the Wind* the day it went on sale. It went through thirty-one printings and sold one million copies in 1936 alone. At this writing, twenty-eight million copies have been sold in more than thirty-seven countries.

NIGGERATI AND WHATNOT

While Dixon and Mitchell were unreconstructed Southerners, Carl Van Vechten was a Northern liberal who frequented Harlem nightspots and counted blacks among his closest friends. And although his novel *Nigger Heaven* didn't begin to approach the popularity of *The Clansman* and *Gone With the Wind*, it was a best seller and minor sensation. Other white authors had produced books with similar titles: Clement Wood had published a novel called *Nigger* in 1922, which Sterling Brown called "completely convincing"; the British novelist Ronald Firbank published *Prancing Nigger* in 1924, which was promoted in the States by none other than . . . Carl Van Vechten.

But no other undertaking provoked as much comment as *Nigger Heaven*, perhaps because its author seemed so unlikely to wound black sensibilities. Kenneth Robert Janken, the biographer of Walter White, noted that "when the bestseller appeared, Van Vechten ('Carlo' to his friends) immediately became suspect. Had he taken advantage of Harlem's hospitality to write a pot-boiler chock-full of the most enduring stereotypes? Most of Harlem thought so." According to David Levering Lewis, "it was considered bad form among Afro-Americans to be caught reading *Nigger Heaven.*" Published in 1926, the novel is set in Harlem and revolves around an ill-fated romance between Mary Love, a virtuous young librarian, and Byron Kasson, an aspiring writer.

In *The Clansman,* Dixon wrote disparagingly of "negroes drunk with whisky and freedom." He was talking about Southern blacks, but the phrase could describe Van Vechten's decadent, dispirited Harlemites, who seem to regard their independence as a license to wallow in self-pity while drowning their sorrows in drink. Chief among these is Adora, a warmhearted and wealthy former entertainer with a large entourage and a seemingly endless capacity for ennui. When we meet Adora, she's playing hostess at her oceanside weekend home, which is crowded with sycophants and pleasure-seekers who have worn out their welcome. She tells Mary, the one guest whose company she enjoys, that she's "tired to death of all those Niggers downstairs. Sometimes I hate Niggers."

A helpful footnote from Van Vechten tells readers: "While this informal epithet is freely used by Negroes among themselves, not only as a term of opprobrium, but also actually as a term of endearment, its employment by a white person is always fiercely resented. The word Negress is forbidden under all circumstances."

His note seems to apply to all whites except himself. He includes the N word approximately forty times in the novel, attributing it to a white speaker only once. His perceived audacity infuriated black critics. Du Bois called it "a blow in the face." Writing in the *Amsterdam News,* Hubert Harrison noted, "it seems strange that one of the professional experts on the Negro should select a selling title which gives such offence to all self-respecting Negroes" before going on to condemn the novel as "an 'atmosphere' story of Harlem, flanked by tone-sketches and garnished with a vicious 'nigger dialect' whose sole source must be the author's mind at 4 A.M. after supping." Harry B. Weber of the *Pittsburgh Courier* pointed to *Nigger Heaven* as an unfortunate and unavoidable result of Negro writers' ignoring the story possibilities that Harlem presented. Phil A. Jones of the *Chicago Defender* called the novel "drivel, pure and simple . . . 286 pages of lurid detail about women's undergarments . . . slushy scenes in Harlem cabarets . . . grotesque character names . . . impossible dialect . . . and general confusion."

Not everyone found fault with Van Vechten's work. Nella Larsen, who was close to him, praised it. James Weldon Johnson, also a friend, defended it in *Opportunity Magazine*. Walter White, who in a few years would pressure David O. Selznick to leave the N word out of the screen version of *Gone With the Wind,* also stood up for Van Vechten, telling him: "My only regret . . . is that I didn't think of [the title] first so I could use it." Langston Hughes managed to publish two defenses of the novel without commenting on its literary quality.

Hughes, along with young Harlem Renaissance luminaries such as Zora Neale Hurston and Wallace Thurman, seemed to be far less uptight about the N word than older black writers (an exception was their contemporary Countee Cullen, who found *Nigger Heaven* so offensive that he didn't speak to its author for fourteen years). They even used it among themselves with the reckless wit that characterized much of their interaction. Thurman and Hurston pioneered the use of the term "Niggerati," which Hurston's biographer Valerie Boyd describes as "an inspired moniker that was simultaneously self-mocking and self-glorifying, and sure to shock the stuffy black bourgeoisie." They even called Thurman's apartment, where the New Negroes often gathered, "Niggerati Manor."

A brilliant folklorist, Hurston was seldom if ever troubled by language that may have challenged others' sensibilities. She once sarcastically concluded a letter to Hughes: "P.S. How dare you use the word 'nigger' to me. You know I don't use such a nasty word. I'm a refined lady and such a word simply upsets my conglomeration." She once anointed Van Vechten an "honorary Negro," a title he may have taken a tad too seriously.

Ditto for his pal Hughes, who eventually wrote blisteringly about the N word on more than one occasion. In his 1940 memoir, *The Big Sea,* he wrote the lines that are quoted at the beginning of this chapter. A 1947 essay discussed the hostilities he endured after publishing a poem called "Christ in Alabama," which begins: "Christ is a Nigger, / Beaten and black." One of his last books, *Misery,* published in 1967, includes a passage describing misery as the feeling that comes when "somebody meaning no harm called your little black dog 'Nigger' and he just wagged his tail and wiggled." If he had any such feelings during the uproar over Van Vechten's book, he kept them to himself. Following Hughes's laudatory comments in the April 16, 1927, *Pittsburgh Courier,* Van Vechten thanked him in a letter. "The situation is *easy* to explain," he wrote. "You and I are the only colored people who really love *niggers.*"

In addition to perhaps exploiting his status as an honorary Negro, Van Vechten proved overly fond of what he perceived to be the black communities' most intriguing traits, what he called "the squalor of Negro life, the vice of Negro life." Hence he showed his heroine, the virginal, refined Mary Love, struggling to get in touch with her primitive side: "This love of drums, of exciting rhythms, this naïve delight in glowing colour — the colour that exists only in cloudless, tropical climes — this warm, sexual emotion, all these were hers only through a mental understanding." Unlike the novice legislators in *Gone With the Wind,* who are allegedly just one generation removed from the jungle, poor Mary has been so caught up in education and uplift that she has lost touch with her African roots. Her would-be lover, Byron, has no such difficulties. He dances "with that exotic Negro sense of rhythm which made time a thing in space."

All too often, Van Vechten went overboard in his descriptions of activities that he admiringly regarded as authentic Negro behavior. Like jazz, for instance: "The jazz band vomited, neighed, barked, and snorted and the barbaric ceremony began."

An excessive preoccupation with the "barbaric" and "primitive" aspects of blackness, plus its alleged "squalor" and "vice" — an American version of *le tumulte noir* — obsessed a sizable group of white artists, whom Hurston memorably dubbed Negrotarians. Among them was Sherwood Anderson, whose misguided enthusiasm was typical. "Damn it, man," he wrote in a letter to H. L. Mencken, "if I could really get inside the niggers and write about them with some intelligence, I'd be willing to be hanged later and perhaps would be."

Van Vechten and the others weren't intentionally malevolent, however harmful their efforts turned out to be. Their inability to see black Americans as they truly were, while less pronounced than the shortcomings of many of their peers, illustrates the degree to which "friendly fire" continued to plague the efforts of both African-American artists and private citizens.

KEEPING IT REEL

His allies supported Van Vechten's contention that his title had a double meaning, alluding to Harlem's status as a black paradise that hovered above white Manhattan and to the slang term for the segregated balconies in movie theaters, to which black audiences were usually confined. By 1926, most of Van Vechten's black readers would probably have caught the reference, as African Americans had begun to participate wholeheartedly in the nation's burgeoning love affair with motion pictures. In addition to occupying "nigger heavens" in white movie theaters, they watched movies at all-black cinemas across the country, of which there were more than two hundred.

Most of the early American films portrayed African Americans in much the same manner as minstrel shows or borrowed themes from the racist literature of the preceding century. In a typical one-reeler (fifteen to thirty minutes long) such as *The Nigger in the Woodpile* (1904) or *Dancing Nig* (1907), black characters conformed to prevailing stereotypes, cavorting about as simple-minded, watermelon-craving chicken thieves.

Cinema had picked up where literature, magazines, and other forms of popular culture had left off, further entrenching the image of blacks as bewildered by freedom and prone to comic mischief and "blacker crimes" if left to their own devices. The NAACP attempted a campaign against one such film in 1910, objecting to the title of a forthcoming production about a black man who bumbles his way to the governorship of a Southern state. The organization was largely unsuccessful in its efforts against *The Nigger,* although the film was shown in New England as *The New Governor* as a result of its criticism.*

The racist short films and *The Nigger* set the stage for *The Birth of a Nation,* the three-hour film adapted from *The Clansman.* D. W. Griffith's film shattered precedent with its many technical innovations and its budget, which reached the then-unheard-of sum of $110,000. It debuted in 1915 to widespread acclaim. From many white viewers, that is. The NAACP — counting white dissenters among its ranks — managed to stall the Los Angeles premiere with a court order, but only temporarily. The group tried and failed to stop the premiere in New York, then followed up with clamorous boycotts in Boston and Chicago. Race riots erupted here and there across the country, which was hardly surprising: According to the film historian Donald Bogle, *The Birth of a Nation* was sometimes advertised as designed to "work audiences into a frenzy . . . it will make you hate."

Stage productions of *The Clansman* had already roused vio-

---

* This film should not be confused with Edward Sheldon's 1909 play of the same name, which expressed an essentially liberal message.

lent emotions. The *Iowa State Bystander,* a black newspaper, quoted remarks overheard at a local performance in 1907. "I'd like to kill that nigger," one woman is reported to have said about a black character. "When I came out, I wanted to kill every nigger I saw," a man said.

The black press went to work in support of the NAACP's efforts. The *New York Age* launched an extended campaign, including articles, editorials, and letters to the mayor. The *Chicago Defender,* the *Crisis,* and the *California Eagle* followed suit, while a few papers, such as the *Philadelphia Tribune,* adopted a contrarian stance. "Some of the cooler heads thought it best to go and see the play before making a kick," the *Tribune* wrote.

Some white critics, such as Francis Hackett of the *New Republic,* found much to criticize in Griffith's production. The majority of them, however, found even more to praise. Dorothy Dix of the *New York Post* called it "a war play the like of which has never been presented on any stage before." James Metcalfe of *Life* magazine loved it too: "It is to the advantage of the Negro today to know how some of his ancestors misbehaved and why the prejudices in his path have grown here."

The turmoil often worked against the film's opponents by stirring up more interest. In Bruce Chadwick's words, "Going to see *Birth* became a national obsession." Like the stage version, the movie made more money in the North and West than in the South. Chadwick wrote, "By 1921 at *Birth*'s first reissue, the movie was estimated to have grossed over $20 million, and by 1941, close to $45 million. By 1949, *Variety* estimated *Birth*'s total revenue at slightly over $50 million, close to $1 billion in contemporary revenue, making it one of the most successful movies of all time." With such monumental box office tallies, the film's influence can hardly be overestimated. The historian John Hope Franklin has argued that it "did more than any single thing to nurture and promote the myth of black domination and debauchery during Reconstruction." In so doing, however, it merely held a mirror up to the white popular imagination, which had progressed very little in its conception of African Americans. As the film scholar James R. Nesteby has written, it was part of a body of work that "both reflected and inflamed the prevailing national sentiments."

"'DARKIES' YES, 'NIGGERS' NO"

The movie version of *Gone With the Wind,* directed by Victor Fleming from a screenplay by Sidney Howard, had its premiere in 1939. Like *The Birth of a Nation,* it quickly became a national obsession, raking in $60 million in ticket sales (nearly $1 billion today). Chadwick wrote, "it was estimated that between its first theater showing in 1939 and 1945 more than 120 million Americans, or just about every adult in the country, saw it." According to Chadwick, both *Gone With the Wind* and *The Birth of a Nation* belong among the top five box office films of all time if revenues are adjusted for inflation. Fleming's film is immeasurably gentler in its treatment of African Americans when compared to *Birth.* For one thing, black characters were actually played by black actors instead of whites in blackface (Hattie McDaniel won a best supporting actress Oscar — the first ever for a black performer — for her role as Mammy).

For another, the book's nearly one hundred invocations of the N word have been deleted. That significant change took place after considerable back-and-forth between its producer, David O. Selznick, Walter White of the NAACP, and Joe Breen of the Hays Office, the agency responsible for censoring films. Initially, Breen had decided that whites could not utter the N word, but the black characters could use it among themselves. On further reflection, he decided against blacks using it as well. Selznick was reluctant to go along, fearing the film would lose an element he cherished: its "Negro flavor." But the studio's publicist Victor Shapiro had already struck a bargain with the black cast members. Leonard J. Leff provided details of the negotiations in a 1999 article in the *Atlantic Monthly:*

The actors . . . had expressed their anxiety over racial elements of the production yet agreed to play the slaves more or less as Margaret Mitchell and Sidney Howard had written them. In return, Shapiro vowed that they would not have to say "nigger." Selznick, with mixed feelings, honored Shapiro's promise. The words "darkies" and "inferiors" stayed in the screenplay — but not "nigger."

But that significant deletion didn't appease the critics in the black press — nor should it have. The film's succession of simple, shuffling, fanatically devoted darkies inevitably evoked all the tragically misplaced priorities and self-betrayal associated with "house niggers" — even if they were never addressed as such. The *Chicago Defender,* a particularly strident critic, lambasted the production, calling it "a weapon of terror against black America." The harshest condemnations came from Melvin B. Tolson, a columnist for the *Washington Tribune* who is best remembered today as a gifted poet. In two essays published in 1940, Tolson took the film apart while chastising blacks who enjoyed seeing it. Negro fans who embraced Victor Fleming's production simply because it compared favorably to *The Birth of a Nation* suffered from low expectations, in Tolson's view. "Since *Gone With the Wind* didn't have a big black brute raping a white virgin in a flowing white gown," he wrote, "most Negroes went into ecstasies." A little jubilation can cloud the faculties, he suggested, and make palatable things that would be unacceptable in more sober circumstances. For Tolson, "*The Birth of a Nation* was such a barefaced lie that a moron could see through it. *Gone With the Wind* is such a subtle lie that it will be swallowed as the truth by millions of whites and blacks alike."

"Of Motion Pictures," Lawrence Reddick's important 1944 essay, touched on many of the same points that Tolson raised in 1940, when *Gone With the Wind* was on nearly every moviegoer's mind. His twenty-two-page essay critiqued a "checklist" of 175 films with regard to their treatment of African Americans and included a still-discussed list of pervasive black stereotypes found in the media. Whereas Sterling Brown had identified six distinct black characters portrayed in fiction (see chapter 5), Reddick came up with a few more:

1. The savage African
2. The happy slave
3. The devoted servant
4. The corrupt politician
5. The petty thief
6. The irresponsible citizen
7. The social delinquent
8. The vicious criminal
9. The sexual superman
10. The superior athlete
11. The unhappy non-white
12. The natural-born cook
13. The natural-born musician
14. The perfect entertainer
15. The superstitious churchgoer
16. The chicken and watermelon eater
17. The razor and knife "toter"
18. The uninhibited expressionist
19. The mental inferior

For Reddick, the cumulative effect of such images drove "deeper into the public mind the stereotyped conception of the Negro" and harnesses the enormous potential of motion pictures for nefarious political purposes. "This great agency for the communication of ideas and information, therefore, functions as a powerful instrument for maintaining the racial subordination of the Negro people," he wrote. In this context, there were some tiny victories. In 1945, for instance, Hollywood studios agreed to stop referring to black electrical screens as "niggers," although by 1960 O. Skilbeck's *ABC of Film & TV* included a passage on the "Nigger," defined as "an adjustable Mask on a stand, used on the Floor to shield the camera from, or to achieve effects with, lights." The N word's continued presence in such industry publications showed that a gulf still existed between speech and practice where entertainment was concerned.

"THERE MIGHT BE A NIGGER IN HERE"

In both *The Clansman* and *Gone With the Wind*, a popular tune is performed to soothe troubled Confederate hearts. The tune, "O Johnny Booker He'p Dis Nigger," makes Ben Cameron, confined to a Washington hospital bed, tremble with visions of his beloved South. Its rollicking strains, performed by a Negro band, make young Scarlett O'Hara want to get up and dance. Because "Johnny Booker" is a folk song, there are many variations of it. Most of them contain a reference or two to "niggers," however. A typical verse goes something like this:

> I drove down to Lickburg town
> I broke my yoke to th collar of th' ground
> Drove from there to ole Ike's shop
> I hollered at my driver an' told 'em t' stop
> Do, Johnny Booker won't you help this nigger
> Do, Johnny Booker, do

The persistent nostalgic streak shown by Ben and Scarlett continued to manifest itself among white Southerners deep into the twentieth century. In his biography of the great gospel group known as the Dixie Hummingbirds, Jerry Zolten wrote that audiences still clamored for such anachronistic fare when the singers began their career. The Hummingbirds discovered this firsthand just a few years after Al Bowlly's recording of "Nigger Blues" topped the charts. "Between 1935 and 1939 . . . when they performed for whites, they began with at least one song that conformed to white expectations of what blacks ought to be singing . . . the song they used as a 'placater' was Stephen Foster's 'Old Black Joe,' a melancholy pseudo-hymn about an aged slave yearning for old times and friends long gone." Seventy years after emancipation, "the 1860 song's romanticized vision of slavery was especially popular with white audiences in the South."

In the same period, the use of "nigger" was, for a time, a nickname among American Jews. In *A Right to Sing the Blues,* Jeffrey Melnick discussed the popularity of such nicknames as "Nigger Benny," "Nig" Rosen, and "Niggy" Rutman. While Jews known by such handles were able to "capture some of the masculine cachet stereotypically ascribed to the African-American male," Melnick wrote, they managed to escape "the most debasing conceptions of Blackness . . . still being circulated in public forums as late as the 1920s."

At the same time, other song titles that used the N word — some of them written by African Americans — found an enthusiastic audience among American music lovers. "He's Just a Little Nigger, But He's Mine, All Mine," "You May Be a Hawaiian on Broadway but You're Just Another Nigger to Me," "Nigger-Toe Rag," "Oh You Bantle Shank Nigger," "Nigger, Nigger," "Ten Little Niggers," "Heart of a Nigger," and "I'll Carve Dat Nigger When We Meet" were among the popular songs available through recordings and sheet music.

By the 1940s, "nigger" was seldom spoken in films or sung over the radio waves, although it remained ubiquitous in popular speech and culture. In family parlors, while their parents sat at the piano and sang "nigger" songs, children could play "The Game of Ten Little Niggers" and read picture books about Ned and Nellie Nigger.

But the warmth and comfort of the hearth provided only temporary shelter from the changes in the streets. The NAACP had been formed in 1909 and quickly become expert at conducting nationwide political campaigns. Courtesy of Alain Locke and a host of talented writers, the New Negro had announced his arrival during the 1920s. In the 1930s, the athletic brilliance of Jesse Owens and Joe Louis gave blacks champions to cheer for. The Congress of Racial Equality (CORE) staged its first sit-in at a Chicago restaurant in 1943. Slowly, inexorably, the fight for social and political equality gained momentum as the twentieth century approached middle age.

Few Negroes exemplified the burgeoning confidence and bright promise of the coming era as well as Adam Clayton Powell Jr., the flamboyant New Yorker who was elected to Congress in 1944, only the second black man since Reconstruction to win a seat in the House. His biographer Wil Haygood relates an incident in 1936 that perfectly illustrates the blend of boldness and subterfuge that Powell and others used to combat the niggerizing effects of Jim Crow.

Adam Clayton Powell — so fair-skinned he could have passed as white — was hustling toward a first-class train compartment in Atlanta. A porter who had looked over his shoulder out of curiosity wondered if the man he had just seen stepping into the train was a Negro. Maybe. Maybe not. But damn if he wasn't going to check it out, go fetch a superior. Upon entering the first-class compartment, the superior looked around and yelled out: "Hey, we believe there might be a nigger in here!" Before eyes could rest suspiciously upon him, Powell hopped up. "Where! You better find him and get him the hell out of here! What kind of train are you running?" Then the young minister sat down, like a king, like a rich white man. And the train pulled off. Powell must have been laughing uproariously on the inside. Couldn't laugh on the outside, though. Negro life was too risky to do that.

11

Bad Niggers

The Negro is believed to be stupid, immoral, diseased, lazy, incompetent, and dangerous — dangerous to the white man's virtue and social order.

— Gunnar Myrdal, *An American Dilemma*, 1944

IN ONE OF THE more charitable passages in *Gone With the Wind*, Margaret Mitchell hesitated to blame black "insolence" during Reconstruction solely on "mean niggers," of which, she said, there were few even in slavery days. Blacks were simply conducting themselves "as creatures of small intelligence might naturally be expected to do," like "monkeys or small children turned loose among treasured objects whose value is beyond their comprehension."

The *Kansas City Star*, like many newspapers of the period, strenuously disagreed. In the aftermath of the 1906 race riot in Atlanta, the paper urged blacks to come up with "a determined policy to expose and root out . . . the mean nigger." Previous concepts of the mean or bad nigger often derived from a widespread belief in blacks' irresistible impulse toward barbarism and their failure to evolve from their original state. After the Civil War, such concepts tended to focus on the release of impulses previously restrained and refined by slavery. In the Reconstructed South in particular, Negroes' bestial proclivities had at last overwhelmed their childlike qualities. In their portrayal of rapacious freedmen and surly "free-issue niggers," Mitchell, Thomas Dixon, and others had merely given fictional form to the brute that Charles Carroll had described a few years earlier in *The Negro: A Beast*. Carroll, of course, hadn't been the only one. In 1893, the Southern essayist Charles H. Smith had argued that Negroes were helpless to avoid attacking white women and children. He wrote: "A bad negro is the most horrible creature upon the earth, the most brutal and merciless." His contemporary Clifton R. Breckinridge contended that when the black race produces a desperado, "he is the worst desperado in the world . . . the worst and most insatiate brute that exists in human form."

Free blacks had long been regarded as "bad niggers," uppity troublemakers who exerted negative influences on slaves. Now that all Negroes were free, their potential to cause harm increased exponentially in the minds of resistant whites, and the prospect of black misbehavior became a convenient excuse for vigilante violence and increased calls to protect white racial purity. For many whites, lynching seemed the most feasible way to root out "mean niggers." Although some whites seemed to disapprove of that method, few spoke out. They maintained a discreet and unconscionable silence while more vocal observers made their preferences known. The Atlanta writer and politician Rebecca Latimer Felton was among the latter. "If it needs lynching to protect woman's dearest possession from the ravening human beasts — then I say lynch; lynch a thousand times a week if necessary," she wrote.

Sexual paranoia like Felton's, inseparable from white fears of racial amalgamation, is what prompted such strong audience response to Gus, the "renegade" villain of *The Birth of a Nation* and the most memorable of the first "bad niggers" on the large screen. With all his lusty, bug-eyed creeping around, Gus typifies the kind of character that the literary scholar Jerry Bryant calls "the 'bad nigger' [as] the white man's worst dream: the slave or (after Emancipation) the laborer who refused to knuckle under, who repeatedly ran away, who deliberately slowed down work, surreptitiously or openly throwing sand into the master's machines."

"THE BADDEST NIGGER"

Increasingly, anyone inclined to throw sand or anything else into machines had to make his way north, where the factories were springing up. Black men who left the South to look for industrial work found that the "mean nigger" stereotype followed them to their new homes in squalid hovels and alleys in the expanding cities. Whereas white journalists and novelists in the South had condemned rude blacks who allegedly shoved whites off sidewalks, northern alarmists lamented the swelling ranks of swaggering troublemakers who frequented saloons, brandished razors, and leered at white women.

Black crime rates did soar alarmingly during the first years of the twentieth century, although black predators tended to concentrate on equally dark-skinned prey. When Du Bois, Booker T. Washington, and other black leaders spoke out on the issue, they seemed less concerned with the real dangers that black felons posed than with the myth of the bad nigger, which threatened the fragile respectability of the emerging black middle class. Du Bois, writing about rape in "Notes on Negro Crime," offered the following concession: "making allowance for all exaggeration in attributing this crime to Negroes, there still remain enough well authenticated cases of brutal assault on women by black men in America to make every Negro bow his head in shame." Du Bois usually cast a hard look at black crime and was no doubt aware how easily such comments could be misused by those who opposed black advancement. Yet he nearly bypassed the issue of the physical abuse of women in his rush to address the potential embarrassment of law-abiding black men.

Booker T. Washington took to task the "loafers, the drunkards and gamblers" who "disgrace our race and disturb our civilization." In sharp contrast, Ida B. Wells had never accepted the tales of wide-ranging black rapaciousness. She always challenged such rumors with countercharges about white women's sexuality. "It is certain that lynching mobs have not only refused to give the Negro a chance to defend himself," she once said, "but have killed their victim with a full knowledge that the relationship of the alleged assailant with the woman who accused him, was voluntary and clandestine."

Wells offered her comments in 1892, just three years before the legend of Stagolee was born. A fearless character who bullied and murdered his fellow blacks and inspired fear among whites, Stagolee and his fictional exploits were celebrated in poem and song through the 1950s, '60s, and '70s, and have already been evoked during the first years of the twenty-first century.

Songs, verse, and farcical "toasts" devoted to Stagolee sprang up in all parts of the country during the late 1890s, but Cecil Brown convincingly traced their origins to a brawl in a St. Louis saloon in 1895 in which thirty-one-year-old "Stack" Lee Shelton fatally shot Billy Lyons. Afterward, Brown contended, passages from earlier, similar folklore came together with descriptions of the barroom fight to form a new type of urban ballad. In most versions, Stagolee shoots Lyons with a .44 Smith & Wesson after the two men argue — sometimes during a card game, sometimes during a conversation about politics. The violence usually begins with Lyons either taking or damaging Shelton's white Stetson hat. Insulted, Shelton brandishes his gun. Citing the needs of his wife and children, Lyons begs for mercy, which has no effect on his assailant. If anything, it enrages him even more:

> Don't care nothin' about your chillun,
> And nothin' about your wife,
> You done mistreated me, Billy,
> And I'm bound to take your life.

Invariably, Stagolee proves to be a skilled and cold-blooded killer, cementing his folk status, in the words of Julius Lester, as "undoubtedly and without question, the baddest nigger that ever lived." In subsequent retellings, Stagolee has various fantastical adventures, including dueling the devil in the underworld. Some versions introduce the ghost of Billy Lyons, who haunts his murderer's dreams.

According to Daryl Cumber Dance, the "bad nigger" of folklore is "tough and violent. . . . He asserts his manhood through his physical destruction of men and through his sexual victimization of women." This certainly applies to Stagolee. Many toasts praise his exploits as a charismatic pimp whose prostitutes work ceaselessly — refusing even to stop for lunch — to raise his bail money. In others he is shown cruelly breaking women's hearts. In one version, he tells Lyons's mother that he has just killed "her last and only son." When she refuses to believe him, he says, "Look, bitch, if you don't believe what I said, / Go down there and count them holes in his motherfuckin' head."

Stagolee and other bad niggers are not always cruel, however. Sometimes they are portrayed as Robin Hoods of "the 'hood," generous to the needy and protective of the weak, friend of many unless they are crossed. Although they often exhibit dangerous flaws, they also possess undeniable masculine charms. "The Bad Nigger is and always has been bad (that is, villainous) to whites because he violates their laws and he violates their moral codes," according to Cumber Dance. "He is *ba-ad* (that is, heroic) to the Black people who relish his exploits for exactly the same reasons." This is only partly true, for the exploits of such men could have only distressed Du Bois and others who invested their hopes and energies in less bodacious forms of resistance. For obvious reasons, then, "bad niggers" often were polarizing figures in black communities. Stagolee, however, remains a durable if subdued cultural influence. Inspired by the blues singer Mississippi John Hurt and other Delta balladeers, the pop singer Beck often performs a version of "Stagolee" in concert. The novelist Percival Everett offered a contemporary and ironic twist on the legend when he invented a pseudonymous writer named Stagger Lee in *Erasure*, his wickedly satirical novel of 2001.

SPOILING FOR A FIGHT

The former heavyweight boxing champion Mike Tyson, not known as a collector of folklore, unwittingly echoed Stagolee's words to the begging Billy Lyons when he threatened Lennox Lewis before their bout in 2002. "I want your heart," Tyson said. "I want to eat your children. I am the most ruthless, brutal champion ever. . . . I enjoy hurting people. That is how I make a living. I am in the hurting business." Tyson also brings to mind Mensa and Jake, two characters in E.C.L. Adams's *Nigger to Nigger,* a 1928 folklore collection. Mensa is described as a "bad nigger" who subdues Bo Shoat, another "bad nigger," of whom it is said, "Look like every wey he go he spilin' for a fight." Mensa, like Cumber Dance's characters, operates according to a personal and quirky code of honor. He is generally kind until he feels disrespected and his idea of respect is fragile indeed. One character says of him, "He ain' never change he friendly ways to nobody 'less dey been natu'ally tryin' to find trouble. Mensa was one er dese kind er niggers dat would cut you' tho'at ef you got him wrong, but he wold bow down to de ground an' take he hat off 'fore he done it, but, my brother, ef you got him wrong, he were bad wrong an' he make everything look wrong 'bout him. Mensa would jes cut you' th'oat 'pologizin' for it." His conduct is not very different from that of Tyson, who gently kissed Lennox Lewis's mother on the cheek after his fight with her son.

Notwithstanding Tyson's reputation for brutality, his cartoonish "bad nigger" posturing in this instance seemed designed largely to attract media attention and boost box office receipts. When Jack Johnson exhibited his brutal talents, he always had more to lose than a lucrative purse or his boxing license. The first black heavyweight champion was a notorious "bad nigger" in the eyes of sports-minded whites and "probably the first black man in America with the power and stature to consciously goad whites with behavior deemed 'lynchable.'" His rise and fall seemed all but inevitable given the racist tenor of his time. It also inspires the notion of the "bad nigger" as a romantic and tragic figure, discussed in some detail in Jerry H. Bryant's study of violent characters in African-American fiction and folklore, *Born in a Mighty Bad Land.* Johnson had the misfortune to be born in the wrong era, long before a black man's athletic brilliance could earn the unabashed admiration of whites (à la Michael Jordan), long before a black man could openly romance a white woman (à la Tiger Woods), and long before brashness could be turned into a lucrative marketing gimmick (à la Dennis Rodman, who alluded to the myth of the bad nigger in his provocatively titled memoir, *Bad As I Wanna Be*).

While Jack Johnson was experiencing his spectacular rise and fall and Stagolee was beginning his storied ascent through urban folklore, African-American authors were exploring the idea of the "bad nigger" as a plaything of Fate whose hubris would lead to punishment. Among the most compelling of those efforts was "Blood-Burning Moon," a selection in Jean Toomer's *Cane* (1923). Its central figure, Tom "Big Boy" Burwell, is a basically goodhearted soul, although he settles arguments with his knife and arrogantly believes that he should be free to love whom he chooses. He "is sho one bad nigger when he gets started," a neighbor is heard to say of Tom, who is beginning to lose patience with Bob Stone, a wealthy young white man who has eyes for Louisa, Tom's sweetheart. A veteran of the chain gang who's "already cut two niggers," Tom has warned Louisa that he will cut Stone "jes like I cut a nigger" if he continues to get in the way.

Bob scoffs at the notion of getting "in a scrap with a nigger over a nigger girl," even "a beautiful nigger gal" like Louisa. "Why nigger?" Bob asks himself. "Why not, just gal? No, it was because she was nigger that he went to her."

Louisa tries to calm Tom down, but Bob forces his hand. Under a reddish moon, Tom pummels his white rival with little effort. When Bob flashes a knife, Tom slits his throat. He waits, paralyzed, for the mob that will come and burn him alive. Perhaps the most physically powerful man in his little Georgia town, he is finally, fatally, powerless in the face of white rage.

All bad niggers did not die terrible deaths like Tom, and not all of them were men. Zora Neale Hurston, perhaps best recalled today as the most talented novelist to emerge from the Harlem Renaissance, was also an extraordinary anthropologist. While collecting folklore in Florida, she encountered a number of hard-working, tough-loving women who weren't shy about cutting men's throats. "Negro women *are* punished in these parts for killing men," Hurston assured her readers, "but only if they exceed the quota."

One Polk County lumber camp where she conducted research sounds very much like the violent company town where Tom met his fate. In both *Mules and Men* (1935) and *Dust Tracks on a Road* (1942), Hurston wrote about the code of conduct among black laborers in the camp, where hardly a day passes without tempers flaring, insults exchanged, and challenges thrown down. Evenings are spent in jook joints, dancing, gambling, getting drunk, "knocking the right hat off the wrong head, and breaking it up with a switchblade." It's the kind of place where one woman might say to another: "Fool wid me and I'll cut all your holes into one."

The most notorious of the female gladiators in camp is Big Sweet. "Tain't a man, woman nor child on this job going to tackle Big Sweet," a camp gossip tells Hurston. "If God send her a pistol she'll send him a man. She can handle a knife with anybody. . . . She done kilt two mens on this job and they said she kilt some before she ever come here. She ain't mean. She don't bother nobody. She just don't stand for no foolishness, dat's all."

Big Sweet befriends the young anthropologist and helps her collect "lies" that the laborers like to swap when not going at one another with deadly weapons. Like the "bad niggers" of myth, Sweet has a somewhat fatalistic philosophy. She tells Hurston, "Ah ain't skeered tuh see Mah Jesus neither cause de Bible say God loves uh plain sinner and he's married tuh de backslider. Ah got jus' as good uh chance at Heben as anybody else."

When we last see Big Sweet, she's holding off the hereafter with consummate skill, saving Hurston's life with a timely flash of her knife and preparing to dispatch yet another rival into God's embrace.

FROM NIGGER TO BIGGER

Although Richard Wright was one of Hurston's harshest critics, he was as fond of folklore as she was. His "Blueprint for Negro Writing" (1937) celebrated blues, spirituals, folktales, sexual boasting, streetcorner vernacular, and other forms of black oral culture as "channels through which the racial wisdom flowed." Wright dipped from that same reservoir when writing *Native Son* (1940). The first black title chosen for the Book-of-the-Month Club, Wright's novel was a publishing phenomenon. It sold 250,000 copies in its first month and secured lasting fame for its creator. In Bigger Thomas, its central figure, it features the most complex portrait of a "bad nigger" yet seen in American literature. Violent, lustful, unskilled, and frustrated, the young Chicago tenement-dweller kills a wealthy young white woman and later murders his black girlfriend. In jail and awaiting execution, Bigger arrives at an epiphany: "I didn't know I was really alive in this world until I felt things hard enough to kill for 'em." Like Stagolee, Bigger reaffirms himself through violence.

In his portrayal of Bigger, whose lack of constructive choices leads him to actively choose a life of violence, Wright forcefully condemned his protagonist's unyielding surroundings. The sordid experiences of Bigger and his peers exposed the fallacy of the great migration and its central myth of the North as a fruitful paradise. Bigger, unlike Stagolee and others of his type, never becomes a polarizing figure by acquiring the admiration of any members of his community; he is ultimately feared if not despised by both blacks and whites. His dual marginality, according to Bernard Bell, makes him "a synthesis of white and black myths of the Bad Nigger."

In his essay "How Bigger Was Born," Wright explained that his famous character is based on five individuals he encountered growing up. He explicitly described Bigger No. 3 as the kind of man "whom the white folks called a 'bad nigger,'" although all five individuals easily met the traditional criteria. Each of them can be regarded as a romantic figure in his apparent possession of that peculiar charisma that such men sometimes had. When Wright described Bigger No. 5's refusal to sit in the colored section of a streetcar, coolly reclining with a knife in his hand, he wrote that the other Negroes onboard overhear a white man say to his fellows: "That's that Bigger Thomas nigger and you'd better leave 'im alone." Wright reported that the compliant blacks "experienced an intense flash of pride." Likewise, he confessed of Bigger No. 1, "Maybe it was because I longed secretly to be like him and was afraid. I don't know."

Each is a tragic figure as well. Like Icarus's flight toward the sun, their refusal to acknowledge white supremacy leads to a fatal plunge. Bigger No. 2 goes to jail. Bigger No. 3 is killed by a white cop. Bigger No. 4 goes crazy. Biggers No. 1 and 5 are believed to have died violently. Reflecting on their fates, Wright observed, "The Bigger Thomases were the only Negroes I know of who consistently violated the Jim Crow laws of the South and got away with it, at least for a sweet brief spell. Eventually, the whites who restricted their lives made them pay a terrible price."

In characters such as Tom Burwell, Big Sweet, and (to a lesser extent) Bigger, black authors worked at overturning the damaging stereotype of the oversexed, blade-wielding "bad nigger," occasionally succeeding by replacing it with a fully dimensional human being who regarded violence not as a virtue but as one of many skills required to survive in a hostile world. Similarly, in the Southern shanties and Northern tenements, ordinary people swapped tall tales and chanted rousing odes to Stagolee and others like him, creating beloved folk heroes who were strong and clever and sometimes cruel but whose victories and defeats alike were lessons for living. Through both channels — literature and folklore — a form of racial wisdom flowed.

PART V

Progress and Paradox
1955–Present

12

Violence and Vehemence

> You can only be destroyed by believing that you really are what the white world calls a *nigger*.
>
> — James Baldwin, "My Dungeon Shook: Letter to My Nephew on the One Hundredth Anniversary of Emancipation," 1963

EMMETT TILL WAS ONLY fourteen, but he fit white Southerners' definition of the "bad nigger" as well as anyone. A Northerner by birth, Till was visiting relatives in Sumner, Mississippi, when he ran afoul of local convention. On August 24, 1955, outside a tiny confectionery in the nearby town of Money, Till allegedly showed his friends a picture of a white woman and bragged of his intimacy with her. He reportedly whistled at the white female proprietor of the store, although that allegation has always been in dispute.

On August 27, Till was roused from sleep at his great-uncle's house and hustled away into the darkness. His body was found floating in the Tallahatchie River on August 31. His skull had been bashed in, he'd been shot at close range, and a 125-pound cotton gin fan was tied around his neck. Till's murder helped galvanize the resistance to Jim Crow in the South; it occurred the same year as the arrest of Rosa Parks in Montgomery, Alabama. Till's horrific death and the circus trial of his killers (who were acquitted in just over an hour) perfectly reflected the state of race relations in Mississippi. There, in the words of the reporter Dan Wakefield, "the question of 'nigger-killing' was coupled with the threat to the racial traditions of the South."

Indeed, few of the precedent-shattering changes in the post-

Brown South took place without an audience of frantic whites denouncing their black countrymen as "niggers," arguing that they were unworthy of citizenship and threatening to kill them.

Till's acquitted murderers, Roy Bryant and J. W. Milam, sold their story to *Look* magazine. According to their version of events, they identified Till by shining a flashlight in his face and asking, "You the nigger who did the talking?" During his interview with *Look*'s William Bradford Huie, Milam expressed something like remorse, implying that Till was such a "bad nigger" that he could not be rehabilitated. "We were never able to scare him," said Milam. "They had just filled him so full of poison that he was hopeless. . . . I never hurt a nigger in my life. I like niggers — in their place — I know how to work 'em. . . . As long as I live and can do anything about it, niggers are gonna stay in their place. . . . I stood there in that shed and listened to that nigger throw that poison at me, and I just made up my mind."

Milam's fervent belief in keeping "niggers" in their place differed little from that of influential Mississippians such as Sam Bowers, a local Klan leader who took special pride in his state's commitment to segregation. Such men sometimes portrayed their struggle as a battle against "communists" and "mongrelizers." "We stand almost alone between them and the Total Barbarism which is their goal," Bowers proclaimed. In truth, however, Mississippi had plenty of company.

"WE ARE A PEACEFUL PEOPLE"

In Little Rock, Arkansas, nine black high school students involuntarily performed the role of "bad niggers" for local whites driven rabid by the prospect of integration. Four black reporters covering the arrival of the students at Central High on September 23, 1957, were attacked and beaten by a mob as they approached the school. Relman Morin, a white reporter also on the scene, wrote, "When a man yelled, 'Look, here come the niggers,' the crowd, thinking the Negroes were the students, went into action."

James L. Hicks, one of the black reporters, filed his own account. He recalled that the leader of the mob approached him and his colleagues and forbade them to proceed. "We are not going to let you niggers pass," he warned. "This is our school. Go back where you came from." When Hicks informed the man he was talking to reporters, he replied, "We don't care, you're niggers and we are not going to let you go any further."

Relman Morin reported that after the black students entered the school a man wailed, "They're going in. Oh, God, the niggers are in the school." A woman later told Morin, "Why don't you tell the truth about us? Why don't you tell them we are a peaceful people who won't stand to have our kids sitting next to niggers?"

Ted Poston, a black journalist, filed a report on the Negro student Minnie Jean Brown's experience at Central High that included the following: "For nineteen days, they spat on her, calling her 'Nigger' and 'Nigger bitch,' twice threw hot soup down her neck in the school cafeteria and kicked her to the campus ground in the presence of her mother." According to Poston, one white girl followed Brown from class to class all week, yelling "Nigger bitch, I hate your guts."

The vitriol flung about by hostile whites during this era can be seen as an extension of long-entrenched racial attitudes that were older than the nation itself. The desperate need to regard blacks as "niggers," whose presence poisoned the pristine perfection of the South, was not just a form of willful hallucination; it was also lucrative political capital. Of the post-*Brown* politicians who hitched their aspirations to the segregation bandwagon, perhaps no one did it as flamboyantly as George Wallace. Wallace gained national exposure when he stood at the doors of the University of Alabama in 1963 and challenged the black students' right to enter. Wallace's epiphany of 1958 was memorably recalled by Seymore Trammell, who was Barbour County's district attorney at the time: "George Wallace came back to the district after the defeat, back to our county, and he asked me if I would come over to his office and talk with him. So I did. And he said, 'Seymore, you know why I lost that governor's race?' I said, 'I'm not sure, uh, Judge. What do you think?' He said, 'Seymore, I was outniggered by John Patterson. And I'll tell you here and now, I will never be outniggered again.'"

Wallace had a lot of competition by then, as racial confrontations in Alabama and elsewhere continued to be characterized by whites vigorously attempting to "outnigger" one another. Their frequent use of the N word reflects both a limited vocabulary and a recognition that the word was also an indispensable weapon in their struggle. Ruby Bridges found out firsthand on November 14, 1960, when, as a first-grader, she was chosen to integrate William Frantz Public School in New Orleans. "On the second day, my mother and I drove to school with the marshals," she recalled in a memoir written for children. "The crowd outside the building was ready. Racists spat at us and shouted things like 'Go home, nigger,' and 'No niggers allowed here.'" While Bridges was integrating Frantz, three other black girls were doing the same at another New Orleans school, McDonogh No. 19. A *New York Times* account of the event shows that it was nauseatingly similar to Ruby's ordeal: "Some thirty minutes after the scheduled start of classes the marshals pulled up at McDonogh No. 19 with three pupils accompanied by parents, a man and two women. An angry roar went up from the whites among the mixed crowd of spectators. 'Kill them niggers!' shouted one man."

Everywhere that blacks actively resisted social inequality, they were greeted with violence and vehemence. These confrontations illustrated the complex relationship between language and brute force. On some occasions, such as the clash at McDonogh, language was used to express what the speaker wished to do but could not. At other times, language functioned as an extension of violent acts, as it did in the murder of Andrew Goodman, Mickey Schwerner, and James Chaney. After their bodies were uncovered in Philadelphia, Mississippi, on August 4, 1964, the three activists became martyrs to the civil rights cause. One of their killers, a Klansman named James Jordan, cooperated with authorities and provided details of the trio's final minutes. According to Jordan, one of the murderers asked Schwerner, "Are you that nigger lover?" When Goodman was pulled from the car he was asked, "Are you that other nigger lover?" Jordan himself said after shooting and killing Chaney, "Well, you didn't leave me nothing but a nigger, but at least I killed me a nigger."

Jordan's hateful words reflected the outlook of whites who, frustrated by their failure to keep blacks in their "rightful" place, increasingly turned to terrorism and violence in both deeds and language. For men like Jordan and Bowers, the only thing more desirable than a subservient "nigger" was a dead one. At the same time, the incremental successes of the civil rights movement and the growing influence of progressive whites hinted at a new future in which racial equality was at least possible if not certain. In such a future, casual killings of blacks would not go unpunished, and casual denunciations of them as "niggers" would not meet with general approval. These changes would affect not only the language of social discourse between blacks and whites but also the various ways in which blacks regarded the N word and used it among themselves. In this context, Wallace and Jordan's use of "nigger" appeared as the last gasp of a dying tradition.

"EVERY NIGGER IN THE STATE"

The street-level challenges to racist Southern customs were also being waged in the halls of government. After successfully blocking every piece of proposed civil rights legislation for eighty-two years, the Southern Caucus (the eleven former Confederate states) suffered a significant defeat in the passage of the Civil Rights Act of 1957. The man who played the principal role in that defeat was the Senate majority leader, Lyndon Baines Johnson. After succeeding President Kennedy in 1963, Johnson became, in Robert A. Caro's words, "the greatest champion Americans of color had in the White House during the twentieth century."

Johnson's private views were complicated. Caro noted that Johnson was an intimate of "the 8-F crowd," a group of wealthy Texas oil and business magnates with racist and reactionary views. Caro wrote: "His rise was financed and planned by men so bigoted that to talk to them when their guard was down was to encounter a racism of almost stunning viciousness."

Robert Parker, a black man who worked for Johnson in a number of capacities, wrote in his memoir, *Capitol Hill in Black and White,* that Johnson "called me 'boy,' 'nigger,' or 'chief,' never by my name." If Johnson demeaned his employee to make a political point, it was not clear in private conversations with Parker, when he continued to abuse him verbally. Once, while Parker was chauffeuring Johnson, he wondered aloud why whites never addressed him by name. Johnson "leaned close to my ear," Parker recalled. "'Let me tell you one thing,' he shouted. 'As long as you are black, and you're gonna be black till the day you die, no one's gonna call you by your goddamn name. So no matter what you are called, nigger, you just let it roll off your back like water, and you'll make it. Just pretend you're a goddamn piece of furniture.'"

Johnson was just as frank with high-ranking staffers. Jack Valenti, a trusted aide, recalled a 1964 conversation in which Johnson, discussing his election prospects, said, "I think I can take every Mexican in the state and every nigger in the state."

Johnson was hardly the first president to say "nigger" and certainly not the last. Yet he oversaw the passage of three civil rights acts, helping bring Americans closer to the dream of a free and equal society. His work in this regard probably stemmed more from his unblinking pragmatism — he knew the tide had shifted and he had no intention of being drowned — and his consummate legislative skills than from a sudden, newfound appreciation of colored humanity.

"ALL THE RESPECT IN THE WORLD"

Whereas twentieth-century congressmen routinely used the N word on the House floor before the arrival of Adam Clayton Powell in 1945, public officials have demonstrated considerably more restraint since the passage of the landmark civil rights legislation. Although far fewer political figures have been so foolish as to utter the epithet before audiences, they continue to stumble often enough to make any observer question what they were thinking.

Charles W. Williams, appointed in 1999 by then-Governor George W. Bush to oversee law enforcement training in Texas, testified in a discrimination lawsuit that blacks didn't mind being called "niggers" fifty years earlier. "It wasn't any big deal back then," he said in an October 1998 sworn deposition. Invited to defend himself in April of 2000, Williams, then fifty-seven, said, "I was born and raised with blacks, and back then we had Nigger Charlie and Nigger Sam, Nigger Joe, and we regarded those people with all the respect in the world."

Cruz Bustamante, then lieutenant governor of California, referred to African Americans as "niggers" during a Black History Month speech to black labor activists on February 9, 2001. Bustamente, with a long history of liberal civil rights activism, characterized his usage as a "slip" that he regretted.

On March 4, 2001, Senator Robert C. Byrd (D–W. Va.), who has used the N word on the Senate floor, told a national television audience: "There are white niggers. I've seen a lot of white niggers in my time — I'm going to use that word." He offered a rambling apology the following day, discoursing on such topics as his former membership in the Ku Klux Klan and his belief that "we talk about race too much. I think those problems are largely behind us."

The comments of these powerful men (and those of Marge Schott, the former owner of the Cincinnati Reds, who lamented during a conference call that all her "million-dollar niggers" were hurt) make clear that outright racist language is not limited to poor, "unrefined" whites, as some would have it. Nor, as Bustamente's speech shows, is it the exclusive province of conservatives.

One suspects that Senator Byrd, who thought race-related problems were "largely behind us," would be baffled by the ongoing campaign to persuade Merriam-Webster to redefine "nigger" in its dictionary. This effort began in 1997 when Delphine Abraham of Ypsilanti, Michigan, looked it up in the tenth edition and found "1. a black person, usu. taken to be offensive." Abraham's campaign sought only to have the epithet redefined, not deleted. She was soon joined by thousands of letter-writers and the NAACP. "We believe the word 'nigger' should not be defined as synonymous with a black, Negro or member of a socially disadvantaged class of person," said Kweisi Mfume, the NAACP's executive director and chief executive at the time.

After reviewing its handling of the word, Merriam-Webster decided to stick to its first definition, although it added a helpful usage paragraph, explaining that the epithet "now ranks as perhaps the most offensive and inflammatory racial slur in English. Its use by and among blacks is not always intended or taken as offensive," but, with rare exception, "it is otherwise a word expressive of racial hatred and bigotry." Mfume called Merriam-Webster's decision "unacceptable" and vowed to fight them "until Hell freezes over."

The same year that Bush's appointee Charles Williams was waxing nostalgic over his respectful relations with Nigger Charlie and Nigger Sam, the National Black Family Empowerment Agenda Network was launching an ambitious crusade against the N word. Condemning the epithet — "no matter who uses it" — as the "most harmful and enduring symbol of slavery and Black oppression," it introduced a resolution on May 22, 2000, calling all black leaders and leadership organizations to "renounce and denounce" all usage. The National Black Leadership Roundtable and the Association of Black Psychologists were among the groups endorsing the motion, which has since expanded into something called the N word Eradication Movement. According to the campaign's Web site, RenounceNword.com, "Supporters of the N word Eradication Movement believe that the only purpose for anyone to use the word 'nigger,' its derivatives, or any racial slur, is while educating others about why they should not use them."

By the group's strict criteria, Ron Dellums's quotation, cited in Merriam-Webster's "nigger" entry, would not pass as acceptable usage. As a U.S. congressman from California, Dellums tried to broaden the political discussion during the seventies by describing America as a nation composed of many types of "niggers." "If you are black, you're a nigger," he explained. "If you are blind, you're a nigger. If you are an amputee, you're a nigger." Dellums also included "poor whites" and "all the people who feel left out of the political process."

Nor would Cornel West's remark after the September 11, 2001, assault on the World Trade Center pass muster. "America has been 'niggerized' by the terrorist attacks," he declared. Four months earlier, West had released a spoken word recording in which he said the N word "associates black people with being inferior, subhuman and subordinate, so we ought to have a moratorium on the term. We ought not to use it at all." His contradictory positions illustrate the torturous predicament that many modern African Americans face in their confrontations with the epithet. Convinced of its uselessness, they nonetheless discover it falling from their lips.

13

To Slur with Love

I say the word every morning when I get up. I say it a hundred times. I say nigger, nigger, nigger, nigger, nigger, nigger! It makes my teeth white!

— Paul Mooney, c. 1990s

ARTISTS, WHO TEND to conduct their everyday lives with less self-consciousness than the rest of us, can often be counted on to demonstrate a similar lack of inhibition with language. While we might rarely invoke the N word or even avoid it altogether, some artists are inclined to confront it directly. In the best instances, their forays produce results so successful that they call into question demands that the N word be eliminated. Artists in a variety of genres, such as Richard Pryor, Dave Chappelle, Sterling Brown, and August Wilson, have effectively critiqued the language of oppression even as they invoked it, shining a glaring light on its limitations, its unintended ironies, and its relative uselessness in most settings beyond art. Theirs is a big-picture approach that pulls back the carapace of polite society to show a larger and more revealing view of a culture in which words such as "nigger" can be successfully spawned and popularized. Their performance of the N word consistently alludes — subtly or overtly — to our nation's troubled and complicated past. The art of their less talented peers who invoke the N word often fails precisely because it neglects to acknowledge the word's origin in white supremacy, suggesting instead that it was coined in a vacuum and can be pulled and stretched into new meanings that wipe it clean of centuries of blood and filth.

In his film *Bamboozled* (2000), Spike Lee brilliantly illustrates the danger of the ahistorical approach. His protagonist, a highly educated television executive named Pierre Delacroix, is shown to be suspiciously ignorant about things that matter. He fondly recalls studying French at Harvard but doesn't mention ever having wandered over to the history or African-American studies departments. Hence a videotape his assistant gives him near the movie's climax has a powerful effect. It contains a remarkable, lengthy succession of demeaning images of blacks in live action and animated film. For me, the nauseating footage brought to mind Walter Benjamin's assessment of Nazi propaganda: "The German masses were offered images of themselves as their leaders called upon them to be. Fascism used the power of the art of the past . . . to create its new fascist citizens. For ordinary Germans, the only identity on show, the one that looked back at them from the screen, was a fascist identity in fascist costume and fascist postures of domination or obedience." In the United States, the effect of such an onslaught of potent, suggestive images on blacks (and "ordinary" whites, whose complicity was crucial to the success of American apartheid) could have been no less devastating. Thus Richard Pryor could confidently presume to speak for generations of blacks when he admitted, "I always thought, why do they never have a hero, a black hero?" Through the final decades of the twentieth century, America's image-makers had created comparatively few black heroes for public consumption.

While black artists and performers tried to fill that void, the N word continued to attract notice as a potent symbol of enduring white racism and a barometer of changing social attitudes — especially among blacks themselves. Creative types seeking material didn't have to look very far: flesh-and-blood characters surfaced to rival those in films, plays, and novels. One such figure was the villainous Mark Fuhrman, who as a star witness in the 1995 murder trial of O. J. Simpson coolly deflected a barrage of intense questions from the famous attorney F. Lee Bailey.

> BAILEY: "I want you to assume that perhaps at some time, since 1985 or 1986, you addressed a member of the African-American race as a 'nigger.' Is it possible that you have forgotten that act on your part?"
>
> FUHRMAN: "No. It is not possible."
>
> BAILEY: "Are you therefore saying that you have not used the word in the past ten years, Detective Fuhrman?"
>
> FUHRMAN: "That's what I'm saying, sir."

Bailey had reason to believe that his cross-examination of the rogue detective would mark a crucial turning point in his defense of Simpson. He knew firsthand that "nigger," if wielded skillfully, could be used to expose a hostile witness and pave the way to a favorable verdict. In his book *For the Defense,* Bailey recalled a 1973 case in which a similar courtroom exchange infuriated a black juror and helped bring about the desired result. During that trial, he wrote, he "barked out the word, trying to give it as much meanness and venom as I could. It hung in the air, an all but palpable accusation."

Although the Bailey-Fuhrman faceoff made for titillating television in 1995, it took place in a context already made sensational by the public's apparently evergreen fascination with scandals involving sex and race. And, while the reality of Fuhrman's time on the stand never matched the anticipation of it, his appearance did provide network television with a rare opportunity to air the kind of sensational dialogue easily found on pay channels such as HBO.

In 1973, when Bailey first capitalized on the volatility of the N word, popular culture was considerably more restrained. The next year, the Supreme Court upheld the Federal Communications Commission's indecency judgment against the comedian George Carlin, who had created an uproar during a radio broadcast by reciting "seven words you can't say on television." Carlin's words were all sexual or scatological — "Shit," "Piss," "Fuck," "Cunt,"

"Cocksucker," "MotherFucker," and "Tits." He was right about their being banned at the time (some of them have since been heard on network programs), although the FCC doesn't maintain an official list of specifically prohibited words. Its policies allow some flexibility in interpretation. Indecency, for example, refers to "language or material that, in context, depicts or describes, in terms patently offensive as measured by contemporary broadcast standards for the broadcast medium, sexual or excretory organs or activities." Profanity, according to the FCC, includes language that "denotes certain of those personally reviling epithets naturally tending to provoke resentment or denoting language so grossly offensive to members of the public who actually hear it as to amount to a nuisance."

During the 1970s, the semantic wiggle room in the FCC codes made it possible for words and phrases that had once been frowned on to be spat out with regularity. These included "spook," "spade," "jungle bunny," "hebe," "chink," "dago," and "spic." And they all came out of the mouth of one character: Archie Bunker. The working-class bigot from Queens was the protagonist of *All in the Family*, which debuted on CBS in 1971 and immediately became America's most talked-about show.

Archie's liberal creators, Norman Lear and Bud Yorkin, were ostensibly lampooning racist attitudes. Their show's language and content made the CBS brass so nervous that they hired additional telephone workers to answer the protests they anticipated. What they got instead was a breakthrough hit that soon attracted 50 million viewers a week. But Archie's popularity — bolstered considerably by Carroll O'Connor's masterful performance — sometimes overwhelmed his creators' ironic intentions and seemed to reflect the viewers' attitudes. At one point, CBS commissioned a study, which found that Bunker's posturing indeed appeared to strengthen racial prejudices, not weaken them.

The Harvard psychiatrist Alvin Poussaint, an African American, argued that Bunker's spite was "dangerous because it's disarming." The Northwestern University sociologist Charles Moskos suggested that the show offered "a cheap way for tolerant upper middle-class liberals to escape their own prejudices while the bigots get their views reinforced." The novelist Laura Z. Hobson, writing in the *New York Times*, cast a skeptical eye at Bunker's racial pejoratives. In her view, his use of "spade" and "hebe" instead of terms she considered more outrageous, such as "nigger" and "kike," reflected a calculated attempt to sanitize a racist character. Such efforts were without merit, Hobson argued, because "you cannot be a bigot and be lovable."

Apparently most Americans disagreed: Archie Bunker remained on the air for twelve years.

Curiously, other Yorkin-Lear programs seldom generated as much controversy. *Sanford and Son,* about a black Los Angeles junk dealer and his son, went on the air in 1972. During its five-year run, its hero, Fred Sanford, called whites everything from "honky" to "paleface" while reserving the bulk of his tirades for his black friends and relatives. *The Jeffersons,* a long-running spinoff of *All in the Family,* featured George Jefferson, a jive-talking black loudmouth who seemed to search constantly for an opportunity to denounce his white neighbors as "honkies."

Writing in *Newsweek,* the critic Harry F. Waters expressed little tolerance for George, who in his view hardly compared with Bunker. "George tosses out racial slurs (Tom Willis is 'that honky') and revels in chauvinist piggery ('Where's my breakfast, woman?')," he wrote. "Unlike Archie, he exudes no redeeming warmth other than a flair for boogalooing to his son's rock records."

But Waters was one of the few observers to object. Perhaps Sanford and Jefferson's bigoted remarks passed mostly without comment because Archie Bunker had already prepared audiences for them, or they seemed somehow less ominous than a white man's rants — even to white viewers. Regardless, Archie's rise undoubtedly paved the way for the "blue" language that appeared regularly on network television in the decades that followed. Because Fuhrman's duel with Bailey revolved around a word that even Archie never uttered, it may have been titillating — although hardly shocking — to a few. But, while it influenced network usage of the N word in future dramatic presentations, its impact on American attitudes toward race was ultimately short-term.

BLACKS AND WHITES IN COLOR

The Bunker era is notable for more than its precedent-setting language. It was also a time when more African-American performers appeared on television than ever before. But it was not a case of quantity equaling quality. Buffoonish characters such as those seen weekly on such long-running shows as *The Jeffersons* and *Good Times* vied for public attention with special programs containing more substantial images, such as *Roots* and *The Autobiography of Miss Jane Pittman.* With few exceptions, however, both weekly and special programs were written by whites who, despite their good intentions, often seemed less concerned with the realities of black life and culture than with imposing their own quite different perspectives. The eight episodes of *Roots* were written by white writers, for example, and included white characters not found in Alex Haley's book, such as a compassionate slave-ship captain who seemed designed to protect the sensibilities of white viewers. With his tongue firmly in cheek, *Sanford's* star Redd Foxx spoke to the inadequacies that result from such imbalances in a 1972 interview with *Time* magazine. He told a reporter that he and his co-star Demond Wilson worked with the show's staff to "translate the scripts into spook." "The writers," he said, "are beginning to learn [that] black is another language."

While fewer black roles became available in the 1980s, some of them were quite impressive. Nauseating "mammy" and "buck" roles were still visible too often — Nell Carter's maid on *Gimme a Break* and Mr. T's B. A. Baracus on *The A Team,* to name just two. But comparatively heroic counterimages could be reliably found on police dramas such as *Hill Street Blues,* which included Michael Warren and Taurean Blacque as Bobby Hill and Neal Washington, two intelligent, dignified policemen. On such shows, the dialogue was smarter, the characters more fully rounded, and the storylines reflected the valuable suggestions of black writers and directors. *Hill Street* even included a couple of racists in its cast of regulars. SWAT Lieutenant Howard Hunter frequently objected to blacks but usually through euphemisms and coded language. Hunter and Andy Renko, the ultimately kindhearted white reactionary who was Bobby Hill's partner, were frequently exposed as unrealistic and out-of-touch, absurd figures to be pitied and perhaps ridiculed but seldom taken seriously. But the show had its shortcomings as well, occasionally sliding into stereotypical characterizations in its portrayals of black parents and criminals.

Steven Bochco, the creator of *Hill Street,* pushed the envelope even further with *NYPD Blue,* which debuted in 1993, two years before Mark Fuhrman entered America's living rooms. By that time, more than thirty-seven percent of American households had been wired for cable, and Bochco was determined to compete with the aggressive newcomer. He challenged — and often overcame — network censors with partial nudity and raw language, including such terms as "asshole" and "dickhead." Like Archie Bunker on *All in the Family,* the chief source of such language was a single character. Andy Sipowicz, superbly played by Dennis Franz, was both a racist and a homophobe, although he was allowed to evolve over time. Unlike Bunker, whose bumbling incompetence was as much a part of his character as his general hostility, Sipowicz was a rule-breaker with a reputation for getting results. His talents included getting "perps" to crack during interviews that showcased his colorful way with words. A 1993 episode showed him quickly dismissing a black suspect's reservations in his typically blunt manner: "I'm trying to find some assholes before they murder another innocent family. It happens these assholes are black. Now how do you want me to put the questions? 'I'm sorry for the injustices the white man has inflicted on your race, but can you provide any information?'"

Five months after Fuhrman testified that he hadn't used the N word in ten years, Simpson's attorneys introduced tapes of his conversations with a North Carolina screenwriter over a period of nine years. They showed that, compared to the methodology Fuhrman claimed to use, Sipowicz's fictional investigative techniques were mild. Fuhrman bragged about terrorizing and brutalizing African Americans, peppering his speech with references to "beating niggers" and "dumb niggers" and "niggers [who] run like rabbits." Seeming to revel in his hatred of blacks, Fuhrman spoke of an old police station that "had the smell of niggers who had been beaten and died there." He also held forth on the credibility of black interviewees: "The first thing out of a nigger's mouth, the first six or seven sentences, is a fucking lie."

Fuhrman's uninhibited chats undoubtedly made possible Sipowicz's increased candor in subsequent episodes of *NYPD Blue*. After the Simpson trial, Sipowicz was free to go where previous fictional racist cops, such as Lieutenant Hunter of *Hill Street*, hadn't dared to tread. Thus viewers could hardly have been surprised when Sipowicz used the N word during an exchange with a black activist in a 1996 episode, "The Backboard Jungle." A black activist resists arrest by telling the detective, "You're dealing with that one nigger in a thousand who knows what you can and cannot do." Sipowicz retorts, "I'm dealing with the nigger whose big mouth is responsible for this mess."

Steven Bochco quite likely had the Fuhrman tapes in mind when he told the *Baltimore Sun:* "These are exactly the kinds of conflicts that exist in the police department, and are sort of a paradigm for the society at large."

The widely praised episode was written by David Mills, an African American. He later told the *New York Daily News* that viewers probably got more insight into Sipowicz's beliefs from a different speech in the episode, in which he accuses some "homies" of "acting their color."

"It's really quite silly to spend so much energy on just the six letters," said Mills. "We do a lot better talking about the larger issues — what does this person mean, how do they feel? Is there really a racist attitude there?"

That certainly seemed to be the case with Fuhrman, who used

the N word forty-one times on the tapes. The jury in the Simpson trial apparently concluded that these remarks did indeed reflect a racist attitude, although it is unlikely that the detective's duplicity alone wrecked the prosecution. The jurors had to base their conclusion on only two excerpts of the recordings, the limit imposed by Judge Lance Ito.

Christopher Darden, a member of the prosecuting team, had argued against letting the jurors hear any portion of the tapes, contending that the word would so upset them that it would impair their judgment: "It is a dirty, filthy word. . . . an extremely derogatory and denigrating term, because it is so prejudicial and so extremely inflammatory that to use that word in any situation will evoke some type of emotional response from any African-American within earshot of that word." Darden was grossly overstating the case, but it was, after all, his job to do so.

But Johnnie Cochran, the defense attorney, was determined to poke a hole in Darden's melodramatic conceit. "Not every African American feels that way," he told the judge. "It is demeaning to our jurors to say that African Americans who have lived under oppression for two hundred–plus years in this country cannot work within the mainstream, cannot hear these offensive words."

Jeffrey Toobin wrote that Cochran paused before leaving the court to whisper a "classic rebuke" to Darden: "Nigger, please . . ."

Judge Ito allowed Simpson's defense team to play all of the tapes with the jury absent, enabling broadcasters to air them uncensored.

The African-American journalist Keith Woods quite reasonably observed that censoring Fuhrman's remarks with ellipses or deletions would have been a disservice to the public: "You just can't convey that definition with n-dash-dash-dash-dash-dash," he wrote. "You can't communicate it with bleeps or blurbs or euphemisms. The problem is that sometimes the only way to do your job as a journalist is to say or write the word that furthers the mission of racists."

The tapes probably intrigued the press more than everyday folks, especially blacks accustomed to racism. Many viewers undoubtedly found Fuhrman's comments sickening, but it's hard to imagine that anyone was genuinely astonished. Thus Christopher Reed, covering the trial for London's *Guardian* newspaper, probably exaggerated when he described white Americans as "in shock" after hearing the tapes. He came closer to the mark in describing blacks and Hispanics as "wearily familiar with such police invective" — a stark contrast to the overwrought scenario that Darden tried to portray in court. Reed quoted one black Los Angeles resident, a barber, who said, "I could show you ten customers any day who've been called nigger, and worse, by the cops."

Far more telling was the brevity of Americans' ostensible disgust with Fuhrman, who ultimately was convicted of one count of perjury. He was sentenced to three years' probation with no jail time (in exchange for pleading "no contest") and appeared to reap more profit than punishment from lying on the stand. The man heard saying "nigger" forty-one times on national television parlayed his newfound notoriety into a successful second career as an author of true-crime books.

STANDING UP TO THE MAN

While black television writers remained relegated to the sidelines when Bunker-mania took over television, black artists rebelled against similar restraints in Hollywood by creating movies of their own. The film credited with launching the new black cinema was Melvin Van Peebles's *Sweet Sweetback's Baadasssss Song,* released in 1971, the same year Bunker made his debut. It found an audience that the Hollywood studios seemed to be completely unaware of: made for $500,000, it quickly grossed $10 million. The writer-director Van Peebles played the role of Sweet Sweetback, a pimp–sex worker who is forced to go on the lam after beating two white policemen nearly to death. The production values of the film matched the minimal standards of the day, but the uniformly atrocious acting and monotonous soundtrack have not helped *Sweetback* to measure up well over time. Still, filmgoers in 1971 found something heroic in Van Peebles's laconic, swaggering, and sexually potent buck. A deadpan egotist who spends most of the movie in a crushed-velour leisure suit, Sweetback somehow manages to upend black male stereotypes as he cleverly eludes the authorities. But he is unquestionably a bad nigger: Sweetback is "known not to take no shit from nobody." This quality, along with his outsize confidence, is what makes him a romantic outlaw, a folk hero who can count on the cooperation of the black community as he makes his way toward Mexico and freedom.

Van Peebles emphasizes the distinction between Sweetback and ordinary "good" niggers in a scene near the end of the film, after Sweetback and a young activist whom he has rescued have killed the two cops. At a police meeting, the commissioner refers to the fugitive pair as "cop killers and niggers to boot!"

After the meeting disbands, he asks his two black detectives to remain behind and tells them: "I didn't mean any offense by that word I used. It was just a figure of speaking, you understand." He goes on to say: "You could be a real credit to your race if you brought the guys in."

In contrast to the hapless black detectives, Sweetback harbors no illusions of embrace by the larger white community. His values, however twisted, are his own; because the options for black men in a racist society are woefully limited, he chooses to be a "bad nigger" and willingly suffers for his decision. A chorus of male and female voices reinforces this point as Sweetback, weak and wounded, staggers toward the border. In racist white society, the chorus informs our hero, "Freedom ain't nothin' but a word" and "a nigger ain't shit." The voices urge him on, insisting that embattled blacks have resources as long as "niggers got feet." Van Peebles reinforces his character's "bad nigger" status by blazing a defiant warning across the screen after his successful escape. "Watch Out," the closing titles advise. "A bad ass Nigger is coming back to collect some dues . . ."

Van Peebles told *Time* in 1971: "The message of *Sweetback* is that if you can get it together and stand up to the Man, you can win."

Sweetback's message resounded in the flurry of films that followed in its wake. According to the film historian Donald Bogle, these productions began to peter out around 1975 — but not before *Shaft, Superfly* (a bad nigger who insisted that he was "a pretty nigger too"), *The Legend of Nigger Charley,* and other productions grossed millions of dollars by offering unsubtle variations on *Sweetback*'s theme.

A host of performers — including Fred Williamson, Jim Brown, Pam Grier, and Richard Roundtree — enjoyed brief stardom by bringing "bad niggers" to life on the silver screen. Williamson, who starred in *The Legend of Nigger Charley* and its sequel, *The Soul of Nigger Charley,* claimed credit for creating his character, "a really standup kind of cowboy: A guy who starts off as a slave, beats up his slave master, escapes from the plantation, goes West, and becomes a gunfighter."

Like Sweetback, Nigger Charley quickly proves to be a topnotch sexual performer. Also like Sweetback, he is shown having sex while whites watch with a mixture of resentment and admiration (most of Sweetback's voyeurs, however, are black). Charley is a skilled blacksmith whose dying owner has kindly provided him with manumission papers. The strong but gentle young man never gets to use them, though, because his enraged overseer tears them up almost immediately, saying: "Only a man's got a right to be free, and you're not a man, you're a nigger."

Soon the overseer is dead and Charley's in the wind, relentlessly pursued by a menacing slavecatcher who vows: "I'm gonna get you, Nigger Charley. I'm going to track you down until you fall in your black nigger tracks."

Williamson's muscular hero has none of the comically robust swagger of Sweetback. Soft-spoken and casually confident, he relies on his obviously superior physical skills as he tames a Western settlement, befriends Native Americans, and bonds with his makeshift family of black gunfighters. Although he takes the law into his own hands, Charley appears to do so less out of outright defiance than simple necessity. He doesn't go looking for a fight but will defend himself if attacked. Rather than embrace bad niggerness, his niggerness and outlaw status are thrust upon him. As in *Sweetback,* the soundtrack explicitly links the N word to white supremacy while helping viewers recognize Charley's refusal to acknowledge his "proper" place in white society. While Lloyd Price sings, "Nigger Charley is what they call me / that's my white folks name / Black is what I am," a chorus of admiring female voices chant, "Nigger Charley nigger Charley nigger Charley" ad infinitum.

"I called it *Nigger Charley* because it was controversial," Williamson later recalled. "The word *nigger* in the '70s was hot. Controversy is what sells. . . . The press grabbed on to that nationwide, and it was so controversial that a lot of press called the film 'Black Charley' or 'The Legend of Charley.' The controversy brought a lot of people into the theater, not knowing what the film was about. They came to see it because of the controversy."

Echoing Van Peebles's comments about "the Man," Williamson attributed the consistent popularity of his films to black audiences' hunger for new and liberating images of themselves. "At the time we made our movies, heroes were needed more than they are now. . . . Anytime any black person stood up for themselves, or did anything that involved any kind of physical confrontation, they always lost, they were always taken to jail."

While black characters' use of the N word was common, it was not nearly as prolific as contemporary usage. Perhaps reflecting the developing public conception of "politically correct" speech, white characters in such films tended to pay dearly for their willingness to call black people "niggers." Meanwhile, black heroes such as Williamson's Charley and Ron O'Neal's Superfly seldom failed to invoke the word without a degree of self-conscious irony; for them it became a badge of honor, signifying their willingness to defy the paralyzing constrictions of white racist society. A lot of folks can talk a good game, they seemed to imply, but we back it up. In one of the most famous poems of the period, Nikki Giovanni expressed what much of her audience may have been thinking when she asked, "Nigger, can you kill?" With fists flying and guns blazing, the black film heroes and heroines of the early seventies answered with an emphatic "yes."

TONTO WITH AN AFRO

"From about 1970 to about 1976, the black actor being the winner, being the hero was happening," according to Fred Williamson. By the end of this period, the black hero's rebelliousness was more central to his identity than any other quality he may have possessed, including excellence. The dominance of this idea in popular culture can be seen in Joe Frazier's comment to Muhammad Ali after losing to him in a legendary 1975 heavyweight title fight known as "the thriller in Manila." Frazier's attempt to place himself and Ali properly in history had less to do with their boxing brilliance than their unwillingness "to take no shit from nobody." "You one bad nigger," Frazier said. "We both bad niggers. We don't do no crawlin'."

Black rebels of the sort that Frazier and Williamson alluded to were already on the way out before the thriller in Manila. While "bad nigger" characters continued to rise in boxing (although they shared the spotlight with equally talented but far less threatening fighters such as Sugar Ray Leonard), they were replaced in the popular imagination by more amiable athletes such as the not-yet-infamous O. J. Simpson, who smashed the NFL's single-season rushing record in 1973. On the screen, the bad nigger who stood up to the Man soon gave way to the genial black sidekick who willingly abstained from many conveniences — romance, a life of his own — to help his white pal find happiness and reach his goal. In the best circumstances, he was devastatingly witty and slyly subversive; in the worst, he was merely a Tonto with an Afro. The defanged and desexed black sidekick made popular by Richard Pryor and, later, Eddie Murphy reassured white viewers after the previous half-decade of in-your-face defiance. He performed a kind of wish fulfillment for this audience by dem-

PROGRESS AND PARADOX: 1955–PRESENT

onstrating his willingness to return to a subservient position in society.

Despite this significant shift, the N word continued to be used as a dramatic device in popular films that touched on racial themes and could still be relied on to elicit strong reactions from moviegoers.

Silver Streak, a hit released in 1976, provides an instructive example of the changes that had taken place. The film's successful pairing of Pryor and Gene Wilder was highly influential and presaged the onslaught of mostly forgettable interracial buddy movies that were unleashed on the public during the 1980s and 1990s. As Grover Muldoon, the hip, fast-talking character who helps the bumbling nerd Wilder stay alive, Pryor illustrates the end of the black heroism that Williamson wistfully recalled. Although infinitely clever and an effortless center of attention, Pryor is merely the sidekick (and a thief, don't forget), the attendant who helps keep Wilder out of trouble and waits faithfully in the margins, sexless and alone, while his white partner pursues sexual and romantic love in the midst of terrible danger.

Only briefly is Pryor allowed to be defiant. When the villain (played by Patrick McGoohan) calls him an "ignorant nigger," Pryor brandishes a gun and lashes out verbally. "Who you calling nigger? You don't know me well enough to call me no nigger. I'll slap the taste out your mouth," he threatens. One can't help wondering if, over the course of time, McGoohan did get to know Pryor better, would it then be okay to call him a nigger? But the moment passes quickly and seems to serve little purpose other than to distinguish Wilder's character from that of the whites, who continued to cling to immoral values. Because he does not use the N word, Wilder is shown to be enlightened and worthy of Pryor's friendship and loyalty. Just as important, the scene calms white fears by showing that potentially dangerous blacks such as Grover Muldoon (who, as an outlaw, is still just a few degrees removed from the "bad niggers" who preceded him) can tell the difference between ordinary white men and "the Man" — and respond accordingly.

"A NIGGER WITH A BADGE"

Among the films of the early 1980s, few did better at the box office than those starring the young comic actor widely regarded as the heir to Richard Pryor, Eddie Murphy. Just as verbally dexterous and nearly as charismatic, Murphy had a performance style that lacked the dangerous edge that Pryor frequently displayed, and he often seemed eager to make that difference dramatically clear. His humor, while bold and raunchy, suggested that racial divisions were something to laugh about rather than obsess over. As Donald Bogle and others have pointed out, Murphy's characters were ideally suited to the dominant politics of the Reagan era, which often made a mockery of calls for racial justice. It was "morning in America," and Murphy positioned himself as a kinder, gentler Pryor, ready and eager to greet the dawn. "I'm not angry," he told *Newsweek* in 1983. "I didn't learn this stuff hanging out with junkies on 158th Street. I have never been much of a fighter. If somebody white called me 'nigger' on the street, I just laughed."

Murphy's first film was *48 Hours* (1982), a tale of a hostile black convict named Reggie Hammond (like Pryor in *Silver Streak,* Murphy plays a thief) who is forced into an unlikely alliance with a racist white cop. Murphy does enjoy a brief moment of comic brilliance when he tames a bar full of hostile whites by pretending to be a detective. The high point of this mostly improvised scene occurs when Hammond proclaims himself a white man's "worst fucking nightmare . . . a nigger with a badge." Black audiences loved this bit because it gave Murphy license to vent frustrations that they may have also felt but were unable to express, a cathartic function often performed by black heroes in the films discussed earlier. It also leads to a significant personality change for Hammond's cop "partner," who begins — ever so slowly — to see black people as human beings whose feelings should be respected. Jack Cates, played by Nick Nolte, is a larger, shaggier version of the police commissioner in *Sweetback.* Like that character, he offers a tepid, incredible apology for his use of the N word: he was "just doing my job."

Hammond, to his credit, refuses to let Cates off easy. He "stands up to the Man," getting in a few potshots and even landing a few punches — although he ends up where he began: behind bars.

Trading Places (1983), another black-white buddy movie, was Murphy's second film and also a huge success. Murphy appears as Billy Ray Valentine, a hustler and thief (what else?) who becomes the unwitting subject of a social experiment conducted by two bored money barons. Taken off the street, given the trappings of wealth, and taught to perform parlor tricks for his racist benefactors, Valentine blissfully complies until he overhears the men referring to him as a "nigger." The scene pulls the wool from his eyes and sets him on a path of vengeance that results in the barons' downfall. Unlike Sweetback's badass revenge, Valentine's is nonviolent, accomplished through wit, subversion, and the cooperation of a white accomplice played by Dan Aykroyd. For all its engagement of social issues and talk of upper-class corruption, the film is ultimately forgettable. However, its reliance on the N word as the best way to lend dramatic force to its villains — and seize viewers' attention — demonstrates the epithet's enduring power and significance. It is also emblematic of an ongoing shift in whites' own attitudes about public displays of racist language. In contrast to the recent past, when the men would have been comfortable uttering the N word in the boardroom or on the golf course, they chose to say it only when they believed no one else was around to hear them.

"ALL GOD'S NIGGAS"

During the twilight years of the Reagan administration, the N word still contained enough attention-getting power to be depended on as a revelatory device in film. At the same time, the notion spread that the N word was suitable for conversational use among blacks. August Wilson's *Fences*, which was staged in 1986, features a lead character who utters the word twenty-seven times, almost always as a synonym for "son," "brother," or "buddy." Whites' use of the slur — and blacks' reaction to their usage — continued to figure significantly in the plots of films such as Spike Lee's *Do the Right Thing* (1989), which has at its center a white family who runs a pizzeria in a black Brooklyn neighborhood, and *Die Hard with a Vengeance* (1995), in which a terrorist forces the white hero (Bruce Willis) to stand on a corner in a black neighborhood while wearing a sign that reads: I HATE NIGGERS.

Willis also appeared in the ultraviolent *Pulp Fiction* (1994), an acclaimed film whose controversy stemmed mostly from its apparent fascination with violence rather than from its exuberant use of the N word. Racial insults are flung about (although not by Willis), including derisive references to "old Jews," "gooks," and "wetbacks." But none appears with the regularity of the N word, which is uttered more than twenty times. Black audiences often responded negatively to its presence in the film, especially when spoken by the character played by Tarantino himself. When two hit men (Samuel L. Jackson and John Travolta) show up at his house with the body of a black man in the backseat of their car, Tarantino erupts. He pauses, however, to explain his anger. "It's the dead nigger in my garage," he explains. "Did you see a sign that says dead nigger storage? Did you see a sign that says dead nigger storage? Storing dead niggers is not my business." Tarantino, who wrote the script, lends a palpable irony to the scene by revealing that his character has a black wife whom he claims to love fervently.

Scenes in which other white characters say "nigger" have less subtext, but they seem entirely conventional and reasonable in the racist underworld in which the characters operate. The black characters' use of the N word, however, anticipates the self-consciously ironic patina the word would acquire in subsequent films such as *Training Day*. The black characters played by Ving Rhames and Jackson use the N word most often in the film, usually when addressing white people. When Rhames's crime lord calls Vince Vega (Travolta) "my nigger," he does so with evident affection. Ditto for Jackson's exchanges with Travolta. When Rhames uses the epithet in a tense conversation with the aging boxer played by Willis, the implication is entirely different.

He hands Willis a bribe, then asks, "You my nigger?" "Apparently so," Willis replies. In this context, Rhames has declared his control of Willis and Willis has acquiesced. His agreement to be a "nigger" indicates both his moral corruption and his willingness to be owned.

Tarantino's subsequent film, *Jackie Brown* (1997), also used racist language and aroused still more controversy. Spike Lee was among the most vocal critics of the film, in which the N word is invoked nearly forty times. Most often it is uttered by Samuel L. Jackson, who tends to say things like "Look, I hate to be the kinda nigga does a nigga a favor, then — *bam* — hits a nigga up for a favor in return. But I'm afraid I gotta be that kinda nigga."

While admitting to his own use of the word, Lee said, "I want Quentin to know that not all African Americans think that word is trendy or slick. I don't expect him to change, but I want him to know for future reference."

Jackson vigorously defended Tarantino: "Black artists think they are the only ones allowed to use the word. Well, that's bull." He went on to say that the word was not offensive in the context of the film. Unfortunately, though, the context is not always clear from the film's somewhat muddled plot.

Tarantino told the *Boston Phoenix* in 1998: "Should any word have that much power? I think it should be de-powered. But that's not my job. I don't have any political agenda in my work. I'm writing characters." He went on to say, quite reasonably, that the use of the N word was consistent with Jackson's character. "To not have him say that would be a lie," he argued.

Lee seemed concerned that presenting the epithet as a fashionable, inoffensive expression would confuse whites or, worse, lead them to conclude that racism no longer existed. As a veteran of Hollywood infighting, Lee doubtless based his heated reaction on his own experiences. I thought of him when reading the bizarre comments of *Variety*'s Peter Bart in a 2001 interview in *Los Angeles Magazine*. Claiming a unique knowledge of the true nature of blackness, the longtime editor of the preeminent Hollywood trade publication told a reporter: "You talk to a lot of the better-educated, wealthy black people. You know, they're not very black. The big distinction is between the people they call 'niggers' — who are the ghetto blacks, who can't even speak, can't get a job, and bury themselves in black-itude — and those people who are better looking, better educated, smarter, and who own the world: the black middle class."

The addled editor must have missed Lee's *Bamboozled,* a quite eloquent rejoinder to the kind of liberal myopia displayed by Bart and which Lee claimed to recognize in Tarantino. Lee also seemed to have Jackson in mind when demonstrating that artists' use of the N word shouldn't be haphazard or lightly considered but employed with great care.

Bamboozled, Lee's most fully realized film since *Malcolm X,* is an overlong but mostly masterful send-up of racial stereotyping and its effect on both black and white thinking. Pierre Delacroix (né Peerless Dothan) hopes to get out of his contract by creating a program based on the most hateful and destructive images of blacks in American history. Delacroix (Damon Wayans) is moved to such an extreme after a frustrating exchange with his white boss, Thomas Dunwitty, who challenges his authenticity and cites his own "black wife and two biracial kids" as evidence of his mastery of black culture. After casually using the N word, he tells Delacroix: "I don't give a goddamn what that prick Spike Lee says. Tarantino was right. Nigger is just a word. If Ol' Dirty Bastard can use it every other word, why can't I?"

Nearly everyone uses it in *Bamboozled.* To illustrate its ubiquity in modern American society, Lee puts it in the mouths of characters of every race, economic class, and political persuasion — usually to devastating effect. When Delacroix's ambitious assistant, Sloan Hopkins, argues with her brother Big Blak Afrika (né Julius), a rapper and self-proclaimed revolutionary, the N word functions as a gauge of class conflict in African-American communities. Sloan listens with growing impatience to her brother's mutterings, during which he manages to give the N word three different meanings in the space of a few sentences. Addressing his own lack of status, he asks, "If I had some plantation drawers I'd be the nigga, right?" After Sloan says that Big Blak's rap group is embarrassing, he issues a half-hearted defense of the "niggas in his crew" before conceding that "niggas ain't perfect."

Sloan takes all this in until Big Blak implies that she is a house nigger: "Are you calling your sister a house nigga? How about you take your field nigga ass out of my house nigga house?" Like that of her boss, Sloan's hard-won professional armor can be undone with a single, skillfully wielded "nigger." At the same time, black achievers such as Sloan — self-aware members of Du Bois's talented tenth, who claim to be all about uplift and progress — are not above "nigger"-slinging themselves. Aware of the word's power to cut deeply, Sloan unleashes it during a heated exchange with Delacroix later in the movie.

As illuminating as such exchanges are, they're minuscule in comparison to the emotions aroused by the catastrophe Delacroix cooks up. His new show, *Mantan: The New Millennium Minstrel Show*, features a pair of blackface hosts named Sleep'n Eat and Mantan ("two real coons"), a house band called the Porch Monkeys, and a chorus of dancing stereotypes, among them Topsy, Rastus, Lil' Nigger Jim, Sambo, and Aunt Jemima.

Having underestimated the appetite of his countrymen (black, white, and otherwise) for racist entertainment, Delacroix is staggered when his show is picked up as a midseason replacement and ultimately becomes a national sensation. In the midst of his confusion, he visits his father, a struggling comic named Junebug who seems to specialize in "nigger" jokes. Junebug appears not to understand his son's melancholy. "You know what I always taught you," he says. "Every nigger is an entertainer."

Shortly thereafter, Sloan presents Delacroix with a Jolly Nigger Bank to help him remember "a time in our history in this country when we were considered inferior, subhuman, and we should never forget."

As the show gains popularity, members of the studio audience start attending in blackface. A master of ceremonies named Honeycutt warms them up by going into the seats and asking various individuals, "Is you a nigger?" All of them answer in the affirmative, including blacks, whites, Latinos, and a Sicilian, who proclaims, "I'm more of a nigger than any nigger in here."

"We're all God's niggers," Honeycutt replies. "Even the lost souls who don't know that they niggers. They niggers too. Do you know why?"

"Why?" the audience yells.

"'Cuz niggas is a beautiful thang!"

Honeycutt both revels in his alleged niggerness and shamelessly markets it to his audience, who are as eager as they are clueless. Just as calling themselves niggers helped Jewish musicians take on "some of the masculine cachet stereotypically ascribed to the African-American male" early in the twentieth century, nonblacks in Lee's new millennium are hoping to acquire some of that old black "magic" without paying for it in sweat and blood.

As Honeycutt whips the audience into a niggeristic frenzy, Mantan (Savion Glover) breaks the spell by taking center stage. Suddenly self-aware and embodying Sloan's injunction that blacks "should never forget," he urges his fans: "Go to your windows and yell out, scream with all the life you can muster up inside your bruised, assaulted and battered bodies: I am sick and tired of being a nigger and I'm not going to take it anymore!"

Dunwitty, Delacroix's white boss, has been watching in horror. He interrupts the show and has the rebellious star tossed outside, an act that soon leads to Mantan's murder.

In Lee's intentionally absurdist ending, any major character who has struggled against the dehumanization of blacks (punctuated throughout by the N word) suffers violent physical or psychological damage. Delacroix, Mantan, and Big Blak are dead, Sloan is deranged, and Honeycutt is poised to become the star of the show. As in the minstrel shows of old, blacks in the new millennium are shown functioning as a convenient and eroticized Other while taking on the mantle of "niggerness" enables whites (and, Lee makes clear, Latinos and Asians) to project their vilest emotions and most lurid fantasies onto blackness. Unlike the entertainers, whose blackness remains beneath their burnt-cork masks, members of the studio audience can take their makeup off when they get home and breathe a sigh of relief, thus turning Dunwitty's initial conception of the show — "They're gonna make us laugh, they're gonna make us cry, they're gonna make us feel good to be Americans" — into a triumphant vision of the new century.

Lee's insightful take on the uses and abuses of the N word and its inescapable association with white supremacy benefits from comparison not only with Tarantino's efforts but also with subsequent films such as *Training Day* (2001), which also attracted scrutiny because of its frequent use of the N word. Alonzo Harris, the film's antihero protagonist played by Denzel Washington, would likely have little use for Sloan Hopkins's cautionary reminders. His response to a Jolly Nigger Bank would probably be limited to considering whether it was worth stealing.

"My nigga" is the tagline for Detective Harris, who says it mostly when talking to his young white partner (Ethan Hawke) to assert his control over him much in the manner of a pimp who frequently reminds a prostitute: "You're my bitch." It's also meant to symbolize Washington's corruption of the younger man and sully him with his mentor's dirt. Whereas in *Pulp Fiction* Bruce Willis agrees to be Ving Rhames's "nigger," Hawke struggles throughout to remain pure and, by implication, white. The many "niggers" in *Training Day* seem more of a deliberate attempt to generate notoriety (à la Fred Williamson's *Nigger Charley*) than to make any kind of serious argument regarding the language or images of oppression. The film's enthusiastic use of the N word reflects a commercial sensibility that overwhelms any thought of irony or exposure of societal hypocrisy; "nigger" seems to fall so often from the lead character's tongue because it was sure to set tongues a-wagging — and help generate box office profits. The film's approach in some ways epitomizes the peculiar journey of the N word through the art and popular culture of the late twentieth century; whereas musicians, writers, and directors once treated it as a gauge of racial tension or social inequality, they were now just as likely to consider it a potentially lucrative marketing gimmick. No longer lamented exclusively as the worst of racial insults — as it once was by centuries of black observers, from Ignatius Sancho to Malcolm X — the N word threatened to become, in Spike Lee's nightmarish phrase, "trendy or slick."

14

What's in a Name?

> Societies create vocabularies, devising new terms when they are
> needed and retaining old ones when they serve a purpose. Dictio-
> naries list words as obsolete or archaic, denoting that they are no
> longer used or heard. But one epithet survives, because people want it
> to. . . . That word, of course, is "nigger."
>
> — Andrew Hacker, 1992

JUST AS JEAN TOOMER, Richard Wright, and other writers explored the fate of "bad niggers" in their respective eras, black writers of the sixties and seventies made similar efforts. Wright observed that every "bad nigger" whom he knew eventually paid "a
terrible price" for his obstinacy.

In the literature of the late '60s, that terrible price often took
the form of incarceration. The defender of black freedom who is
burnished by prison epiphanies — whose "badness" ultimately becomes a force for good — arose as a dominant folk figure as well as
a central character in the liberation scenarios favored by some
black poets, memoirists, and fiction writers. Malcolm X, a former
criminal who emerged from prison in 1952 and became one of the
most iconic black personalities of his time, came to embody the
apotheosis of the "bad nigger" as a streetwise messianic figure willing to sacrifice himself for his people.

In his best-selling memoir, Malcolm cemented his reputation as
a fearless black man who was more inclined to fight than grin. Published shortly after his death in 1965, his autobiography charts the

spiritual and intellectual evolution of a man whose enduring influence continues to inspire. With the help of his coauthor Alex Haley, Malcolm describes his transformation from a thief with such an evil reputation that his fellow inmates called him Satan into a devout Muslim with little patience for sinners.

Some of the most telling sections of the book deal with his troubled childhood in East Lansing, Michigan. In several episodes, he discusses the ways in which encounters with racist language helped shape his identity; indeed, he posts such interactions as virtual landmarks along his road to full social and political awareness. He reports that white children called him and his siblings "'nigger' and 'darkie' and 'Rastus' so much that we thought those were our natural names." Describing his father's confrontations with a Klanlike group called the Black Legionnaires, Malcolm writes that his father was reviled everywhere he went as "an 'uppity nigger' for wanting to own a store, for living outside the Lansing Negro district, for spreading unrest and dissension among 'the good niggers.'"

Malcolm recalls that the whites in East Lansing were almost uniformly racist, although some of them didn't appear to be aware of it. The white foster couple who took him in after the breakup of his biological family "would talk about me, or about 'niggers,' as though I wasn't there, as if I wouldn't understand what the word meant," he remembered. "A hundred times a day, they used the word 'nigger.' I suppose that in their own minds, they meant no harm; in fact they probably meant well." Malcolm's teachers used the N word as well, as did hostile white audiences when he traveled and competed as the sole black on the school basketball team. He was seldom bothered by it, although he later reflected: "Mine was the same psychology that makes Negroes even today, though it bothers them down inside, keep letting the white man tell them how much 'progress' they are making. They've heard it so much they've almost gotten brainwashed into believing it — or at least accepting it."

He proved far more sensitive during an exchange with Mr. Ostrowski, his eighth-grade English teacher. After Malcolm confessed to wanting to become a lawyer, Ostrowski told him, "We all here like you, you know that. But you've got to be realistic about being a nigger. A lawyer — that's no realistic goal for a nigger. You need to think about something you *can* be." It was a turning point for Malcolm, much like a scene Richard Wright describes in *Black Boy*. While working as an errand boy, Wright tells his employer that he wants to be a writer. "You'll never be a writer," she replies. "Who on earth put such ideas into your nigger head?"

Like Wright's fateful conversation, the encounter with Ostrowski changed Malcolm significantly. He writes, "Where 'nigger' had slipped off my back before, wherever I heard it now, I stopped and looked at whoever said it. And they looked surprised that I did."

Frustrated that his top marks and model citizenship had failed to exempt him from the taint of presumed inferiority that seemed to engulf all blacks, young Malcolm began to turn his back on what is commonly called the American dream. His newfound enlightenment and considerable anger became an incentive to leave East Lansing and begin an intensely personal — and often unlawful — pursuit of happiness. Reflecting later on his exchange with Ostrowski, Malcolm writes, "Whatever I have done since then, I have driven myself to become a success at it."

Malcolm's and Wright's experiences suggest that the repeated use of racial epithets may temporarily reduce their sting without permanently removing their power. They both discovered that a word shrugged off in calm circumstances becomes a wounding insult in other contexts. The lingering effect of the eighth-grade incident on Malcolm was detectable in one of his most memorable debates, held years later. During an intense duel with a black university professor, he unleashed what became one of his most famous ripostes: "Do you know what white racists call black PhD's?" When the professor demurred, Malcolm reports in the *Autobiography*, "I laid the word down on him, loud: '*Nigger!*'"

The influence of *The Autobiography of Malcolm X* is nearly immeasurable. It has sold more than 3 million copies. In addition to updating and adding a redemptive gloss to the archetypal "bad nigger," it anticipated a decades-long flood of books, films, and pop culture products that have borrowed from, expanded, and even parodied Malcolm's model. Among the best-known is *Soul on Ice,* a disjointed assemblage of memoir and critical commentary by Eldridge Cleaver, a one-time criminal who became a high-ranking member of the Oakland branch of the Black Panthers. Published in 1968, his book is notable for its author's self-conscious attempt to position himself in the tradition of "bad niggers," which, in his view, includes Bigger Thomas, Emmett Till, and Malcolm X. He writes, "I have, so to speak, washed my hands in the blood of the martyr, Malcolm X, whose retreat from the precipice of madness created new room for others to turn about in, and I am now caught up in that tiny space, attempting a maneuver of my own."

Cleaver, too, reaches an epiphany in prison, a new state of awareness that requires his reinvention as a "bad nigger" before his return to the outside world. The literate Cleaver portrays his transformation as a peculiar blend of noble defiance and romantic longing: "The term *outlaw* appealed to me and at the time my parole date was drawing near, I considered myself to be mentally free — I was an 'outlaw.' I had stepped outside of the white man's law, which I repudiated with scorn and self-satisfaction. I became a law unto myself — my own legislature, my own supreme court, my own executive."

For Cleaver, his rebellion is a necessary response to white Americans' systematic attempts to cast black men as "Supermasculine Menials." During slavery, Cleaver argues, the black man "was conceived in terms of his ability to do [backbreaking] work — 'field niggers,'" etc. Although he has been allowed to gradually loosen the bonds of the "complex, all-pervasive myth which at one time classified the black man as a subhuman beast of burden," he remains trapped in a limbo of second-class citizenship. One must become a "bad nigger," then, to leave the "field nigger" behind.

Like Cleaver, Robert H. DeCoy also grappled with the elusive nature of genuine black identity in *The Nigger Bible* (1967), an oddball collection of rants that reads as if it were written by a drunk and disillusioned black Christian clergyman. DeCoy offers his pulp philosophy as a "Black Blueprint," which, if followed, will help his fellow blacks to escape the "futility of Caucasian existence." He addresses his readers as "my Nigrite Beings," "niggerons," and "niggerupes," to whom he has given "the Nigger words, forgotten somewhat, perhaps. . . . For Language, your own Nigger Words, could well be a final means to your Salvation and Survival."

In DeCoy's universe, salvation requires abandoning Christianity and making the right choice between being a Negro and being a "nigger." Negroes are a creation of white people (the Alabaster Ones), while "being a Nigger is closer to your inherent black nature." (Ironically, DeCoy claims the word "niggerology" without acknowledging its origin in scientific racism, instead defining it as "the study of being Niggers.") DeCoy warns, "By teaching you to forsake your Niggerness and Niggerism, he, the Caucasian, thus teaches you to forsake your birthrights." He never makes it clear exactly what blacks' birthrights actually are, but he comes close to Cleaver in suggesting that embracing one's "niggerness" is perhaps the only legitimate form of rebellion against white racism. Featuring an effusive foreword by Dick Gregory — himself the author of a memoir called *Nigger* — *The Nigger Bible* is still in print.

While *The Autobiography of Malcolm X* continues to sell and *The Nigger Bible* remains a staple of street vendors, *Soul on Ice* has faded from circulation, and it was out of print when this book was written. While *Soul* was much discussed and often debated during its time, it has been completely surpassed by yet another jailhouse memoir, this one published in 1969. *Pimp* by Iceberg Slim (a.k.a. Robert Beck), in which Beck recalls his life of crime, remains popular enough to challenge even Malcolm's legendary volume. According to its publisher, *Pimp* has sold 2.5 million copies.

Reflecting on his own cutthroat past, Malcolm X observed: "The hustler, out there in the ghetto jungles, has less respect for the white power structure than any other Negro in North America. The ghetto hustler is internally restrained by nothing. He has no religion, no concept of morality, no civic responsibility, no fear — nothing. To survive, he is out there constantly preying upon others, probing for any human weakness like a ferret."

Beck, who died in 1992 at the age of seventy-three, would probably have agreed wholeheartedly. Written in florid, slang-laden prose, *Pimp* is both gruesome and compelling, like pictures of a car wreck. Beck frequently describes himself as a "nigger" and hints that he is a "bad nigger" who has to create his own rules in order to survive. While in prison, he dreams of turning white and wreaking revenge on the judge who gave him his first jail sentence, but decides to face reality: "Well Nigger, you're pretty, but a bleach cream will never be invented that will make you white. So, pimp your ass off and be somebody with what you got."

After making parole, Beck becomes the protégé of Sweet Jones, the "baddest nigger" in the book and the self-proclaimed "greatest Nigger pimp in the world." Sweet taught Beck the history of black pimping, a practice he said was begun by black men, "slick Nigger heroes" who escaped the depravity of the South only to find that cities were little different from plantations. "The first Nigger pimps and sure-shot gamblers was the only Nigger big shots in the country," says Sweet.

During a subsequent prison stint after years of pimping, Beck experiences a jail cell epiphany similar to those described by Malcolm and Cleaver. "I came to a decision in that awful cell," he writes. "I was through with pimping and drugs. I got insight that perhaps I could never have hoped to get outside. . . . I had spent more than half a lifetime in a worthless, dangerous profession." He asks himself, "Can I learn to be proud of my black skin? Can I adjust to the stark reality that black people in my lifetime had little chance to escape the barbed-wire stockade in the white man's world?" For Beck, the answers to those questions are ultimately to be found in the ordinary comforts of a wife and children. He becomes a "square" and turns his back on his "bad nigger" past.

Beck continued to write about race, crime, and politics in a series of hard-bitten novels and a best-selling essay collection, *The Naked Soul of Iceberg Slim*. The essays are dedicated to the "heroic memory" of Malcolm X, Jack Johnson, and a host of others in the black rebel tradition, including Jonathan and George Jackson, Angela Davis, and "all street niggers and strugglers in and out of the joints." In paying homage to these individuals, Beck seems to suggest that his previous notion of "bad niggers" was unfairly limited and should be expanded to include those who flout convention in pursuit of a better life for all blacks. In an essay about the Black Panthers, he comments on the "good niggers" who "had remained silent when Panthers and other black people were being beaten, shot and killed" by police. The "good niggers," according to Beck, were outraged by the police department's deadly raid on the Panthers' Los Angeles headquarters, but only because they had not been told in advance and thus had to "suffer humiliating surprise" like everyone else. But the raid taught a valuable lesson: "the 'good nigger' realized that in the final analysis a nigger is a nigger is a nigger, and that his genuflective ass has no immunity from threat, terror and death."

Beck stuck to that assessment throughout his many works. Ever remorseful of his criminal past, he remained grateful for the opportunity to redeem himself through writing. "What a joyously painful transport it is to be part of that struggle," he wrote, "to be a besieged black man, an embattled nigger, in racist America."

The Naked Soul of Iceberg Slim was published in 1971, just as novelists and writers began to be overshadowed by the new wave of aggressive black actors and filmmakers already discussed. Sometimes dubbed the "blaxploitation" generation, they took such durable concepts as the "bad nigger" and subjected them to their own fertile imaginations. Many of these tortured tussles seemed to — or at least wanted to — confirm the controversial observations of the black social scientists Price M. Cobbs and William H. Grier. In their seminal book *Black Rage* (1968), they boldly asserted, "Every black man harbors a potential bad nigger inside him."

"A NOD TO THE PANGS OF HISTORY"

In her classic study of American humor, Constance Rourke quoted a white traveler who in 1795 observed: "The blacks are the great humorists of the nation. . . . Climate, music, kind treatment act upon them like electricity." The statement is certainly patronizing on its surface (toss a Negro a compliment and he'll start shuffling and tapping with a smile), but it is notable for its enthusiastic endorsement of blacks' comic talent. Toss aside the condescension, and the statement could even refer to the black comics who became popular in the sixties. They rose to fame in part by taking advantage of the changing political climate to woo mainstream audiences — and earn hefty paychecks — at the kinds of venues that had formerly been closed to black entertainers.

Performers such as Bill Cosby and Godfrey Cambridge gently but consistently challenged black stereotypes by presenting a different kind of Negro, warm, witty, and even somewhat cerebral. Dignified but still wearing the "mask" that Paul Laurence Dunbar immortalized — the serene countenance that "grins and lies" while mouthing "myriad subtleties" — their routines featured droll observations of humanity that applied smoothly and easily to all races.

Dunbar had advised: "Why should the world be overwise, / In counting all our tears and sighs? / Nay, let them only see us, while / We wear the mask." But black comedians were eager to doff their masks and, as other forms of black art became more confrontational, so, too, did standup. Dick Gregory was prominent among those who gradually introduced racial bits into their routines. Promoting his autobiography, Gregory told a mixed-raced audience at a Mississippi civil rights rally: "Take a *Nigger* to bed with you tonight." Wil Haygood, noting that the line was received with exuberant applause, wrote that the joke was "all at once, publicity and a sexual joke and a nod to the pangs of history."

Gregory disarmed potentially hostile white audiences by telling them that his contract included a clause awarding him $50 each time a heckler hurled the N word at him. He would explain, "I'm only making ten dollars a night, and I'd like to put the owner out of business. Will everybody in the room please stand up and yell nigger?" In his memoir, Gregory described these types of jokes as quick and sophisticated, a slick kind of protective camouflage: "Cool. No bitterness. The audience would never know I was mad and mean inside. And there would be no time to feel sorry for me."

"THAT NIGGER'S CRAZY"

In a poem called "Slim in Atlanta," Sterling Brown sends his everyman, Slim Greer, down to that city, where he discovers to his amazement a law that prohibits "all de niggers / From laughin' outdoors." Says Brown's narrator: "Hope to Gawd I may die / If I ain't speakin' truth / Make de niggers do deir laughin' / In a telefoam booth." Slim is so taken aback that he runs into the booth and nearly laughs himself to death. As the poem ends, Slim is still laughing while a long line of three hundred antsy "niggers" await their chance to enter the booth and let some laughter loose. The problem, the poem suggests, is that there is insufficient space in which blacks can laugh and joke and comfortably be themselves. Nor should the reader confuse blacks' need to laugh with an inordinate degree of mirth; unlike, say, Thomas Jefferson, Slim has never labored under the delusion that the "numberless afflictions" of his people are "less felt and sooner forgotten." Rather, he encounters in Atlanta an example of the limitations Ralph Ellison described as resulting from "the heritage of a people who for hundreds of years could not celebrate birth or dignify death, and whose need to live despite the dehumanizing pressures of slavery developed an endless capacity for laughing at their painful experiences."

Ellison persuasively suggested that blacks responded to the lack of opportunities to heal themselves with humor by funneling much of their wit into art forms such as the blues. In the manner of a Muddy Waters or a Charlie Parker, Richard Pryor determined to use his art not only to get into that metaphorical "booth" but bust it wide open and dance on its shattered remains. The boundaries that Pryor challenged were not caused solely by white racism. There was also what we might call the black politics of respectability at work. Pryor chafed against all such restraints. About a decade before George Clinton would offer funk fans a chance to dance their way out of their constrictions, Pryor chose to laugh his way out of his.

He discovered his voice in the late 1960s, having already enjoyed considerable success as an amiable Cosby-esque performer. Thumbing his nose at the self-imposed bourgeois pretensions that inhibited many black entertainers, Pryor devised a new style that was raw, obscene, and often delivered while its creator seemed to teeter on the verge of weeping or violence. Countering Dunbar, Pryor made "tears and lies" a hallmark of his appearances. To blacks with middle-class sensibilities, he presented a frustrating conundrum: he was as embarrassing as he was funny, like a witty but uncontrollable cousin who you just knew was going to act up in front of company. Pryor's escape from conformity undoubtedly motivated lines such as "I was a nigger for twenty-three years. I gave it up. No room for advancement."

He looked and sounded tentative in the initial performances of his new material, as if anticipating a hostile reaction from folks offended by his off-color recitations and almost mantra-like repetition of the N word. The first memorable routine of this nature was "Super Nigger" (1968), a monologue solidly within the "bad nigger" tradition, in which Pryor astutely blended cultural criticism with his fantasy of possessing extraordinary powers. "I always thought, why do they never have a hero, a black hero? I always wanted to go to the movies and see a black hero. I figured out maybe someday on television they'll have it, man, like you see on television. He'll come out: Look, up in the sky! It's a crow. It's a bat. No, it's Super Nigger! Yes, friends, Super Nigger. Able to leap tall buildings with a single bound, faster than a bowl of chitlins."

Pryor went on to tell us that Super Nigger has X-ray vision that enables him to see through "everything except whitey" and disguises himself as "Clark Washington, mild-mannered custodian." Super Nigger takes off in flight when he learns that the warehouse where he's hidden his drugs has caught fire.

Ralph Ellison once wrote, "One of the first epithets that many European immigrants learned when they got off the boat was the term 'nigger' — it made them feel instantly American." Pryor arrived at a similar conclusion in "New Niggers," a routine from 1975: "White folks tired of our ass, too. They getting them some new niggers: the Vietnamese. 'Bring em over, bring all of 'em over. Niggers won't mind.' They didn't ask us *shit*. We the muthafuckas got to give the jobs up for 'em. . . . Got all the Vietnamese in army camps and shit, taking tests and stuff, learning how to say nigger so they can become good citizens."

Pryor signaled his disapproval of whites' using the N word by putting it in the mouths of racist authority figures such as cops and employers of the sort played by Chevy Chase in the notorious "job interview" sketch that aired on *Saturday Night Live* in 1975. With the help of his fellow comic Paul Mooney and cast member Chevy Chase, Pryor created an exchange of insults that becomes humorously and imminently combustible.

CHASE: "Jungle Bunny!"
PRYOR: "Honky."
CHASE: "Spade!"
PRYOR: "Honky-honky!"
CHASE: "Nigger!"
PRYOR: "Deeead honky."

Chase later recalled, "I remember asking Richard for as many slang words for white people as he could come up with. He hesitated and then realized that there were many more for African Americans than he could think of for 'whities.'"

Pryor's most powerful routine involving the N word contained unusually few laughs. "Bicentennial Nigger," from the 1976 album of the same name, traces the origins of black humor from the slave ships to a hypothetical "200-year-old nigger in blackface," who's been trotted out to express blacks' gratitude to whites for allowing them to be a part of the American dream. In less than three minutes, Pryor touched on many of the most painful aspects of the historical black experience, including the Middle Passage, slavery, and the intentional dissolution of black families in the name of profit. Throughout, he punctuates the bizarre, blistering piece with a strange and vaguely ominous high-pitched chuckle.

He ends with an atypically somber last line that functions effectively as a cautionary note for all blacks who want to believe that what happened in the past should remain there. "Y'all probably done forgot about it," he says, "but I ain't gon' never forget it."

While brandishing unsavory language like a loaded magnum, Pryor was also self-deprecating. Complaining about his declining sexual prowess or his lack of boxing skills, he deftly punctured the destructive myths of the black stud and the hyperathletic Negro who is incapable of feeling pain. Magnetic and oracular, Pryor established himself as a modern Bert Williams, the best in his field. I found many of his monologues so mesmerizing that I laughed helplessly, so caught up in his uproarious scenarios that the N words flowed past my ears with ease, even with repeated listenings. As adept as any poet or playwright if not more so, Pryor skillfully manipulated the meanings and connotations of "nigger," using it to illustrate everything from the limits of black power to the objectification of black humanity. (If his fantasy hero were named Super Black Man, for example, one would be inclined to question why he was working in such a low position, but his remaining a "nigger" explains it all.) Pryor proved emphatically that "nigger" in the hands of a brilliant artist was not a liability but a weapon. And a highly effective one at that.

After years of presenting what was essentially an eloquent argument against eliminating the N word altogether, Pryor famously abandoned the epithet. A 1979 trip to Africa led to a dramatic change of heart. Pryor described his epiphany on his "Live on the Sunset Strip" recording (1982):

> One thing that happened to me that was magical. I was sitting in a hotel lobby and a voice said look around you. What do you see? I looked around and I saw people of all colors and shapes. And the voice said, "Do you see any niggers?" I said "naw." It said, "you know why? 'Cuz there aren't any." 'Cuz I'd been there three weeks and I hadn't said it. And it started making me cry. I said, "Holy shit. All the acts I've been doing as an artist and comedian and all the speaking I've been doing and I been trying to say something and I've been saying that. And that's a devastating fucking word. That has nothing to do with us."

Although Pryor's subsequent routines are full of "bitches" and "motherfuckers," "niggers" are seldom if ever found.

CONJURING UP DEMONS

Although the eighties and nineties have spawned a plethora of best-forgotten Pryor wannabes, his ultimate antipathy toward the N word has not been reflected in their material. These pretenders have retained Pryor's freewheeling approach to profanity, but it is mostly gratuitous — typical of an era in which performers shy away from the comedy of ideas and wallow instead in a kind of cesspool where vulgarity replaces insight and profanity for wit.

A notable exception has been Paul Mooney, Pryor's longtime colleague and quite possibly the most talented satirist in the land. Mooney's act has included such routines as "Nigger History Lesson," "1-900-Blame-A-Nigger," "Nigger Vampire," and "Niggerstein." A staunch defender of the N word, he told Regina R. Robertson: "I'm not bothered by it. The word is going nowhere, it's not leaving this planet. I'm going to use it because it conjures up demons and I like that. It comes from the word Negro, Negroid — it all means black. When it was powerful and offensive, people called me 'nigga' enough, so much so that I feel like I own it." In December 2006, following white comedian Michael Richards's meltdown at a Los Angeles nightclub in which he denounced black hecklers as "niggers," Mooney had a surprising change of heart. He appeared at a press conference calling for a moratorium on the N word. Echoing Pryor's epiphany, Mooney pledged to abandon the slur. "I'm free of it," he told the *Washington Post*. "I won't be using that word on-stage, and I won't be using the B word. We're asking the rappers and all the people on earth to stop using the word."

While Mooney commands respect as the keeper of the Pryor flame, Chris Rock is widely regarded as the successor to Pryor's comic dominance. By 2001, *Time* magazine had anointed him "the funniest man in America" and Pryor had damned him with faint praise ("Does he remind me of me? I'm afraid so"). In March 2004, *Entertainment Weekly* crowned Rock as the nation's number one funnyman once again. "Watching Rock in 2004," the magazine enthused, "is like watching a great prize-fighter in peak condition."

Rock first reached the pinnacle in 1996 after *Bring the Pain*, an HBO special that featured a controversial and attention-getting routine commonly referred to as "Niggas vs. Black People": "Everything white people don't like about black people, black people *really* don't like about black people. . . . There's like a civil war going on with black people and there's two sides: there's black people and niggas — and niggas have *got* to go. . . . I love black people but I hate niggas."

Rock's roster of "nigga" misbehavior could have come right out of *Notes on the State of Virginia*. Rock argued that "niggas" are violent, lazy, ignorant, prone to theft, and suffer from a perverse lack of ambition. Whereas Thomas Jefferson thought a Negro "could scarcely be found capable of tracing and comprehending the investigations of Euclid," Rock observed that "Niggas hate knowledge, shit. Niggas break into your house — you want to save your money, put it in a book." In fairness to Rock, he doesn't even use the N word that often. And while his scathing criticism resembles Jefferson's, it seems to derive less from the wizard of Monticello than from Booker T. Washington, who denounced the "loafers, the drunkards and gamblers" who "disgrace our race and disturb our civilization." The routine is relatively brief and memorable mostly for its almost defiant endorsement of the notion of a culture of poverty afflicting members of the black underclass, an idea made more troublesome by its positioning as a punch line for a mixed audience to laugh at. It's not particularly humorous once the initial shock wears off, which is a pity because most of the rest of the show is hilarious. Ultimately, "Niggas vs. Black People" is among the least funny aspects of a very funny performance.

Paul Mooney occasionally appeared on *Chappelle's Show*, a cable program that featured the comedian Dave Chappelle. Like Rock, Chappelle insists on holding a mirror up to America's many contradictions and inconsistencies, an act that inevitably involves race. His sketch comedy targeted Americans of all colors, whom he lampooned while playing dangerously with stereotypes. One character, for example, was Clayton Bigsby, a blind white supremacist who has never been told that he's black. During the second season of *Chappelle's Show*, the most talked-about sketch was "The Niggars," a parody of 1950s family comedies such as *Leave It to Beaver*. The all-white Niggars (pronounced "nigger") are introduced as "everyone's favorite family" while a whimsical theme song sets up the sketch. It begins with Mr. and Mrs. Niggar engaging in friendly banter at the breakfast table as they wait for their son to wake up.

DAD: "Is Tim still asleep?"
MOM: "I think so."
DAD: "He sure is one lazy Niggar."

After Tim arrives and mentions that he has a date with Jenny, we are taken to Jenny's house, where a similar breakfast table exchange is taking place.

MOM: Jenny has a date with that Niggar boy across the street."
DAD: "What? Oh god, no!"
JENNY: "No, Daddy, that's his *name*, Timmy Niggar."
DAD (RELIEVED): "Oh, of course."

Chappelle eventually enters the Niggar household as Clifton, the milkman. He reminds them that they haven't paid their bill and declines an offer of bacon. "I know better than to get between a Niggar and his pork," he says with a smile. "Might get my fingers bit off." In many respects, the scene is a typical Chappelle performance, fearless, abrasive — even outrageous — but reliably funny. Not surprisingly, Chappelle shrugs off comments from offended critics. "I'm not so concerned when black intellectuals say the N word is awful," he told the *New York Times*. "If people stop saying the N word, is everything going to be equal? Is a rainbow going to come out of the sky, and all of a sudden things will be better for black people?"

Chappelle's response is more than a little disingenuous, as his comedy is often self-consciously cerebral and can be as intellectual as anything produced by a lineup of black scholars from Harvard — even something as deceptively simple as a riff about marijuana often contains nuggets of provocative insight. Yet I think he is right. Suggesting that Chappelle refrain from using racial language (to parody racist attitudes, after all) is to profoundly miss the point. It would be like asking Jonathan Swift to lay off the talk about eating children.

Nigger vs. Nigga

It's okay to have that Nigga in you. . . . Ain't nothing wrong with bein'
a Nigga. There's somethin' wrong with being a "nigger" — but not a
Nigga.

— Bernie Mac, 2001

IN *JUBA TO JIVE: A Dictionary of African-American Slang,* Clarence Major wrote that the N word can function as a term of endearment when exchanged by blacks, whose usage reflects "a tragicomic sensibility that is aware of black history." That tragicomic sense continues to infuse defendable usage, and not just during black-black dialogue. In "Time Haters," one of my favorite sketches from Dave Chappelle's show, the comic meets Major's requirements in a skit that is only indirectly about the N word.

According to its ludicrous premise, Chappelle and his squad of righteous colored avengers invade historical scenarios on behalf of ethnic minorities who have suffered unjustly. The scene begins with their arrival at a Southern plantation, where a white slaveholder is abusing his black captives. When Silky (Chappelle) orders the slaveholder to cease and desist, the white man asks him who he is.

"We are the time haters," Silky explains. "We've traveled all the way back through time . . . to call you a cracker."

The white man brandishes a whip, but Silky produces a pistol and issues an order: "Reach for the sky, honky!"

"Honky?"

"Honky is a racial epithet used for white people made popular by a man named George Jefferson in the 1970s," Silky says. He goes on to declare that in the future, all black people will be free, before he shoots the slaveholder many times.

The whole scene is self-consciously preposterous but manages to show that for slaves, racial oppression not only included forced servitude and crippling social inequality but extended to language itself. As we have seen, slaves were not even allowed the luxury of silence — they were forced to sing on command, to laugh when not amused. Only through superhuman intervention are the slaves in Chappelle's sketch given leave to say what's on their mind. While challenging, albeit in comic terms, the dominant narrative of blacks as debased "niggers," Chappelle demonstrates that calling a white man "honky" does nothing to change the balance of power. He has to explain what the epithet means because, unlike "nigger," it has no tradition of "racial folklore grounded on centuries of instinct, habit and thought" to give it weight and substance. While "nigger" has traveled smoothly through the centuries, "honky" has no significance outside the era in which it briefly flourished. As outrageous as the comedian's performance is, it is charged throughout with an awareness of history. In this sense Chappelle confirms Greg Tate's observation that young black men can at times "ironically respond to language as a tool of oppression by disempowering it with crazed black wit."

"QUEER THEORY"

In *Do You Speak American?*, a 2005 survey of national speech habits, Robert MacNeil and William Cran noted that "queer" has "lost some of its homophobic sting in the general culture." They asked the black gay activist Calvin Gibson whether gays' use of queer is "analogous to blacks' using 'nigger' but being offended if white people did."

"That's exactly what it's like," Gibson replied. "I believe it's because people feel disempowered and this is one way to empower themselves. If we can use the word *queer* so many times that it just becomes a normal word in our language without any consequences, then I think we see ourselves as being more empowered. So — it sort of proves the point that you can change the meaning of words."

Does it indeed? I'm not at all suggesting that such change is impossible, but in this instance it is a romantic conclusion at best. The proposed analogy of "queer" and "nigger" is equally wistful. To begin with, homosexuals don't insist that heterosexuals refrain from using "queer" to describe homosexuals, hence the substantial popularity of mainstream television programs such as *Queer as Folk* and *Queer Eye for the Straight Guy*. Need I describe the reaction to a program called "Nigger Eye for the White Guy"?

Second, the N word doesn't appear to have lost much of its "sting in *the general culture*." If anecdotal evidence is any indication, liberal white professionals often react as strongly to it as their black counterparts do. One white colleague told me it is still "the only word that produces visceral unease. . . . I cringe inwardly when I hear it on a hip-hop record." Outside hip-hop's boundaries, it remains an underground word. Whereas, for instance, "queer studies" is a generally accepted colloquialism among (gay and straight) intellectuals interested in lesbian, gay, and transgender issues, few if any academics devoted to the study of African-American life and culture have seen fit to describe their work as "nigger studies."

"Queer" and "gay" didn't emerge as commonly used epithets until the 1900s. By the 1950s, "gay" had been embraced by those whom it was formerly used to condemn; "queer" followed in the 1980s, when it was taken up by gay rights and AIDS activists. Compare the short shelf lives of those insults to the seemingly immortal N word, which was used to describe blacks in America as far back as 1619. As seen in our discussion of "honky," we find that "queer" and "gay" are not attached to a commensurate folklore grounded on "centuries of instinct, habit and thought."

In addition, "queer" and "gay" have always had other meanings that have nothing to do with sexual identity. "Queer," for instance, has meant odd ("My little horse must think it queer / to stop without a farmhouse near"), and "gay" has meant lively or merry ("gay Paree," "when our hearts were young and gay"). "Nigger," in stark contrast, is not one of those words of innocuous meaning that morphed over time into something different and harmful; it has always been tethered to notions of race and racial inferiority.

What's more, to regard all members of lesbian, gay, bisexual, and transgendered communities (LGBT) as "queer" could be a well-intentioned but ignorant misstep — the type of mistake we'd quickly condemn in a racial context. "Queer" as an identity "is only accepted by a fraction of the LGBT community and rejected by the majority," Matthew Frederick Streib argued in a January 2004 column in the *Cornell Daily Sun*. "Many people who are supposed to be included under the queer umbrella do not identify with the word and may even detest it," he wrote. For this reason, "calling the LGBT movement 'the queer movement' is like calling the NAACP the NAAN."

Michelangelo Signorile, a well-known gay journalist, has also observed that "not all gay people are happy to be called queer. Many would rather stick with the GLBT terminology than be called something that was once a slur and that literally means they're unusual. As in the past, these differences seem to occur along generational lines. No major gay and lesbian political group uses the word queer. They don't want to alienate anyone, let alone confuse the politicians they're lobbying."

Finally, there is the question of whether "queer" and "gay" are in fact as defanged as we'd like them to be. Despite the rise of positive homosexual characters in films, literature, and television — and despite the gradual growth of school clubs for gay teens and school programs promoting tolerance — "that is so gay" ranks among the most venomous insults one American teenager can sling at another.

"IF NIGGERS COULD FLY"

In his debut novel, *White Boy Shuffle* (1996), Paul Beatty performs an act of linguistic dismantling that evokes "the crazed black wit" celebrated by Greg Tate. Beatty's youthful protagonist, Gunnar Kaufman, fails to navigate his new neighborhood until he decodes the local lingo, a fluid glossary of slang, insults, and curses fairly crackling with sarcasm and nervous energy. A self-described "cultural alloy, tin-hearted whiteness wrapped in blackened copper plating," young Gunnar had lived happily in Santa Monica, "where Black was being a nigger who didn't know any other niggers." Fearing that her children are being deprived of a "traditional black experience," Gunnar's mom moves the family to an inner-city Los Angeles community. In Hillside, Gunnar discovers, "Language was everywhere. Smoldering embers of charcoal etymology so permeated the air that whenever someone opened his mouth it smelled like smoke."

He might have added that every time someone opened his mouth, the N word fell out. Hostile cops seek Gunnar's gang affiliation by asking him to identify "your crimeys, your homies, your posse? You know, yo' niggers." Friends are greeted with "my nigger." Enemies, on the other hand, get "Nigger, what the fuck you looking at?" A little neighbor girl calls herself Vamp a Nigger on the Regular Veronica. The prevailing neighborhood philosophy allows no brooding over small tragedies because "niggers got to get up and go to work tomorrow."

Gunnar realizes that he's finally beginning to fit in after a conversation with a popular student. "He called me 'nigger,'" Gunnar reflects. "My euphoria was as palpable as the loud clap of our hands colliding in my first soul shake." Only by mastering the many meanings of "nigger" — and being welcomed into "niggerness," as it were — does Gunnar begin to acclimate himself to the new black world he has entered.

Because Gunnar casts a skeptical eye toward anyone who tries to make it through life without acknowledging the absurdity of it all, he recognizes and occasionally revels in the inescapable conundrums attached to issues of identity and belonging. Beatty flirts with farce as he takes his hero to adulthood and life as a celebrated writer. The grown-up Gunnar continues to wrestle with the idea of blackness and whether membership has its privileges. One of his best-known poems is called "If Niggers Could Fly":

> If niggers could fly, where would we alight? We orbit a treeless world, nest on eaveless clouds, unable to stop flapping our wings for even a second, in constant migration to nowhere.

Much later in the book, a deeply disillusioned Gunnar urges his fellow blacks to abandon America, to "toss our histories overboard" along with our expectations that justice and equality will ever be ours among a people who refuse to behave toward us in a principled manner. Before he arrives at that somber realization, he leads readers on a wild and wordy ramble (one of his nicknames is "the underground neologist") through urban L.A. and exclusive Boston academia, puncturing pretensions and providing a poet's-eye view of the unlikely clash and merge of various subcultures, including street gangs and creative writing workshops. Life is ludicrous, he seems to suggest, and our preoccupation with "niggers" and other forms of smoldering etymology is a defining symptom that distracts us from more meaningful concerns.

As we have seen, comics and writers have not been the only black artists to address the N word as metaphor and symbol of this nation's failure to make satisfactory amends for its long tradition of racial injustice. The multimedia specialist Faith Ringgold's *The Black Light Series: Flag for the Moon: Die Nigger* (1969) is an especially well-executed example of such encounters. At first glance, the 36 x 50-inch oil on canvas appears to be a straightforward if mildly stylized portrait of an American flag. A second glance reveals the word "die" hidden in the stars. The stripes, meanwhile, are shown to be made from the word "nigger." It's a simple but effective piece that appears to warn blacks to beware the trap of uncritical patriotism or face deadly consequences. Created after the assassinations of Medgar Evers, Malcolm X, and Martin Luther King Jr. and in the midst of escalating calamities in Vietnam, the painting suggests a sense of fatalism commensurate with the mood of the country.

Quite similar in spirit and tone is "I Wants *You*, Nigger," a mock recruitment poster (circa 1970) that parodies the famous Uncle Sam image created by James Montgomery Flagg in 1916. In this version, Sam encourages potential recruits to "become a member of the world's highest paid black mercenary army." Enlistees will receive "valuable training in the skills of killing off other oppressed people!" Finally, Sam urges his quarry "Die Nigger Die — you can't die fast enough in the ghettos. So run to your nearest recruiting chamber!"

A contemporary form of such pointed satire can be found in Tana Hargest's installations *Bitter Nigger, Inc.* (2001) and *New Negrotopia* (2003), both of which offer knowing, sardonic comments on the commodification of blackness. They revolve around a fictional corporation whose "products" include pharmaceuticals aimed at blacks and situation comedies featuring black themes (courtesy of a subsidiary, the Bitter Nigger Broadcast Network). The "products" are introduced through a mock trade show booth advertising the virtues of Tominex ("the go along to get along pill") and garnished with reassuring slogans such as "Bitter Nigger Pharmaceuticals is committed to alleviating the bothersome effects of racism." There is also a mission statement from "Chairwoman and CEO" Tana R. Hargest that proudly informs potential stockholders, "in the last 8 months Bitter Nigger's ideas have doubled, viewer investment in Bitter Nigger, Inc. has more than tripled, and the value of our relevancy stock has grown eightfold." Meanwhile, *New Negrotopia* touts the delights of a planned amusement park that will include such entertainments as Atlantic Adventure, a 3-D interactive experience of the Middle Passage, and a Cotton Bales on the Mississippi water ride.

In varying degrees, the work of Chappelle, Beatty, Ringgold, the anonymous poster artist, and Hargest can be said to represent that crucial tragicomic sense that Major described, approaching the N word and its attendant baggage with an appropriate consideration of context and history.

Picking up on an idea from Albert Camus, the African-American writer Chester Himes once observed: "Racism introduces absurdity into the human condition. Not only does racism express the absurdity of the racists, but it generates absurdity in the victims. . . . Racism creates absurdity among blacks as a defense mechanism. Absurdity to combat absurdity." The work of artists such as Ringgold, Hargest, and Beatty confirms the prescience and validity of Himes's statement.

GANGSTA-ASS NIGGAS

When I was growing up, calling someone a "nigger" was only slightly less offensive than talking about his mother. I still remember a typical comeback that girls would deliver with a snap of their fingers and a toss of their pigtails: "I'm not a nigger. I'm a nigger-o." ("Negro" was never pronounced with a long e in my neighborhood.) Even kids in kindergarten, new to the world of "the dozens" and dirty jokes, seemed to instinctively grasp that the N word had about it a stench of powerlessness that was to be avoided at all costs. It so perfectly embodied a life full of futility, empty of purpose. Young as we were, we understood that it carried a hate strong enough to turn on us and consume us. "When you're called a nigger," James Baldwin wrote, "you look at your father because you think your father can rule the world — every kid thinks that — and then you discover that your father cannot do anything about it. So you begin to despise your father and you realize, oh, that's what a nigger is."

But times have changed. Back then, we imitated the cool teenagers and proud young men who greeted one another on the street with elaborate handshakes and "What it is?" or "What's happenin', brother?" These days, most young men I see greet one another with "Whassup, nigga?" All they've kept is the handshake.

Other developments may be contributing to this epochal shift, but none has done so as emphatically as the hip-hop subgenre known as gangsta rap. From 1979, when "Rapper's Delight" was released, until 1988, when "Straight Outta Compton" went gold, the N word was seldom uttered on hip-hop recordings.

All that changed when N.W.A. (short for Niggas Wit Attitude) became a national sensation with "Straight Outta Compton." This record was not the earliest example of gangsta rap, but it was the first to attract large numbers of converts from all over the country. Essentially a collection of hip-hop odes to urban dysfunction, "Straight" mixes infectious beats with vicious imagery and often clever lyrics. With his obsessive focus on drugs, double-crossing "bitches," and hardcore violence, the lyricist Ice Cube emerged as the poet laureate of ghetto pathology and spawned an apparently endless horde of imitators. Atop Dr. Dre's groove-heavy production, Cube and his colleagues recite the N word approximately 46 times, only slightly more than it is uttered in *Jackie Brown* and far less than the 215 times it occurs in *Huckleberry Finn*. Multiple listenings nullify such comparisons, of course, although the tally provides some measure of the group's move toward even more hardcore lyrics on its follow-up CD, *Efil4Zaggin*. Released in 1991 to widespread acclaim (and controversy, too), it contains approximately 185 utterances.

More important than how many times the N word was said is how it was used. N.W.A.'s ideas about being "a nigga" are largely derivative of Iceberg Slim (whose influence on Ice Cube isn't limited to his choice of a rap moniker) and could be assembled and loosely described as the Gangsta's Guide for Real Niggas. Little of the gangsta rap produced in the years since N.W.A.'s emergence differs much from the guidelines they laid down. In many instances, they use "nigga" to refer to mere ordinary, law-abiding men or to lowlifes unworthy of respect. "Real niggas" is an appellation reserved for those who have earned it. In the N.W.A. cosmos, life is only about "bitches and money." To get plenty of both, real niggas must run the streets, smoke weed, guzzle malt liquor, trust no one except members of their clique, and be prepared to kill without a moment's hesitation. This is the model that has been slavishly adhered to for the past eighteen years in such gangsta rap anthems as "Strictly 4 My N.I.G.G.A.Z." by 2Pac, "Hurt Niggas" by Mobb Deep, "Jigga My Nigga" by Jay-Z, and "Niggas Bleed" by the Notorious B.I.G.

The hustler plots described in these songs usually unfold in an insular world. The villains tend to be disrespectful "niggas," or "bitches runnin' game," and the racial realities of the surrounding universe are limited mostly to references to prison and oppressive police. In stark contrast to the "bad nigger" tales of previous generations, the protagonists are seldom portrayed as rebels against an unfair system whose "standing up to the Man" inspires both fear and admiration in their timid neighbors. There are notable exceptions, such as the Geto Boys' "Damn It Feels Good to Be a Gangsta" (1999), which enlivens a typical litany of dysfunction with a barbed political twist. While the first three verses relate the adventures of a "real gangsta-ass nigga" making deals and "ridin' around town in a drop-top Benz," the last verse takes listeners out of the 'hood and into the White House. There the new president of the United States hints at a Republican conspiracy, boasts of his Mafia ties, and pledges to allow "a big drug shipment" to pass undisturbed into a poor community in exchange for the Mob's help in fixing the election. Whereas the typical gangsta merely flexes his gat when he feels disrespected, the president has more dramatic means at his disposal. He warns, "Other leaders better not upset me or I'll send a million troops to die at war." Unlike many similar raps, this offering presents an aerial view that reveals the Geto Boys' small-time shenanigans as the delusional fantasies they are; real power is shown to be beyond the reach of "real niggas."

Another striking departure comes from N.W.A.: "Why do I call myself a nigger, you ask me?" So begins "Niggaz 4 Life," which tries to answer that question. While the group often presents a grandiose view of themselves, they also see themselves as both targets of white oppression and agents of their own destruction. In their view, blacks will be called "niggers" by the larger society no matter what they accomplish in terms of wealth, education, or professional status, so there's little purpose in trying to shake off the word. Striving for progress through the few legitimate channels available to them is a waste of time, so instead they choose to embrace the absurdity of life by becoming a nigga, "a young brother who don't give a fuck about another." In a world without compassion, it's every nigga for himself.

In this instance, while the group's logic is questionable, their treatment of the N word is not. Their use of it is overtly self-conscious and infused with macabre wit and an awareness of history. This is positively Ellisonian in comparison to lesser, derivative raps that have also tried to address what has become gangsta rap's existential riddle. Consider, for example, "Niggaz Theme" by the rapper Ja Rule. For him the question "What is a nigga?" has but one answer: "Rob a bitch, slap a bitch."

Supporters defend such lyrics as keeping it real, or merely reflecting accurately what is said and done in urban neighborhoods on a daily basis. But that explanation fails to account for other rappers, whose "reports" on the same conditions use far different language. "Nigger" and/or "nigga" appear far less frequently in the work of socially conscious rappers such as Chuck D of Public Enemy, Mos Def, Common, and Lauryn Hill, although they also address such potentially explosive issues as inner city poverty, racial discrimination, and relations between black men and women. Just as much of black cultural output can be considered as a counternarrative to the majority culture's enduring myth of black inferiority, the work of intellectually astute hip-hop artists can be heard as a counternarrative to gangsta rap's legacy of rampant nihilism. Because much of gangsta rap turns a blind eye to history, it often abets a white supremacist agenda by keeping alive dangerous stereotypes linking African Americans to laziness, criminal violence, and sexual insatiability. Instead of standing up to "the Man," gangsta rappers serve as his henchmen.

The greater tragedy may very well lie in majority audiences' preference for the more titillating and bloodthirsty material, an affinity confirmed by gangsta rap's regular reign at the top of the pop charts. Like the voyeuristic whites peering in the window while Nigger Charley made love, mainstream audiences continue to overlook the positive and the thoughtful in favor of the illicit and the sensational. By cavorting colorfully in the margins of modern life, gangsta rappers reinforce a sense of belonging in members of their audience who have deep roots in society's snug interior. Like the modern minstrels in *Bamboozled*, self-proclaimed "real niggas" make majority audiences laugh, they make them cry, they make them feel glad to be Americans.

WARRING IDEALS

Concomitant with the rise of gangsta rap is the notion that incorporating the N word into everyday speech somehow deconstructs it and removes its power to offend. The great poet Sonia Sanchez has written of her own efforts in this direction. Learning that a group of her young black students had been chased home by a group of older white students who called them "niggers," she wrote a poem about it. "That word ain't shit to me," the poem declares. "I'll say it slow for you — niiiigggger."

Sanchez intended to help the students arm themselves against such insults by stripping the words of their old meanings. "If they could chase someone with just one word, then they have the power, but if you could stop the word's importance by replacing it with something new, then you had the power," Sanchez wrote. "I tried to reinvent the word to give them the new power. And that's what you have to do. I empowered those children . . . when they stopped and turned with their interpretation of the word nigger, they were at a new place with themselves."

Mos Def is one of the most impressive rappers currently working. Aside from "Mr. Nigga," a trenchant comment on the limits of wealth and fame, his body of work shows no particular interest in the N word. But he sympathizes with rappers who, like Sanchez, believe the epithet can be disinfected. As he sees it, "If you define hip-hop as a survival mechanism, as a means of making something from nothing, then the act becomes compulsory. It's an act of empowerment. When we call each other 'nigga,' we take a word that has been historically used by whites to degrade and oppress us, a word that has so many negative connotations, and turn it into something beautiful, something we can call our own. I know it sounds cliché, but it truly becomes a 'term of endearment.'"

Rappers and others with similar views about "nigger" have chosen to indicate their efforts to turn insult into affection by giving it a new spelling, helpfully provided by N.W.A. in "I Ain't the One": "I'm a ruthless N-I-double-G-A." According to such thinking, "nigga" can be used without malice between blacks and also to distinguish acceptable forms of black behavior from uncouth ones, which shall remain the exclusive province of "niggers." How this new concept can be reconciled with the "real niggas" who gleefully commit rapes, murders, assaults, and thefts in countless rap songs — or with those "niggas" who hate knowledge and torment black people in Chris Rock monologues — has thus far gone unexplained. Should we, for instance, disregard N.W.A.'s "One Less Bitch," which declares: "A nigga is one who believes that all ladies are bitches"?

The logic behind the new spelling breaks down further when one recalls that racist whites have used "nigga" nearly as often as they've used "nigger." To accept the validity of "nigga," we'd have to forget those lovely "nigga songsters" that used to grace the music parlors of respectable white families in nineteenth-century America. We would also have to wink at all those segregationist senators — Helms, Thurmond, Stennis, et al. — who used to insist that "Negro" sounded just like "nigga" when pronounced with a Southern accent.

Not everyone in the hip-hop community sees a distinction between "nigga" and "nigger." In the opinion of Davey D, a respected critic and writer in the San Francisco Bay area, "the use of the word with either spelling is disparaging." In March 2002, he posted an article on his Web site about a spat between the Philadelphia rappers

Shortyo and Beanie Siegel. Shortyo, who is white, refused to retract his use of the N word in a rap he created to ridicule Siegel, who is black. He told Davey D that he used the n-i-g-g-a version of the term, which, in his opinion, is merely slang and nothing more. According to a very skeptical Davey D, Shortyo "emphatically insisted that he is not a racist and he did not want to send out the wrong message." Jennifer Lopez, who is Puerto Rican, offered a similar defense when she was chastised for using the N word in "I'm Real," a hit song released in July 2001. Davey D predicts that future entanglements stemming from the two spellings will surely follow, complicating everything from racial harassment complaints to court proceedings involving hate crimes.

Tupac Shakur, the celebrated gangsta rapper who continues to attract a huge following several years after his violent death, devised an unusual attempt to give "nigga" a positive spin. N-I-G-G-A, he said, was an acronym for Never Ignorant and Getting Goals Accomplished. To my knowledge, few if any of his followers have endorsed his proposed innovation. Perhaps Tupac's effort, like Bernie Mac's revisionist comment quoted at the beginning of this chapter, was prompted by that same irrational mixture of attraction and repulsion that many African Americans feel toward the unlikeliest of words. As with so many other tensions animating our hard and tedious journey on this storied continent, the roots of those conflicting impulses can likely be found in W.E.B. Du Bois's durable concept of double-consciousness. "One ever feels his twoness — an American, a Negro; two souls, two thoughts, two unreconciled strivings; two warring ideals in one dark body, whose dogged strength alone keeps it from being torn asunder." It makes sense if you think about it: Why wouldn't our language also reflect that bifurcated vision?

WITTGENSTEIN'S LABYRINTH

The new spelling has continued to loosen the inhibitions of non-blacks, who apparently feel free to write or utter the N word in the name of comedy or camaraderie, even though their approaches are more likely to produce confusion. The ever-watchful Davey D has reported receiving "letters from white kids who tried to explain that they only use the word when they rap."

Ongoing attempts to tinker with the N word will undoubtedly yield new and unpredictable consequences, the very thought of which brings to mind Wittgenstein's labyrinth. Wittgenstein described language as a maze: "You approach from one side and know your way about: you approach the same place from another side and no longer know your way about." If we follow the N word into the labyrinth, where will it lead?

It may point the way to outlandish conceits: the convicted white traitor John Walker Lindh, for example, who as a teen was fond of posing on the Internet as an African American. "It [the N word] has, for hundreds of years been a label put on us by Caucasians," he once posted, "and because of the weight it carries with it, I never use it myself." It may lead to movies like Larry Clark's *Kids*, a 1995 film in which white and Latino adolescents sling "nigger" among themselves with a breezy lack of concern and nary a nod to the possibility of offense.

Or it could lead to the humor Web site Onion.com, which has parodied hip-hop cosmology in an article headlined "God Finally Gives Shout-Out Back to All His Niggaz: "'Right about now, I want to send a shout-out to each and every nigga who's shown Me love through the years,' said the Lord, His booming voice descending from Heaven." Later God is quoted giving a ghetto-fabulous blessing: "All y'all niggaz, y'all be My niggaz."

It can lead to approval. For Dave Chappelle, non-black usage of the N word is just another convincing demonstration of the dominance of black culture. "I love the irony of it," he said. "Every time I hear one white kid call another white kid 'nigger,' it makes me smile. And I think that it might be one of the best things that's happened to race relations in quite a long time." As much as I admire Chappelle, I can't help wondering if, say, an Asian-American man would be similarly encouraged by the sight of one black kid calling another black kid a "gook" or a "jap." Would he see the exchange as a sign of racial progress?

It can lead to vigilance. Raye Richardson, a bookstore owner in the Bay Area, told *Savoy* magazine: "I don't give white people the right to use the word until they clean up the conditions they made that attempted to relegate me to a nonhuman status. I believe racial equality will make the word powerless. At that time, yes, but until that time, don't even say it. You have not earned the right."

It can lead to indignation. A'Lelia Bundles, an African American reviewing Edward Ball's *Sweet Hell Inside* for the *New York Times,* took issue with the white author's alleged fascination with the term "nigger rich." She explained that it is "used ironically among some middle-class African-Americans to describe their affluence relative to truly wealthy whites and much poorer whites and blacks." But, she wrote, "one wishes he had provided more context in his explanation of the phrase and employed more editorial sensitivity by not using it as a section title."

It can lead to shock, as it did for David Sylvester, an African American from Philadelphia. Bicycling across Africa in 2004 to raise money for a memorial scholarship fund, he encountered a hip-hop clothing store in Lilongwe, Malawi, called Niggers. When he asked the two black male proprietors about the name, they responded to his American accent. One of them thumped his chest proudly, Sylvester recalled, and said, "P-Diddy New York City! We are the niggers!"

Deeply disturbed by the incident, Sylvester wrote an essay about it and sent it to thirty–five friends on the Internet. They passed it along to others, and Sylvester soon received 600 responses from all over the globe. "I rode over 12,000 miles on two continents through 15 states and 13 countries and broke two bikes in the process to get to a store in Africa called Niggers," Sylvester lamented in his essay. He went on to blame himself and other African Americans who have casually allowed the N word to enter everyday discourse. "I was wrong. We are wrong," he contended. "There is no justification for an infraction of this magnitude. The word and the sentiment behind it are flat out wrong. We have denigrated and degraded ourselves to the point that our backwards mindset has spread like a cancer and infected our source, our brothers, our sisters, our Mother Land."

It can lead to unexpected encounters. Writing in the November 1999 issue of the *Idaho Observer,* an antifederalist paper, the white editorial writer Hari Heath presented a bold proclamation. "Times have changed and we need a new definition for nigger," he declared. "It ain't about black and white any more. . . . 'Nigger,' under a new definition for our current times, is any one who files a 1040 form."

It can also lead right back to the ugliness we started with. The tenuous present met the irresistible past in Heath, who couldn't conclude his column without inserting a bit of racist badinage: "We is all niggers now. Dat's right, whitey, yo got chains an shackles keeping yo down, an yo is such a fool dey got you thinking it's jewelry!"

To exhibit any flexibility about the slur is to risk getting lost and frustrated, which is probably why members of the N word Eradication Movement have adopted a zero-tolerance platform. Rather than wander through the blind alleys and hairpin turns of the labyrinth, they'd prefer to step outside its boundaries and blow the whole thing up. The movement's call for total elimination seems perilously narrow to me. It doesn't include an explanation of how our artists and scholars can tell our story — the American story — without the N word. Should the work of artists such as Stevie Wonder, Faith Ringgold, and yes, N.W.A. — all of whom have skillfully used the epithet — be summarily dismissed because they failed to meet such strict criteria or would they be grandfathered in?

To most observers, those who oppose any use of the N word are wasting time and energy on a quixotic campaign that distracts us from other issues that could benefit from organized activism. George Orwell would disagree. In "Politics and the English Language," he wrote that "the decadence of our language is probably curable. Those who deny this would argue, if they produced an argument at all, that language merely reflects existing social conditions, and that we cannot influence its development by any direct tinkering with words and constructions. So far as the general tone or spirit of a language goes, this may be true, but it is not true in detail. *Silly words and expressions have often disappeared, not through any evolutionary process but owing to the conscious action of a minority*" (emphasis mine).

His point is well taken, but the conscious action to which he alludes would require something close to unanimity among blacks, a seemingly insurmountable obstacle given the dramatic diversity of black reactions to the N word. I cannot imagine, for instance, Jay-Z and DMX joining an effort to rid the world of "nigger" or "nigga." But I will never say never because I'm aware that any forecast made while navigating the American racial landscape is a foolhardy exercise. The ground has been known to shift without warning, forming fissures capable of opening up and swallowing boulders whole. When the dust clears, fertile vistas are sometimes revealed where rocky, unyielding terrain had once stretched toward the horizon. For example, twenty years ago, could anyone have predicted that the earth would move enough to enable the stern visage of Malcolm X — once the most reviled black man in America — to stare back at us from a postage stamp?

PRIVATE SPEECH, PUBLIC SPEECH

"Language is also a place of struggle," bell hooks reminds us. Ultimately, struggles involving the N word and other forms of toxic language become intensely personal conflicts, waged and decided within our individual selves. Alone with our thoughts, impulses, and emotions, we are at liberty to weigh the arguments and make a choice at a protective remove from the clamor and heat of Orwellian crusades. The primacy of individual choice and the esteem with which we Americans regard freedom of expression complicates our attitudes toward the N word. Like most of us, I embrace the sanctity of personal space. The thought of language police (or any other kind of police) patrolling our kitchens, bedrooms, and parlors for evidence of rude chatter chills me to my marrow. No speech is improper under one's own roof.

My concern is with the public square, where I believe the N word and other profane expressions have no rightful place. Out in public is where we depend on polite speech, in the words of the linguist Edward Sapir, to "act as a socializing and uniforming force." In a public space, say on a subway train, I should not expect my fellow commuters' tacit permission to assault their ears with "nigger"-laden speech any more than I should expect their acceptance of my shouting into a cell phone or scrawling obscenities on the windows and seats. But my obligations to others regarding civility and decency end at my doorstep, where I'm free to enter and sing along with my Ja Rule CDs as exuberantly as I please. Conversely, if you are white, whether you refer to me as a "nigger" when you're at home is of little consequence to me. Unlike blacks who wonder how commonly the term is used among white people when there are no black people around, or Mos Def, whose song "Mr. Nigga" voices the suspicion that whites who refrain from public utterances of the N word will "say it out loud again / When they deal with their close associates and friends," I'm willing to acknowledge a distinction between private speech and public behavior.

Abraham Lincoln reportedly was fond of telling "nigger" jokes in private. In public he issued the Emancipation Proclamation. Audiotapes confirm that Lyndon Johnson frequently spoke of "niggers" in private conversations. In public he presided over civil rights legislation that helped transform the daily lives of black Americans. Talking privately with Alex Haley, Malcolm X expressed his disgust with his former associates by denouncing them as "niggers." In public he demonstrated by example the importance of blacks conducting themselves with courage and dignity. "A man may have as bad a heart as he chooses," said Oliver Wendell Holmes Jr., "if his conduct is within the rules." It seems to me that the same reasoning should apply to language.

REMEMBERING

As we have noted, most whites now adhere to post–civil rights notions of public decorum, while increasing numbers of blacks — especially younger ones — go about blissfully heedless of them. Their fondness for calling one another "nigger" (ostensibly in the spirit of friendship or defiance) marks what Ralph Ellison would call "an odd swing of the cultural tide." One of the most curious paradoxes of the past few decades is the phenomenon of blacks, only recently allowed to romp freely in a language that has often betrayed them, dallying with that language in a way that threatens the legacy of all those whose words and deeds challenged the national narrative — those whose efforts, as I suggested earlier, wrote black Americans into existence.

I suppose there's nothing wrong with attempting, however erratically, to transform a word that has so long demeaned us. What's more troubling is the lack of imagination such attempts seem to suggest. Our slave ancestors made the most of limited means when they prepared meals from pork entrails deemed inedible by the whites they served; now, in the twenty-first century, to subsist on our former masters' cast-off language — even in the name of revising it — strikes me as the opposite of resourcefulness. Our modern vocabularies, unlike the empty larders of slaves, are well stocked.

Some have argued in defense of the N word that the gratuitous use of it may be ill-considered and inappropriate, but it is not illegal and therefore should be tolerated as one would a boor who repeats the same tiresome anecdote at every cocktail party he attends. This reasoning may work for some. But for me, even more significant than the law and the freedoms it guarantees is the purposeful example of my forebears. It is on their instructive standard that I attempt to model my own conduct, in and out of doors.

When Lemuel Haynes composed "Liberty Further Extended" in 1776, he wrote: "I think it not hyperbolical to affirm, that even an African, has Equally as good a right to his Liberty in common with Englishmen." He made no mention of "niggers." When David Walker published his remarkable *Appeal* in 1829, he addressed it to "my dearly beloved Brethren and Fellow Citizens." He did not mention "niggers." When W.E.B. Du Bois published his landmark collection of essays in 1903, he called it *The Souls of Black Folk* — not "niggers." When Marcus Garvey formed his organization in 1916, he called it the Universal Negro Improvement Association. He made no mention of "niggers." In his speech at the March on Washington in 1963, Martin Luther King Jr. said, "America has given the Negro people a bad check"; he did not say America has given "niggers" a bad check. A year later, Malcolm X began his "Ballot or the Bullet" speech with a greeting to "Brothers and Sisters and Friends," not "niggers" and friends. In her 1971 lecture at Tougaloo College, Fannie Lou Hamer urged, "Stand up, black men, this nation needs you." She did not say "Stand up, niggers."

"Africans." "Negroes." "Black men." "Brothers." "Sisters." "Fellow Citizens." Each falls off the tongue with ease. None is hard to pronounce.

If the epic struggle of blacks in the United States — a quest that the national narrative of white supremacy has often tried to distort — teaches me anything, it is that there is no god higher than history. To ignore its commandments seems not only blasphemous but also counterproductive.

DREAMING WORLDS

"Negro, Seen in Dream, Causes Death of Girl." So screamed a headline in the *Atlanta Constitution* during the hysterical September of 1906. I repeat it here to illustrate the space that the stereotypical monstrous black male has often occupied in the collective white American imagination. The easy credibility of Caucasian killers such as Charles Stuart, a Bostonian who in 1989 murdered his pregnant wife and blamed it on a mythical black man, and Susan Smith, who in 1994 attributed the drowning deaths of her children to a nonexistent black carjacker, demonstrates the extent to which imaginary black marauders still stalk the dark alleys of the Caucasian mind. By no means do they wander there alone: they keep strange company with the legion of counterimages that have recently jostled into view of newscasters and CEOs, of college presidents and secretaries of state — but few if any of those latecomers has yet shown the power to provoke equally strong, durable, and dramatic responses.

Because we are a vastly outnumbered minority, our image as African Americans will always be to some extent determined by the majority's capacity and willingness to evolve beyond its hallucinatory and crippling prejudices. Even so, it is the African-American imagination that concerns me most. What of our capacity to imagine? I for one can still visualize the "nigger," and perhaps because I'm a man, I usually see him as a man, odious and shiftless, violent and stupid, contemptuous of black women and obsessed with white ones — a self-hating, devilish phantom whose footsteps can still be heard as we tread through the tentative early years of the twenty-first century. Like the "nigger" in that dead girl's dream, he continues to haunt my sleep.

"The American image of the Negro lives also in the Negro's heart," James Baldwin observed, "and when he has surrendered to this image life has no other possible reality." While I don't share Baldwin's extreme pessimism, I'm drawn to his evocation of "surrender." As we have seen, "nigger" rightly belongs to the realms of art, scholarship, journalism, and history, none of which can be effectively pursued without critically engaging the word. For us ordinary folk, however, mindlessly uttering the epithet may very well be a form of giving in. As long as we embrace the derogatory language that has long accompanied and abetted our systematic dehumanization, we shackle ourselves to those corrupt white delusions — and their attendant false story of our struggle in the United States. Throwing off those shackles would at least free us to stake a claim to an independent imagination.

"To imagine a language is to imagine a way of life," Wittgenstein wrote.

"I dream a world," wrote Langston Hughes. I entertain similar visions in which the language we use helps us determine a new and invigorating reality. I imagine a way of life derived from our purest, wisest, fiercely loving selves. I dream of a world where "nigger" no longer roams, confined instead to the fetid white fantasy land where he was born.

Epilogue

> We African Americans are perceived as acceptable in a token amount, toxic beyond it. This is a devastating commentary on the majority's perception of our nature.
>
> — Arthur Ashe, 1992

"OUR COUNTRY SHALL be peopled," Patrick Henry observed, "shall it be with Europeans or with Africans?" As we noted in the first chapter, Henry spoke for many of his peers when he expressed concern that blacks would someday outnumber them. They needn't have worried: a few years into the twenty-first century, African Americans make up a little more than twelve percent of the U.S. population. However, our outsize public image — or our image in the minds of whites — often leads whites to overestimate our numbers. In national polls, some whites estimate that blacks make up as much as fifty percent of the populace.

This exaggerated perception doubtless also derives in part from African Americans' disproportionate influence on many aspects of popular culture, ranging from movies, television, and popular music to the wide world of sports. Bolstered also by the unprecedented explosion in technology that makes popular culture more ubiquitous and accessible than ever, black athletes and entertainers are aggressively pursuing roles that would have been unthinkable even a mere thirty years ago. Whereas, for example, black sports stars and celebrities were routinely shut out of lucrative endorsement deals in the past, Michael Jordan and Tiger Woods are the dominant product pitchmen of recent years.

In the world of big-screen entertainment, the lascivious, dim-witted Gus of *The Birth of a Nation* has given way to black characters played by genuine black actors, accepted and even embraced in heroic roles such as savior of the world (Will Smith in *Independence Day*) and ruler over all Creation (Morgan Freeman in *Bruce Almighty*).

The new mass media, while helping to perpetuate damaging images of African Americans, have often been used to counter the most virulent stereotypes. While Willie Horton and O. J. Simpson were exploited to sustain the old negative images in the 1980s and '90s, respectively, during that same period blacks in very disparate fields emerged to set forth new images of profound impact. In addition to celebrity endorsers and box office champions, Oprah Winfrey and Jesse Jackson were just two of the prominent blacks who made masterful use of television exposure. Winfrey parlayed her talk show popularity into profitable forays in movie and theater productions and magazine publishing, resulting in her being nicknamed "the queen of all media." While Jackson's media moment was considerably briefer, it remains historically significant. His speech at the 1988 Democratic convention elevated his own image as a statesman of stature and skill and helped paved the way for future political aspirants on both sides of the political divide, including Condoleezza Rice, Colin Powell, and Barack Obama. Obama's own turn in the spotlight at the 2004 Democratic convention promoted a new image of wise, committed black leadership capable of organizing and speaking on behalf of all Americans.

During the civil rights era, black visionaries had taken similar advantage of the advent of the mass media to promote the image of nonviolent, spiritually inclined seekers of justice maintaining their dignity and courage in the face of violence and madness. The televised pictures of peaceful, patient African Americans in their Sunday best, forthrightly arrayed against violent, ragtag, and raging mobs of whites, changed hearts and minds and brought about a permanent, *significant* transformation of American culture.

Civil rights activists claimed the moral high ground, a meaningful stance in a nation that has always fancied itself as morally astute, despite a bloody and hypocritical history that suggests a far less noble existence. The public profile of the civil rights vanguard was not adopted by succeeding generations of African Americans, who kept alive the notion of creative rebellion but dressed it up in dramatically different clothing. Somewhere along the line, the romantic rebel in the Bigger Thomas–Stokely Carmichael–Sweet Sweetback tradition became a "gangsta," a self-absorbed sellout who peddles everything from cognac to sneakers to vitamin water while pushing tall tales of sex, drugs, and destruction. While it is true that Jordan, Woods, and other post–civil rights celebrities have carefully nurtured clean-cut personae reminiscent of the marchers of yesteryear, they have done so at the risk of losing credibility in the eyes of their African-American peers. The apparent abandonment of the high ground, exacerbated by the 24-7 display of choreographed black dysfunction through cable television, cell phone, ring tone, iPod, and Web site, elevates a misbegotten philosophy of "street-cred" nihilism while obscuring African Americans who do their utmost to uphold the finest traditions of our past. The forces of uplift and excellence continue their steady tread, but beneath the shadow of a commoditized "gangsta" culture that both titillates mainstream audiences and keeps alive the very images of black depravity that white supremacy feeds on.

Retreat from the high ground probably can also be attributed in part to moral fatigue, weariness derived from staggering under the load of conscientious example — of proving, in the words of Martin Luther King Jr., that "almost always, the creative dedicated minority has made the world better."

Centuries of demonstrating to the majority culture that Americans can conduct themselves with decorum, intelligence, and faith in building a community based on fairness, compassion, and mutual trust is enough to wear out any minority group. That's no excuse for corrupt and immoral behavior, but it must at least be considered.

Some blacks have also acknowledged a feeling that nothing can be done to change whites' view of African Americans; hence there is nothing wrong with giving in and cashing in. That kind of thinking, of course, is a willful disregard of history and a failure to recognize that a minority group so overwhelmingly outnumbered will always depend at least partly on the vision and imagination of the majority; this is a distasteful but unavoidable reality. The failure to acknowledge it results in exuberantly dysfunctional conduct, best exemplified by "gangsta" culture that celebrates underachievement and criminality; the popularity of its products — both inside and outside black communities — complicates our measured rise.

The stagnation of African-American images can't be blamed on thug love alone. Ironically, black entrepreneurs have also played a key role. In recent years, we have witnessed a precipitous descent from the brave pioneering of our earliest media purveyors, savvy, activist businessmen such as John Russwurm and Samuel Cornish, the founders of *Freedom's Journal,* and Frederick Douglass and Martin Delany, the founders of *The North Star.* Consider the sordid example of Robert Johnson's Black Entertainment Television. Aside from its few substantive shows (e.g., *Lead Story* and the occasional business show), its lurid, sexist programming mostly spat in the face of those illustrious ancestors. While Johnson accumulated his wealth and embodied a heretofore radical concept — the fruition of Booker T. Washington's dream — the black billionaire, he did so by demeaning blacks and especially black women. If white-operated networks had persisted in unleashing so many derogatory images, they would have attracted legions of placard-bearing black protesters. Under new, and ironically white, ownership, BET may someday realize its vast potential.

THE MOSAIC

With the number of Latinos in the United States steadily increasing, the character of racial conflict will undoubtedly change. However, given the long history of black-white discord and the deeply rooted nature of hostility against blacks, it's difficult to predict the extent of the newcomers' impact. The September 11, 2001, terrorist attack also confounded blacks' traditional place as the target of white racism by allowing men of Arab extraction to displace African-American males as the most reviled in the culture. With the weight of history on their backs, few black observers dare hope that such a historic shift — despite its intensity — will be anything more than temporary.

THE TWO TWONESSES

Far more durable is the majority culture's invocation of "timeless American values," such as individual rights, religious freedom, and equal justice — and its simultaneous ignorance of other traditional American traits, such as greed, duplicity, and intolerance. This contradiction at the core of our nation, stretching back to its beginning, derives from the double-consciousness of whites. Just as blacks struggle with the "twoness" that Du Bois spoke of, white society often wrestles with similarly split and unreconciled strivings, between a belief in a genuine democracy in which talent, energy, and initiative lead to power and privilege — and a subtle yet tenacious clinging to another tradition, which holds that whites are superior and entitled to the best of America's bounty while others most emphatically are not. Despite some blacks' relatively recent embrace of detrimental behavior, African-Americans' ability to overcome the effects of white supremacy still depends as much if not more on whites' willingness to resolve their own "warring ideals." In the meantime, we continue our own epic struggle, constructing narratives to oppose the toxic mythology that still hinders our striving, writing ourselves into existence.

NOTES

SELECTED BIBLIOGRAPHY

INDEX

Notes

Introduction

2   "failure of nerve": Ralph Ellison, *The Collected Essays* (New York: The Modern Library, 1995), 777.

    "personal disrespect": W.E.B. Du Bois, *The Souls of Black Folk* (New York: Penguin Books, 1996), 10.

3   "radiate a qualifying influence": Ellison, *The Collected Essays,* 776.

1. Founding Fictions

10   However, little other than Sewall's discourse: Mason Lowance, ed., *Against Slavery: An Abolitionist Reader* (New York: Penguin, 2000), 11. Lowance wrote, "The full text of *The Selling of Joseph* [Sewall's best-known writing], shows clearly that Sewall condemned chattel slavery, however, it also reveals a writer who was familiar with contemporary race theory and who accepted the inherent inferiority of the Negro to the white."

    Merchant Nicholas Crisp: Hugh Thomas, *The Slave Trade* (New York: Simon & Schuster, 1997), 176.

    In 1651: Ibid., 198.

11   Others, most notably: J. E. Lighter, ed., *Random House Historical Dictionary of American Slang* (New York: Random House, 1994), 657.

    "I am one of those": Ignatius Sancho, *Letters of the Late Ignatius Sancho, An African* (New York: Penguin, 1998), 73.

    The rebel clowns: Gail Buckley, *American Patriots: The Story of Blacks in the Military from the Revolution to Desert Storm* (New York: Random House, 2001), 21.

    An item in the *Virginia Gazette:* Winthrop Jordan, *White over Black: American Attitudes Toward the Negro, 1550–1812* (Baltimore: Penguin, 1969), 303.

    By then it was reasonable: Hugh Rawson, *Wicked Words: A Treasury of*

Curses, Insults, Put-Downs, and Other Formerly Unprintable Terms from Anglo-Saxon Times to the Present (New York: Crown, 1989), 266.

12 He speculated that Africans': Winthrop Jordan, *The White Man's Burden: Historical Origins of Racism in the United States* (New York: Oxford University Press, 1974), 9.

"Blackness had become": Jordan, *White over Black*, 258.

13 In 1705, Virginia assembled: Robin D. G. Kelley and Earl Lewis, *To Make Our World Anew: A History of African Americans* (New York: Oxford University Press, 2000), 73. Slave codes were enacted in northern colonies as well. A law passed in 1731 forbade any "Negro, Mulatto or Indian slave" older than fourteen to go outside at night without a lantern. The penalty for breaking the law was up to forty lashes at a public whipping post.

15 Rebuffed, they returned: Ira Berlin, *Many Thousands Gone: The First Two Centuries of Slavery in North America* (Cambridge, Mass.: Harvard University Press, 1998), 193. One wonders if Massachusetts patriots had referred to their mistreatment at the hands of the king as a form of slavery, as had George Washington, George Mason, and other prominent Virginians. This surely would have struck the petitioners as the most tragic of ironies.

16 "Our country shall be peopled": Jordan, *White over Black*, 544.

17 To make matters worse: Eric Foner, *The Story of American Freedom* (New York: W. W. Norton, 1998), 16.

18 Charleston fell soon after: Buckley, *American Patriots*, 27.

2. *Niggerology, Part 1*

20 "the logic of subordination": Berlin, *Many Thousands Gone*, 9.

"the most influential utterances": Jordan, *White over Black*, xii.

21 "a staunch believer": Joseph Ellis, *American Sphinx: The Character of Thomas Jefferson* (New York: Knopf, 1998), 297.

22 "more ardent after their female": Thomas Jefferson, *Notes on the State of Virginia* (New York: Penguin, 1999), 146.

23 "Where Mr. Jefferson learnt": Jordan, *White over Black*, 496–504.

"That the PENIS": Ibid., 501.

24 Back in the late eighteenth century: Foner, *Story of American Freedom*, 34.

"Their griefs are transient": Jefferson, *Notes*, 146.

25 At Monticello he surrounded: Ellis, *American Sphinx*, 149–50.

"the slaveholder watches every move": Kelley and Lewis, *To Make Our World Anew*, 180.

All of these shortcomings: Jefferson, *Notes*, 147.

26 most extensive private library: Guy McElroy. *Facing History: The Black Image in American Art, 1710–1940* (San Francisco: Bedford Arts, 1990), xxx.

In his explanatory comments accompanying the *Notes,* Frank Shuffelton
wrote that Jefferson owned copies of Wheatley's and Sancho's books.

26 By the time *Notes* was published: William L. Andrews. *African American Biography: A Collection of Critical Essays* (Englewood Cliffs, N.J.: Prentice
Hall, 1993), 19. In addition to the authors mentioned above, Henry Louis
Gates Jr. identifies Juan Latino, Jacobus Capitein, and Wilhelm Amo as
blacks who published during this period.

"If Oppression be so hard to bear": Jordan, *White over Black,* 273.

27 "Slavery is so foreign": Ibid., 281.

"brutish, ignorant, idle": Ibid. (quoting Edward Long).

"from the first dawn of reason": Ibid., 276.

28 the very apogee of irony: Don Higginbotham et al. *George Washington Re-
considered* (Charlottesville: Univ. Press of Virginia, 2001).

At Monticello: Rawson, *Wicked Words,* 59.

"an-Other Negro": McElroy, *Facing History,* xxix.

29 "The earliest plays": Sterling Brown, *Negro Poetry and Drama and the Negro in American Fiction* (New York: Atheneum, 1969), 104.

"were more widely read": Jordan, *White over Black,* 429.

courtesy of the three-fifths compromise: Foner, *Story of American Freedom,*
44. Foner wrote: "Had three-fifths of the South's slaves not been counted in
apportioning electoral votes, John Adams would have won reelection in
1800."

3. No Place to Be Somebody

34 As for blacks mixing: Jordan, *White over Black,* 568.

It all amounted: George M. Fredrickson, *The Black Image in the White
Mind: The Debate on Afro-American Character and Destiny, 1817–1914* (Hanover, N.H.: Wesleyan University Press, 1987), 41.

Through the ideology of manifest destiny: Foner, *Story of American Freedom,* 77.

35 during the 1830s: Fredrickson, *Black Image in the White Mind,* 47.

36 "If the free states have passed no law": Deirdre Mullane, ed., *Crossing the
Danger Water: Three Hundred Years of African-American Writing* (New
York: Anchor Books, 1993), 70.

"The justification for [racial] discrimination": Leon F. Litwack, *North of
Slavery: The Negro in the Free States, 1790–1860* (Chicago: University of Chicago Press, 1961), viii.

"there does not exist": Ibid., 39.

37 "The prejudice of race": Alexis De Tocqueville, *Democracy in America* (Indianapolis: Hackett, 2000), 155. It must be said, however, that Tocqueville

was hard on Southerners as well. In his view, the pro-slavery legislation of the Southern states presented "a kind of unprecedented atrocity, which by itself shows some profound disturbance in the laws of humanity."

37 "the heaviest of curses": Litwack, *North of Slavery*, 40, 169.
"the bondman is disfranchised": Mullane, *Crossing the Danger Water*, 124.
Those stereotypes prevailed: Litwack, *North of Slavery*, 157, 196.

38 "have a little of the plantation speech": Ibid., 225.

39 "pseudoscientific racism or its equivalent": Fredrickson, xviii.
These and similar comments: Litwack, *North of Slavery*, 225.
"branded by the hand of nature": Ibid., 224.

40 "If they cowered": Sterling Stuckey, *Going Through the Storm: The Influence of African American Art in History* (New York: Oxford University Press, 1994), 16.
"those who rose above depravity": Litwack, *North of Slavery*, 103.
"a most disastrous" effect: Ibid., 98.

41 "a simple representation of facts": Mullane, *Crossing the Danger Water*, 65.
"Negroes often reproached": Litwack, *North of Slavery*, 186.
"Neber mind him, Sa": Ibid., 182.

42 "no contemptuous intonation": Stuckey, *Going Through the Storm*, 10.
"Look, missis!": Simmons, *Star-Spangled Eden*, 84.
"with glowing affection": Stuckey, *Going Through the Storm*, 10.

43 "Whites might distinguish": Litwack, *North of Slavery*, 179.

4. Niggerology, Part 2

45 "the most degraded of human races": Stephen Jay Gould, *The Mismeasure of Man* (New York: W. W. Norton, 1981), 36.
"the brain of the Bushman": Ibid.
"The break will be then rendered": Ibid.
"'hardliners' held that blacks": Ibid.

46 Some Ethiopian tribes: William Stanton, *The Leopard's Spots: Scientific Attitudes Toward Race in America, 1815–1859* (Chicago: University of Chicago Press, 1960), 41.
In Maine, for instance: Litwack, *North of Slavery*, 41.

47 "a curse instead of a blessing": Stanton, *Leopard's Spots*, 61.
"those primeval attributes of mind": Ibid., 41.

48 "polygenism is the more radical theory": Louis Menand, *The Metaphysical Club: A Story of Ideas in America* (New York: Farrar, Straus, 2001), 105.
"precious poor opinion of niggers": Stanton, *Leopard's Spots*, 82, 193.

49 Their main opponent: Gould, *Mismeasure of Man*, 70.
"two distinct species": Stanton, *Leopard's Spots*, 67.

50 "the angry and senseless discussions": Ibid., 81.

50 "the brain of the Negro": Ibid., 100.
At the time, however: Menand, *Metaphysical Club*, 103.
51 "His later support": Gould, *Mismeasure of Man*, 44–47.
A legitimate expert: Menand, *Metaphysical Club*, 99.
"the public mind is at present": Stanton, *Leopard's Spots*, p. 122.
Immediately following his address: Ibid., 148.
"probably no scientific man": Gould, *Mismeasure of Man*, 51.
"For the present": Stanton, *Leopard's Spots*, 144.
52 Though it was essentially: Ibid., 163.
"exercise a great influence": Ibid., 164.
Squier was right: Gould, *Mismeasure of Man*, 36; Menand, *Metaphysical Club*, 111.
He made it clear: Stanton, *Leopard's Spots*, 172.
Gobineau's book: Fredrickson, *Black Image in the White Mind*, 69.
In 1857: Menand, *Metaphysical Club*, 112.
53 "The grounds I have taken": Fredrickson, *Black Image in the White Mind*, 85.
Therefore, he deduced: Stanton, *Leopard's Spots*, 151.
54 Slaves with this bizarre: Gould, *Mismeasure of Man*, 71.
The failure of Cartwright's Negro: Fredrickson, *Black Image in the White Mind*, 87.

5. Life Among the Lowly

55 "the first full-length portrait": Catherine Juanita Starke, *Black Portraiture in American Fiction: Stock Characters, Archetypes, and Individuals* (New York: Basic, 1971), 31.
56 "The calves were neither before": Ibid.
distinct types of black characters: McElroy, *Facing History*, xxix.
57 "buxom, glistening, smooth-faced": Starke, *Black Portraiture*, 35.
Once seduced: Gould, *Mismeasure of Man*, 49.
Five million copies: Simmons, *Star-Spangled Eden*, 73.
"Scott had so large a hand": Ibid.
58 "swollen lips": Brown, *Negro in American Fiction*, 11.
59 "supported by the myth": Starke, *Black Portraiture*, 30.
"the grown-up slaves": Brown, *Negro in American Fiction*, 18.
"I never meet a Negro": Ibid., 19.
"is in his moral constitution": Starke, *Black Portraiture*, 30.
60 "wrinkled decrepit old men": Brown, *Negro in American Fiction*, 19.
"'Tis onpossible, maussa": Ibid., 7.
"Wha da debbil dat!": Starke, *Black Portraiture*, 46.
"Let every darkey look his best": Ibid., 42.

61 A revised edition: Brown, *Negro in American Fiction*, 32.

It quickly sold: Ibid., 35.

"He was a large, broad-chested": Harriet Beecher Stowe, *Uncle Tom's Cabin* (New York: New American Library, 1998), 26.

62 "Mas'r always found me": Starke, *Black Portraiture*, 108.

"I's willin' to lay down my life": Ibid., 109.

"What a fuss": Stowe, *Uncle Tom's Cabin*, 454.

63 In her preface: Lowance, *Against Slavery*, 298.

"I never dreamed": Brown, *Negro in American Fiction*, 24.

An author's note: Stowe, *Uncle Tom's Cabin*, 475.

69 "some novelists depart": Brown, *Negro in American Fiction*, 45.

"Mrs. Stowe showed": Ibid., 38.

"Apart from her lively procession": James Baldwin, *Notes of a Native Son* (Boston: Beacon Press, 1984), 14–16.

70 "that good, faithful creature": Stowe, *Uncle Tom's Cabin*, 38–39.

"the Negro mind": Ibid., 34.

"the soft, impressible nature": Ibid., 160.

"There is no more use": Ibid., 82.

71 "Certainly they will": Ibid., 197.

By 1862: Lowance, *Against Slavery*, 292.

6. Jim Crow and Company

72 "the boy commenced": Stowe, *Uncle Tom's Cabin*, 7.

73 "the most imperturbable": Ibid., 83.

"The black, glassy eyes": Ibid., 259.

"they glorified the Negro's": Brown, *Negro in American Fiction*, 109.

"While Uncle Tom": Eric Lott, *Love & Theft: Blackface Minstrelsy and the American Working Class* (New York: Oxford Univ. Press, 1995), 217.

74 "My Old Kentucky Home": Lowance, *Against Slavery*, 291.

"they have but one coat": Lott, *Love & Theft*, 120.

"addicted to the use of big words": Brown, *Negro in American Fiction*, 106.

75 "Dar's dandy niggers": William J. Mahar, *Behind the Burnt Cork Mask* (Urbana: Univ. of Illinois Press, 1999), 211.

76 "sports and pastimes": Ibid., 337.

"straight-up faux anthropology": W. T. Lhamon Jr., *Raising Cain: Blackface Performance from Jim Crow to Hip Hop* (Cambridge, Mass.: Harvard Univ. Press, 1998), 31.

"became gibberish": Brown, *Negro in American Fiction*, 106.

"went hand in hand with another linguistic innovation": Shane White,

Stories of Black Freedom in Black New York (Cambridge, Mass.: Harvard Univ. Press, 2002), 109.

76 "Den yoa see de meanin": Mahar, *Behind the Burnt Cork Mask*, 81.

77 "To be called an 'Irishman'": Litwack, *North of Slavery*, 163.
"Antebellum native whites": Lott, *Love & Theft*, 71.
"Down with the Nagurs!": Litwack, *North of Slavery*, 163.
"niggerology": Lott, *Love & Theft*, 96.

78 "imitating the motions of birds": Bessie Jones and Bess Lomax Hawes, *Step It Down: Games, Plays, Songs, and Stories from the Afro-American Heritage* (New York: Harper & Row, 1972), 55.
"stirred men with a mighty power": W.E.B. Du Bois, *The Souls of Black Folk* (New York: Penguin Books, 1996), 205.
"sneaked onto the lips": Lhamon, *Raising Cain*, 39.

79 "I'm a full blooded niggar": Lott, *Love & Theft*, 23.
"crowded with offshoots, parodies": Ibid., 212, 215.

80 "veering between the devoted and the daft": Ibid., 217.
"Nigga in de Cornfield": Ibid., 218.
"Oh, I does hate a nigger": Ibid., 162.

81 "The best-loved songs": Alan Lomax, *The Folk Songs of North America* (Garden City, N.Y.: Dolphin Books, 1975), 81.
"an abject Negro": Brown, *Negro in American Fiction*, 85.

82 "Firth and Pond": Lott, *Love & Theft*, 171.

7. The World the War Made

85 "the language": Eric Foner, *The Story of American Freedom* (New York: W. W. Norton, 1998), 131.

86 "We want you damn niggers": Michael Lee Lanning, *The African-American Soldier: From Crispus Attucks to Colin Powell* (Secaucus, N.J.: Birch Lane Press, 1997), 34.
"This Department has no intention": Ibid.
"not only caught supposed fugitives": Louis Menand, *The Metaphysical Club: A Story of Ideas in America* (New York: Farrar, Straus, 2001), 39.
"What is to be done": William Stanton, *The Leopard's Spots: Scientific Attitudes Toward Race in America, 1815–1859* (Chicago: Univ. of Chicago Press, 1960), 187.

87 "I will be damned": Lerone Bennett Jr., "Did Lincoln Really Free the Slaves?" *Ebony* (February 2000).

88 "And I may as well remark": J. E. Lighter, *Random House Historical Dictionary of American Slang* (New York: Random House, 1994), 656.

88 "In *every respect*": John David Smith, *Black Soldiers in Blue*, (Chapel Hill: Univ. of North Carolina Press, 2002), 39.

"We don't want to fight": Ibid., 6.

"I never believed in niggers": Leon F. Litwack, *Been in the Storm So Long: The Aftermath of Slavery* (New York: Random House, 1980), 101.

"When this war is over":Smith, *Black Soldiers*, 10.

89 "Put those damn niggers": Lanning, *African-American Soldier*, 43.

"It is a War": Smith, *Black Soldiers*, 6.

"the shrine of the great nigger": Menand, *Metaphysical Club*, 48.

"I don't see why": Smith, *Black Soldiers*, 6.

90 "fighting against your master": Ibid., 154.

"had enemies in his rear": Ibid., 39.

"I have given the subject": Lanning, *African-American Soldier*, 46.

"There will be some black men": George M. Fredrickson, *The Black Image in the White Mind: The Debate on Afro-American Character and Destiny, 1817–1914* (Hanover, N.H.: Wesleyan Univ. Press, 1971), 168.

"The African race": Ibid., 124.

91 "Africans have more": Ibid., 164.

"The American Negroes": Lanning, *African-American Soldier*, 61.

92 "No sooner did": W.E.B. Du Bois, *The Souls of Black Folk* (New York: Penguin, 1996), 22.

"The nigger is going": Richard Wormser, *The Rise and Fall of Jim Crow* (New York: St. Martin's Press, 2003), 15.

In Texas: Eric Foner, *A Short History of Reconstruction, 1863–1877* (New York: Perennial Library, 1990), 95.

93 "without morals": Stanton, *Leopard's Spots*, 187.

94 "the negro is not": Fredrickson, *Black Image*, 191.

"We hold this to be a government": James G. Hollandsworth, *An Absolute Massacre: The New Orleans Race Riot of July 30, 1866* (Baton Rouge: Louisiana State Univ. Press, 2001), 33.

"semi-barbarous race": David W. Blight, *Race and Reunion: The Civil War in American Memory* (Cambridge, Mass.: Belknap Press, 2000), 101.

95 "I'm a Democrat": Mark Bauerlein, *Negrophobia: A Race Riot in Atlanta, 1906* (San Francisco: Encounter Books, 2001), 15.

"You niggers": Wormser, *Rise and Fall*, 29.

"Why is it": Ibid., 30.

"just the same as birds": Foner, *Short History*, 235.

96 "the slave went free": Ibid., 254.

"As the war": Philip S. Foner, *Frederick Douglass: Selected Speeches and Writings* (Chicago: Lawrence Hill Books, 1999), 657.

"White folks didn't": Wormser, *Rise and Fall*, 60.

97 "'What's that nigger'": Ibid., 75.
"The man who says": Guy McElroy, *Facing History: The Black Image in American Art, 1710–1940* (San Francisco: Bedford Arts, 1990), xxxii.
"The Confederacy": Blight, *Race and Reunion*, 311.
98 "For the first time": Hollandsworth, *Absolute Massacre*, 150.

8. Nigger Happy

99 "realism and custom": Sterling Brown, *Negro Poetry and Drama and the Negro in American Fiction* (New York: Atheneum, 1969), 62.
100 "the devoted slave": David W. Blight, *Race and Reunion: The Civil War in American Memory* (Cambridge, Mass.: Belknap Press, 2000), 220.
Songs and Sayings: Blight, *Race and Reunion*, 228.
"made to express admiration": Stowe, *Uncle Tom's Cabin*, xxii.
"Put a spellin'-book": Brown, *Negro in American Fiction*, 54.
"'Tain't wid niggers": Starke, *Black Portraiture*, 52.
101 "In virtually every": Blight, *Race and Reunion*, 222.
"an old Negro": Brown, *Negro in American Fiction*, 51.
"Dem wuz good ole times": Blight, *Race and Reunion*, 222.
"sentimental, imaginative": Ibid., 211.
102 "What American artist": Litwack, *North of Slavery*, 99.
103 "repeatedly as a trade name": Larry Vincent Buster, *The Art and History of Black Memorabilia* (New York: Clarkson Potter, 2000), 47.
105 "had ingrained in its imagination": Blight, *Race and Reunion*, 236.
106 "One night Tanner": Romare Bearden and Harry Henderson, *A History of African-American Artists: From 1792 to the Present* (New York: Pantheon, 1993), xi.
109 "the spoken idiom": Ralph Ellison, *Shadow and Act* (New York: Vintage, 1995), 51.
110 "It is sometimes said": Fredrickson, *Black Image in the White Mind*, 115.
111 "If one is not willing": Shelley Fisher Fishkin, *Lighting Out for the Territory: Reflections on Mark Twain and American Culture* (New York: Oxford Univ. Press, 1997), 143.
"First of all": Ibid., 100.
112 "the boldness and cleverness": Harriet E. Wilson, *Our Nig; or, Sketches from the Life of a Free Black* (New York: Vintage, 1983), xxvii.
"The book's title": Ibid., li.
113 "Git out, Pete": Ibid., 10.
"good enough for a nigger": Ibid., 26.
"religion was not meant": Ibid., 68.
"niggers are just like black snakes": Ibid., 88.

113 "discuss the prevalent opinion": Ibid., 7.
"Work as long as I can stand": Ibid., 75.
"watched by kidnappers": Ibid., 129.

114 "Dis nigger's too cute": Harriet Jacobs, *Incidents in the Life of a Slave Girl* (Mineola, N.Y.: Dover, 2001), 87.
"Dat nigger allers": Ibid., 93.
"I knowed de debbil": Ibid., 157.

115 "This trading in niggers": Ibid., 90.
"I admit": Ibid., 40.
"either do not sufficiently take": Menand, *Metaphysical Club*, 386.
"a venereal impulse": Mark Bauerlein, *Negrophobia: A Race Riot in Atlanta, 1906* (San Francisco: Encounter, 2001), 58.

116 "false beliefs": Blight, *Race and Reunion*, 139.

9. Different Times

120 "Until the South": Bauerlein, *Negrophobia*, 20.
"the thought of the older South": W.E.B. Du Bois. *The Souls of Black Folk* (New York: Penguin, 1996), 75.

121 "with freedom": Blight, *Race and Reunion*, 112.
"We took them": Bauerlein, *Negrophobia*, 58.

122 black sexual hunger: Ibid.
"necessitate our killing": Philip Dray. *At the Hands of Persons Unknown: The Lynching of Black America* (New York: Modern Library, 2002), 161.

123 "a dozen reported assaults": Ibid., 164.
"Oh, go home": Ibid., 165.
"the cumulative provocation": Bauerlein, *Negrophobia*, 177.
"no other remedy": Dray, *At the Hands*, 168–69.

124 "Wilson allowed various": Charles Paul Freund, "Dixiecrats Triumphant," *Reason Online* (March 2003).
"the recent episode": Dray, *At the Hands*, 199.

125 "They shot & yelled": Lisa Grunwald and Stephen J. Adler, *Letters of the Century: America, 1900–1999* (New York: Dial Press, 1999), 117.
The most notorious conflict: Dray, *At the Hands*, 255.

126 "There's an organization": Steven Barboza, *The African American Book of Values* (New York: Doubleday, 1998), 871.
"Sit down, niggers": Dray, *At the Hands*, 266.
"They had names": Jerry Zolten, *Great God A'Mighty!: The Dixie Hummingbirds Celebrating the Rise of Soul Gospel Music* (New York: Oxford Univ. Press, 2003), 54.

10. From House Niggers to Niggerati

131 The stage version: Bruce Chadwick, *The Reel Civil War: Mythmaking in American Film* (New York: Knopf, 2001), 98.

134 *The Clansman* takes place: Ibid., 120.

136 "strong and fleshy": Alexandra Ripley, *Scarlett* (New York: Warner, 1991), 13.

"Almost everything best about me": Alice Randall, *The Wind Done Gone* (Boston: Houghton Mifflin, 2001), 84.

137 "One way of looking": Ibid., 177.

"proved how much": Grace Elizabeth Hale, *Making Whiteness: The Culture of Segregation in the South, 1890–1940* (New York: Vintage, 1999), 263.

138 "when the bestseller": Kenneth Robert Janken, *White: The Biography of Walter White, Mr. NAACP* (New York: New Press, 2003), 117.

"it was considered bad form": David Levering Lewis, *When Harlem Was in Vogue* (New York: Penguin, 1997), 181.

"tired to death": Carl Van Vechten, *Nigger Heaven* (New York: Knopf, 1926), 26.

"While this informal": Ibid., 26.

"it seems strange": Jeffrey B. Perry, ed. *A Hubert Harrison Reader* (Middletown, Conn.: Wesleyan University Press, 2001), 341–42.

139 "drivel, pure and simple": Ibid., 350.

"My only regret": Emily Bernard, ed. *Remember Me to Harlem: The Letters of Langston Hughes and Carl Van Vechten, 1925–1964* (New York: Knopf, 2001), 41.

"an inspired moniker": Valerie Boyd, *Wrapped in Rainbows: The Life of Zora Neale Hurston* (New York: Scribner, 2002), 116.

"Niggerati Manor": Lewis, *When Harlem*, 193.

140 "P.S. How dare you": Carla Kaplan, *Zora Neale Hurston: A Life in Letters* (New York: Doubleday, 2002), 205.

"Christ is a Nigger": Gerald Early, ed. *Speech and Power: The African-American Essay and Its Cultural Content from Polemics to Pulpit, Vol. 1* (Hopewell, N.Y.: Ecco Press, 1992), 121–27.

"The situation is *easy*": Bernard, *Remember Me*, 46.

"the squalor": Lewis, *When Harlem*, 177.

"This love of drums": Van Vechten, *Nigger Heaven*, 90.

"with that exotic": Ibid., 163.

141 "The jazz band": Ibid., 212.

"Damn it, man": Lewis, *When Harlem*, 99.

all-black cinemas: Chadwick, *Reel Civil War*, 92.

142 "work audiences into a frenzy": Donald Bogle, *Toms, Coons, Mulattoes,*

Mammies, & Bucks: An Interpretive History of Blacks in American Films (New York: Continuum, 2002), 15.

143 "I'd like to kill": Anna Everett, *Returning the Gaze: A Genealogy of Black Film Criticism, 1909–1949* (Durham, N.C.: Duke Univ. Press, 2001), 61.
"Some of the cooler heads": Ibid., 81.
"It is to the advantage": Chadwick, *Reel Civil War*, 132.
Birth's total revenue: Ibid., 132.
"did more than any single thing": Bogle, *Toms, Coons*, 15.

144 "both reflected and inflamed": James R. Nesteby, *Black Images in American Films, 1896–1954: The Interplay Between Civil Rights and Film Culture* (Washington, D.C.: Univ. Press of America, 1982), 40.
"it was estimated": Chadwick, *Reel Civil War*, 187.

145 "The actors": Leonard J. Leff, "*Gone With the Wind* and Hollywood's Racial Politics," *Atlantic Monthly* (December 1999): 106–14.
"a weapon of terror": Ibid.
"Since *Gone With the Wind*": Everett, *Returning the Gaze*, 293.
"such a barefaced lie": Ibid., p. 292.

146 "deeper into the public mind": Everett, *Returning the Gaze*, 288.

147 "Between 1935 and 1939": Zolten, *Great God A'Mighty*, 29.

148 "capture some of the masculine": Jeffrey Melnick, *A Right to Sing the Blues: African Americans, Jews, and American Popular Song* (Cambridge, Mass.: Harvard Univ. Press, 1999), 101.

149 Adam Clayton Powell: Wil Haygood, "Why Negro Humor Is so Black," *American Prospect* (December 18, 2000).

11. Bad Niggers

150 "as creatures of small intelligence": Margaret Mitchell, *Gone With the Wind* (New York: Warner, 1993), 645.
"a determined policy": Bauerlein, *Negrophobia*, 230.

151 "A bad negro": Fredrickson, *Black Image in the White Mind*, 278.
"he is the worst": Ibid.
"If it needs lynching": Bauerlein, *Negrophobia*, 63.
"white man's worst dream": Jerry H. Bryant, "*Born in a Mighty Bad Land*": *The Violent Man in African American Folklore and Fiction* (Bloomington: Indiana Univ. Press, 2003), 2.

152 "making allowance": Bauerlein, *Negrophobia*, 124.
"loafers, the drunkards": Ibid., 113.
"It is certain": Dray, *At the Hands*, 68.

153 "undoubtedly and without question": Julius Lester, *Black Folktales* (New York: Richard W. Baron, 1969), 113.

154 "her last and only son": Daryl Cumber Dance, *Shuckin' and Jivin': Folklore from Contemporary Black Americans* (Bloomington: Indiana Univ. Press, 1978), 224.

155 "Look like every wey he go": E.C.L. Adams, *Nigger to Nigger* (New York: Charles Scribner's, 1928), 43.
"He ain' never change": Ibid., 43–46.
"probably the first": Dray, *At the Hands*, 194.

156 "sho one bad nigger": Jean Toomer, *Cane* (New York: Modern Library, 1994), 43–49.

157 "Negro women *are*": Zora Neale Hurston, *Folklore, Memoirs, & Other Writings* (New York: Library of America, 1995), 63.
"knocking the right": Ibid., 693.
"Fool wid me": Ibid.
"Tain't a man": Ibid., 697.
"Ah ain't skeered": Ibid., 172.

158 "channels through which": Angelyn Mitchell, *Within the Circle: An Anthology of African American Literary Criticism from the Harlem Renaissance to the Present* (Durham, N.C.: Duke Univ. Press, 1994), 99.
"I didn't know": Richard Wright, *Native Son* (New York: HarperPerennial), 429.
"a synthesis": Bernard W. Bell, *The Afro-American Novel and Its Tradition* (Amherst: Univ. of Massachusetts Press, 1987), 166.

159 "That's that Bigger Thomas": Wright, *Native Son*, 437.
"Maybe it was": Ibid., 435.
"The Bigger Thomases": Ibid., 437.

12. Violence and Vehemence

163 "the question of 'nigger-killing'": *Reporting Civil Rights. Part One: American Journalism, 1941–1963* (New York: Library of America, 2003), 218.

164 "You the nigger": Ibid., 237–39.
"We stand almost alone": Dray, *At the Hands* 445.
"When a man yelled": *Reporting*, 374.

165 "we are not going to let you": Ibid., 379.
"They're going in": Ibid., 375–77.

166 "On the second day": Ruby Bridges, *Through My Eyes* (New York: Scholastic, 1999), 22.
"Some thirty minutes": Ibid., 31.

167 "Are you that nigger lover?": Dray, *At the Hands*, 447–48.
"the greatest champion": Robert A. Caro, "The Compassion of Lyndon Johnson," *New Yorker* (April 1, 2002): 56–77.

168 "called me 'boy'": Ibid., 61.
"I think I can take": Connie Bruck, "The Personal Touch," *New Yorker* (August 13, 2001), 42.

13. *To Slur with Love*

174 "I want you to assume": Lawrence Schiller et al. *American Tragedy* (New York: Avon 1997), 514.
"barked out the word": Jeffrey Toobin, *The Run of His Life: The People v. O. J. Simpson* (New York: Random House, 1996), 324.
180 "It is a dirty, filthy word": Toobin, *Run of His Life*, 292.
183 "a really standup kind of cowboy": Gerald Martinez et al. *What It Is . . . What It Was: The Black Film Explosion of the '70s in Words and Pictures* (New York: Hyperion, 1998), 88.
184 "The word *nigger* in the '70s": Ibid.
"At the time we made our movies": Ibid, 92.
185 "You one bad": Deirdre Mullane, *Words to Make My Dream Children Live* (New York: Anchor 1995), 159.
191 "You talk to": Amy Wallace, "Peter Bart Is on the Phone and He's Threatening to Sue," *Los Angeles Magazine* (August 23, 2001).

14. *What's in a Name?*

197 "'nigger' and 'darkie'": Malcolm X, *The Autobiography of Malcolm X: With the Assistance of Alex Haley* (Secaucus, N.J.: Castle Books, 1965), 9.
"would talk about me": Ibid., 27.
"Mine was the same": Ibid., 31.
198 "We all here like you": Ibid., 38.
"Do you know": Ibid., 290.
199 "I have, so to speak": Eldridge Cleaver, *Soul on Ice* (New York: Dell, 1968), 66.
"The term *outlaw*": Ibid., 13.
"was conceived": Ibid., 78.
200 "futility of Caucasian": Robert H. DeCoy, *The Nigger Bible* (Los Angeles: Holloway House, 1967), 251, 117, 18.
"the study of": Ibid., 35.
"by teaching you": Ibid., 97.
"The hustler": X, *Autobiography of Malcolm X*, 318.
201 "Well Nigger": Iceberg Slim, *Pimp: The Story of My Life* (Los Angeles: Holloway House, 1969), 141.
"The first Nigger pimps": Ibid., 195.
"I came to a decision": Ibid., 305.

202 "the 'good nigger'": Iceberg Slim, *The Naked Soul of Iceberg Slim* (Los Angeles: Holloway House, 1971), 248.

204 "all at once": Haygood, "Why Negro Humor Is so Black."
"I'm only making": Dick Gregory, *Nigger* (New York: Washington Square Press, 1964), 130–35.

211 "I'm not so concerned": Lola Ogunnaike, "A Comic Who Won't Hold Back," *New York Times* (February 18, 2004), 1E.

15. Nigger vs. Nigga

214 "That's exactly what it's like": Robert MacNeil and William Cran, *Do You Speak American?* (New York: Nan Talese/Doubleday, 2005), 175.

216 "Language was everywhere": Paul Beatty, *The White Boy Shuffle* (Boston: Houghton Mifflin, 1996), 48.
"niggers got to get up": Ibid., 51.
"My euphoria": Ibid., 67.

217 "If Niggers Could": Ibid., 178.

219 "Racism introduces": Chester Himes, *My Life of Absurdity* (New York: Thunder's Mouth Press, 1976), 1.

223 "That word ain't shit": Medina, Tony, and Louis Reyes Rivera, *Bum Rush the Page: A Def Poetry Jam* (New York: Three Rivers Press, 2001), xvi–xvii.
"If you define hip-hop": Mos Def, "Does the 'N' Word Belong in Hip-Hop?" *Blaze* (March 1999).

226 "I love the irony": Nick A. Zaino, "Ask a Black Dude: Meet Comedian Dave Chappelle," *Progressive* (November 2003).

227 "I don't give white people the right": Cheo Tyehimba, "Nigger? Please," *Savoy* (November 2001), 69–71.
"used ironically": A'Lelia Bundles, "Family Tree," *New York Times* (November 18, 2001), 62.

233 "The American image": Baldwin, *Notes of a Native Son*, 38.

Epilogue

235 "our outsize public image": Malcolm Gladwell, "Reality Check: Attitudes and Anxieties About Race," *Washington Post* (October 8, 1995), A26.

Selected Bibliography

Adams, E.C.L. *Nigger to Nigger*. New York: Scribner's, 1928.

Andrews, William L., ed. *African American Autobiography: A Collection of Critical Essays*. Englewood Cliffs, N.J.: Prentice Hall, 1993.

Ashe, Arthur. *A Hard Road to Glory: A History of the African-American Athlete 1619–1918*, Vol. 1–3. New York: Amistad Press, 1988.

Baker, Houston A. *Turning South Again: Re-Thinking Modernism/Re-Reading Booker T.* Durham, N.C.: Duke Univ. Press, 2001.

Baldwin, James. *Notes of a Native Son*. Boston: Beacon Press, 1984.

Barboza, Steven, ed. *The African American Book of Values*. New York: Doubleday, 1998.

Bauerlein, Mark. *Negrophobia: A Race Riot in Atlanta, 1906*. San Francisco: Encounter Books, 2001.

Bearden, Romare, and Harry Henderson. *A History of African-American Artists: From 1792 to the Present*. New York: Pantheon, 1993.

Beck, Robert. *The Naked Soul of Iceberg Slim*. Los Angeles: Holloway House, 1971.

———. *Pimp: The Story of My Life*. Los Angeles: Holloway House, 1969.

Bell, Bernard W. *The Afro-American Novel and Its Tradition*. Amherst: Univ. of Massachusetts Press, 1987.

Berkeley Art Center. *Ethnic Notions: Black Images in the White Mind*. Berkeley Art Center, 2000.

Berlin, Ira. *Many Thousands Gone: The First Two Centuries of Slavery in North America*. Cambridge, Mass.: Harvard University Press, 1998.

Bernard, Emily, ed. *Remember Me to Harlem: The Letters of Langston Hughes and Carl Van Vechten, 1925–1964*. New York: Knopf, 2001.

Blassingame, John W. *The Slave Community: Plantation Life in the Antebellum South*. New York: Oxford Univ. Press, 1972.

Blight, David W. *Race and Reunion: The Civil War in American Memory*. Cambridge, Mass.: Belknap Press, 2000.

Blockson, Charles L., and Ron Fry. *Black Genealogy.* Englewood Cliffs, N.J.: Prentice-Hall, 1977.

Bogle, Donald. *Toms, Coons, Mulattoes, Mammies, & Bucks: An Interpretive History of Blacks in American Films.* New York: Continuum, 2002.

Botkin, B. A. *Lay My Burden Down: A Folk History of Slavery.* New York: Dell, 1973.

Boyd, Valerie. *Wrapped in Rainbows: The Life of Zora Neale Hurston.* New York: Scribner, 2002.

Brown, Cecil. *Stagolee Shot Billy.* Cambridge, Mass.: Harvard Univ. Press, 2003.

Brown, Sterling. *Negro Poetry and Drama and the Negro in American Fiction.* New York: Atheneum, 1969.

Bryant, Jerry H. *"Born in a Mighty Bad Land": The Violent Man in African American Folklore and Fiction.* Bloomington: Indiana Univ. Press, 2003.

Buckley, Gail. *American Patriots: The Story of Blacks in the Military from the Revolution to Desert Storm.* New York: Random House, 2001.

Buster, Larry Vincent. *The Art and History of Black Memorabilia.* New York: Clarkson Potter, 2000.

Carretta, Vincent, ed. *Unchained Voices: An Anthology of Black Authors in the English-Speaking World of the 18th Century.* Lexington: Univ. Press of Kentucky, 1996.

Chadwick, Bruce. *The Reel Civil War: Mythmaking in American Film.* New York: Knopf, 2001.

Cleaver, Eldridge. *Soul on Ice.* New York: Dell, 1968.

Clinton, Catherine, and Michele Gillespie. *The Devil's Lane: Sex and Race in the Early South.* New York: Oxford Univ. Press, 1997.

Dance, Daryl Cumber. *Shuckin' and Jivin': Folklore from Contemporary Black Americans.* Bloomington: Indiana Univ. Press, 1978.

DeCoy, Robert H. *The Nigger Bible.* Los Angeles: Holloway House, 1967.

Dixon, Thomas, Jr. *The Clansman: An Historical Romance of the Ku Klux Klan.* Lexington: Univ. Press of Kentucky, 1970.

Dray, Philip. *At the Hands of Persons Unknown: The Lynching of Black America.* New York: Modern Library, 2002.

Du Bois, W.E.B. *The Souls of Black Folk.* New York: Penguin, 1996.

Ellis, Joseph J. *American Sphinx: The Character of Thomas Jefferson.* New York: Knopf, 1998.

Ellison, Ralph. *Shadow and Act.* New York: Vintage, 1995.

Everett, Anna. *Returning the Gaze: A Genealogy of Black Film Criticism, 1909–1949.* Durham, N.C.: Duke Univ. Press, 2001.

Fishkin, Shelley Fisher. *Lighting Out for the Territory: Reflections on Mark Twain and American Culture.* New York: Oxford Univ. Press, 1997.

Foner, Eric. *A Short History of Reconstruction, 1863–1877.* New York: Perennial Library, 1990.

——. *The Story of American Freedom*. New York: W. W. Norton, 1998.

Foner, Philip S., ed. *Frederick Douglass: Selected Speeches and Writings*. Chicago: Lawrence Hill Books, 1999.

Fredrickson, George M. *The Black Image in the White Mind: The Debate on Afro-American Character and Destiny, 1817–1914*. Hanover, N.H.: Wesleyan Univ. Press, 1987.

Giscombe, C. S. *Into and Out of Dislocation*. New York: North Point Press, 2000.

Gould, Stephen Jay. *The Mismeasure of Man*. New York: W. W. Norton, 1981.

Grunwald, Lisa, and Stephen J. Adler. *Letters of the Century: America 1900–1999*. New York: Dial Press, 1999.

Hadden, Sally E. *Slave Patrols: Law and Violence in Virginia and the Carolinas*. Cambridge, Mass.: Harvard Univ. Press, 2001.

Hale, Grace Elizabeth. *Making Whiteness: The Culture of Segregation in the South, 1890–1940*. New York: Vintage, 1999.

Hietala, Thomas R. *The Fight of the Century: Jack Johnson, Joe Louis, and the Struggle for Racial Equality*. London: M. E. Sharpe, 2002.

Hollandsworth, James G. *An Absolute Massacre: The New Orleans Race Riot of July 30, 1866*. Baton Rouge: Louisiana State Univ. Press, 2001.

Hurston, Zora Neale. *Folklore, Memoirs, & Other Writings*. New York: Library of America, 1995.

Jacobs, Harriet. *Incidents in the Life of a Slave Girl*. Mineola, N.Y.: Dover, 2001.

Janken, Kenneth Robert. *White: The Biography of Walter White, Mr. NAACP*. New York: New Press, 2003.

Jefferson, Thomas. *Notes on the State of Virginia*. New York: Penguin, 1999.

Jones, Bessie, and Bess Lomax Hawes. *Step It Down: Games, Plays, Songs, and Stories from the Afro-American Heritage*. New York: Harper & Row, 1972.

Jordan, Winthrop D. *The White Man's Burden: Historical Origins of Racism in the United States*. New York: Oxford Univ. Press, 1974.

——. *White over Black: American Attitudes Toward the Negro, 1550–1812*. Baltimore: Penguin, 1969.

Kelley, Robin D. G., and Earl Lewis, eds. *To Make Our World Anew: A History of African Americans*. New York: Oxford Univ. Press, 2000.

Lanning, Michael Lee. *The African-American Soldier: From Crispus Attucks to Colin Powell*. Secaucus, N.J.: Birch Lane Press, 1997.

Lester, Julius. *Black Folktales*. New York: Richard W. Baron, 1969.

Lewis, David Levering. *When Harlem Was in Vogue*. New York: Penguin, 1997.

Lhamon, W. T., Jr. *Raising Cain: Blackface Performance from Jim Crow to Hip Hop*. Cambridge, Mass.: Harvard Univ. Press, 1998.

Litwack, Leon F. *Been in the Storm So Long: The Aftermath of Slavery*. New York: Random House, 1980.

——. *North of Slavery: The Negro in the Free States 1790–1860*. Chicago: Univ. of Chicago Press, 1961.

————. *Trouble in Mind: Black Southerners in the Age of Jim Crow.* New York: Knopf, 1998.

Lomax, Alan. *The Folk Songs of North America.* Garden City, N.Y.: Dolphin, 1975.

Lott, Eric. *Love & Theft: Blackface Minstrelsy and the American Working Class.* New York: Oxford Univ. Press, 1995.

Lowance, Mason, ed. *Against Slavery: An Abolitionist Reader.* New York: Penguin, 2000.

Mahar, William J. *Behind the Burnt Cork Mask: Early Blackface Minstrelsy and Antebellum American Popular Culture.* Urbana: Univ. of Illinois Press, 1999.

Maier, Pauline. *American Scripture: Making the Declaration of Independence.* New York: Knopf, 1997.

McElroy, Guy. *Facing History: The Black Image in American Art 1710–1940.* San Francisco: Bedford Arts, 1990.

Melnick, Jeffrey. *A Right to Sing the Blues: African Americans, Jews, and American Popular Song.* Cambridge: Harvard Univ. Press, 1999.

Menand, Louis. *The Metaphysical Club: A Story of Ideas in America.* New York: Farrar, Straus, 2001.

Mitchell, Angelyn. *Within the Circle: An Anthology of African American Literary Criticism from the Harlem Renaissance to the Present.* Durham, N.C.: Duke Univ. Press, 1994.

Mitchell, Margaret. *Gone With the Wind.* New York: Warner Books, 1993.

Morgan, Thomas L., and William Barlow. *From Cakewalks to Concert Halls: An Illustrated History of African American Popular Music from 1895 to 1930.* Washington, D.C.: Elliott & Clark, 1992.

Mullane, Deirdre. *Crossing the Danger Water: Three Hundred Years of African-American Writing.* New York: Anchor, 1993.

Murray, Albert. *From the Briarpatch File: On Context, Procedure, and American Identity.* New York: Pantheon, 2001.

Nesteby, James R. *Black Images in American Films, 1896–1954: The Interplay Between Civil Rights and Film Culture.* Washington, D.C.: Univ. Press of America, 1982.

Perry, Jeffrey B., ed. *A Hubert Harrison Reader.* Middletown, Conn.: Wesleyan Univ. Press, 2001.

Phillips, Caryl. *The European Tribe.* New York: Vintage, 2000.

Rampersad, Arnold. *Jackie Robinson: A Biography.* New York: Ballantine, 1998.

Randall, Alice. *The Wind Done Gone.* Boston: Houghton Mifflin, 2001.

Rawson, Hugh. *Wicked Words: A Treasury of Curses, Insults, Put-Downs, and Other Formerly Unprintable Terms from Anglo-Saxon Times to the Present.* New York: Crown, 1989.

Ripley, Alexandra. *Scarlett.* New York: Warner, 1991.

Sancho, Ignatius. *Letters of the Late Ignatius Sancho, An African.* New York: Penguin, 1998.

Simmons, James C. *Star-Spangled Eden: An Exploration of the American Character in the 19th Century*. New York: Carroll & Graf, 2000.

Smith, John David, ed. *Black Soldiers in Blue: African American Troops in the Civil War Era*. Chapel Hill: Univ. of North Carolina Press, 2002.

Spears, Richard A. *Slang and Euphemism*. New York: Signet, 1991.

Stanton, William. *The Leopard's Spots: Scientific Attitudes Toward Race in America 1815–1859*. Chicago: Univ. of Chicago Press, 1960.

Starke, Catherine Juanita. *Black Portraiture in American Fiction: Stock Characters, Archetypes, and Individuals*. New York: Basic Books, 1971.

Stowe, Harriet Beecher. *A Key to Uncle Tom's Cabin*. Bedford, Mass.: Applewood Books, 1998.

———. *Uncle Tom's Cabin*. New York: New American Library, 1998.

Stuckey, Sterling. *Going Through the Storm: The Influence of African American Art in History*. New York: Oxford Univ. Press, 1994.

Taylor, Yuval, ed. *I Was Born a Slave: An Anthology of Classic Slave Narratives*, Vol. 1. Chicago: Lawrence Hill, 1999.

Thomas, H. Nigel. *From Folklore to Fiction: A Study of Folk Heroes and Rituals in the Black American Novel*. New York: Greenwood Press, 1988.

Tocqueville, Alexis de. *Democracy in America*. Indianapolis: Hackett, 2000.

Twain, Mark. *Adventures of Huckleberry Finn*. New York: Fawcett Columbine, 1996.

Van Vechten, Carl. *Nigger Heaven*. New York: Knopf, 1926.

White, Deborah Gray. *Ar'n't I a Woman? Female Slaves in the Plantation South*. New York: W. W. Norton, 1999.

White, Shane. *Stories of Black Freedom in Black New York*. Cambridge, Mass.: Harvard Univ. Press, 2002.

Wideman, John Edgar. *My Soul Has Grown Deep: Classics of Early African-American Literature*. Philadelphia: Running Press, 2001.

Wilkins, Roger. *Jefferson's Pillow: The Founding Fathers and the Dilemma of Black Patriotism*. Boston: Beacon Press, 2001.

Wilson, Harriet E. *Our Nig; or, Sketches from the Life of a Free Black*. New York: Vintage, 1983.

Wormser, Richard. *The Rise and Fall of Jim Crow*. New York: St. Martin's Press, 2003.

Wright, Richard. *Black Boy*. New York: HarperCollins, 1966.

X, Malcolm, with Alex Haley. *The Autobiography of Malcolm X*. New York: Ballantine, 1987.

Zolten, Jerry. *Great God A'Mighty!: The Dixie Hummingbirds Celebrating the Rise of Soul Gospel Music*. New York: Oxford Univ. Press, 2003.

Index

CPSIA information can be obtained at www.ICGtesting.com
Printed in the USA
BVOW08s1826230716

456614BV00001B/2/P